John L. Tomkinson comes from Stoke-on-Trent in the English Midlands. He was educated at the University of Wales (Lampeter) and the University of Keele in Staffordshire. He holds an MA in History and an MA and a PhD in Philosophy from the University of Keele.

A British qualified and trained teacher, he has thirty-five years experience teaching History to students from primary to undergraduate level, the latter for the University of Maryland, and has experience of the British and US systems of education, and of teaching in international schools. He has taught IB History for fifteen years and has been an assessor for the International Baccalaureate since 1995.

Today he teaches at the Moraitis School in Athens, and writes on various subjects.

D1091900

Themes in Twentieth Century World History for the International Baccalaureate

In the same series and by the same author:

Wars and Warfare

Single-Party States

The Cold War

John L. Tomkinson

Anagnosis
Athens, Greece

Anagnosis
Deliyianni 3
15122 Maroussi
Athens, Greece
Website: www.anagnosis.gr

First published 2003
Reprinted 2005
Second edition 2006
Reprinted 2006
Reprinted 2007

ISBN 978-960-88087-4-4
Third Edition
© Anagnosis 2008

Photoset and printed by:
K. Pletsas - Z. Karadri O.E.
Harilaou Trikoupi 107
Athens
www.typografio.gr

Teachers' Preface

The teacher of history for the course of the International Baccalaureate has a very difficult task. Some problems are shared with teachers of other subjects, while some are unique to history.

The IB course is a short one: two academic years means considerably less time than two calendar years, when the final examinations are held in May or November. In addition, many of the students are studying in a language which is not their mother tongue.

Unlike the "newer" Group Three subjects, where it is assumed that students enter the course knowing nothing about the subject at all, and where the standards of examination are based entirely upon what can reasonably be accomplished in such a short time, it is assumed that history students will already have a long background in the subject when they enter on the course, and the standard of the examination is necessarily set high, because the grades awarded have to be comparable with those of long-established university entrance examinations, which are themselves the final stage in a long period of education and training in the discipline.

Yet in practice IB History students, particularly those in international schools, come to the subject from very different backgrounds. Their experience of history in their previous schools may not provide any useful foundation for their IB studies at all; and it may even be counterproductive. In his book *Lies My Teacher Told Me: Everything Your American History Textbook Got Wrong*, James W. Loewen quotes a colleague teaching history in college as saying that he sees his first job as disabusing his charges of what they learned in high school. "In no other field does this happen. Mathematics professors, for instance, know that non-Euclidian geometry is rarely taught in high school, but they don't assume that Euclidian geometry was *mistaught*. Professors of English literature don't presume that *Romeo and Juliet* was misunderstood in high school. Indeed, history is the only field in which the more courses students take, the stupider they become." In many countries, the study of history in schools has been reduced to the rote of learning selective "basic facts" and stories ,or it is so imbued with nationalist ideology as to be worse than useless.

The history teacher is thus pulled from both ends. On the one hand his/her pupils may have no useful background in the subject at all, or one which is actually counterproductive, and they may not be working in their mother tongue. On the other hand, he/she has to prepare students in a very short period of time for examinations which are marked to a standard which matches those of students who have usefully studied history in their mother tongue over many years. This means that the history teacher has very speedily to instill in his/her students a new way of looking at the subject, teach new skills and provide basic facts, yet at the same time provide a level of analysis which will enable the students to obtain the best grades of which they are capable.

There is no shortage of excellent texts for school history, but few are designed to provide for the wide range of levels and backgrounds which the IB course needs to encompass. Either they are designed for lower level examinations, and provide basic facts and an elementary introduction to analysis, or they provide adequate analysis, but assume knowledge of basic facts.

This small series of books is an attempt to fill that void, by providing both basic facts and a range of analysis, which will enable the students to make the transition to an appropriate level as quickly as possible.

The books may usefully be employed as an accompaniment to a course taught in class, the numbered paragraphs providing ready references. Students may use the text as a model upon which to construct their own notes. The texts may also function as revision notes for examinations. Each individual note usually contains a single idea which can be identified by a key word or phrase. If the student identifies these key words by highlighting or underlining them, then the very mental process of making the decision about which word(s) to highlight will ensure that he/she will have actively considered the points, and the process of committing facts and theories to memory will have already taken place. Running the eye over the highlighted words will then quickly enable recall of the entire set of ideas. As examples, the key words in the notes have sometimes been highlighted in bold; but most have been left for the students themselves to do.

The unusual format of these texts is an attempt to combine the condensation of notes with the readability of a text, giving the student some idea both of the depth of knowledge which needs to be acquired and the level of analysis which needs to be aimed at.

Like many books designed for use in schools, these do not have detailed footnotes. Students should be warned that this makes them unsuitable for use as sources for internally assessed studies or extended essays; although used as initial reading they may provide the student with some initial idea of the background to be mastered, and the issues to be confronted, in approaching a particular topic.

A lot of attention has been paid to the development of the students' vocabulary, with the needs of those not working in their mother tongue in mind. Science students spend much of their time becoming acquainted with the technical vocabulary of their subject. By contrast, students of history are frequently quite unaware of the need to assimilate a special vocabulary at all, because history books do not have the immediate opacity that science texts present to the uninitiated. Teachers are sometimes unaware of the burden of new vocabulary required of their students because they themselves assimilated it imperceptibly over many years, and fail to realise how unfamiliar it may be to their students.

A good grade in one of today's university entrance examinations such as the IB, requires that the student demonstrate evidence of wide reading. Without an adequate command of the terminology of history, such reading may be superficial, ill-assimilated, and of limited use. Even those students who understand such terms in context may be unable to use them confidently, if at all, in their own essays and examinations, without some explicit focus upon their meaning. Dictionaries have their uses as works of reference, but there are few students so highly motivated, or so Spartan in character, as to work their way through a dictionary of relevant terms. I have tried to focus upon the meaning of key terms which dominate the study of the themes covered in each volume. This should make the students more aware of the complex conceptual issues at stake in the subjects they are studying, and might also go some way towards dragging students away from narrative, and focusing their attention upon ideas and issues.

Finally, History should never be a "dead subject" concerned entirely with the past, with no relevance to the burning issues of the day. These books are offered to help students see the relevance of what they study to understanding today's world, to be more intelligent and critical in their reading of contemporary situations, and so come to grips with the living issues of the day in a confident and thoughtful manner.

John L. Tomkinson
Athens 2005

Contents

Acknowledgements

My thanks are due to Aris Karey of *Anagnosis Books* for encouraging and fostering the project. For the lists of US military interventions on pp. 10-11 and p. 169, I am indebted to Dr. Zoltan Grossman.

Author's Note

IB teachers will be aware that the various options on the IB History course overlap considerably. For this reason, a considerable amount of material relevant to the study of the Cold War may be found in the other volumes in this series. For example, there are chapters on the Soviet Union under Khrushchev and Brezhnev, and China under Mao Zedong, in the companion volume, *Single-Party States;* while the Arab-Israeli Wars, which also have a Cold War dimension, are to be found in *Wars and Warfare*.

Theodore Roosevelt

1. Dominance and Dependency

"I spent thirty-three years and four months in active service in the country's most agile military force, the Marines. I served in all ranks from second lieutenant to major general. And during that period I spent most of my time being a high-class muscle man for Big Business, for Wall Street and the bankers. In short, I was a racketeer, a gangster for capitalism.

"I suspected I was just part of a racket at the time. Now I am sure of it. Like all members of the military profession I never had an original thought until I left the service. My mental faculties remained in suspended animation while I obeyed the orders of the higher-ups. This is typical with everyone in the military service.

"Thus I helped make Mexico, and especially Tampico, safe for American oil interests in 1914. I helped make Haiti and Cuba a decent place for the National City Bank boys to collect revenue in. I helped in the raping of half-a-dozen Central American republics for the benefit of Wall Street. The record of racketeering is long. I helped purify Nicaragua for the international banking house of Brown Brothers and Co. in 1909-1912. I brought light to the Dominican Republic for the sugar interests in 1916. I helped make Honduras 'right' for American fruit companies in 1903. In China in 1927 I helped see to it that Standard Oil went its way unmolested.

"During those years, I had, as the boys in the back room would say, a swell racket. I was rewarded with honours, medals, and promotion. Looking back on it, I feel that I might have given Al Capone a few hints. The best he could do was to operate a racket in three city districts. The Marines operated on three continents." (Major General Smedley Butler, former Commandant, US Marine Corps)

1. The lands acquired by the most powerful European states were called empires, and the states which acquired them **imperial powers**.* The areas which they acquired and administered were called **colonies**.*

2. There were many reasons for acquiring colonies, which included:
    (a) Economic reasons. Colonies provided:
        (i) sources of raw materials for factories;
        (ii) labour for production, where costs were lower;
        (iii) captive markets for manufactured goods.

(b) Strategic reasons: Some colonies were strategically located for the protection of the homeland or for the defence of its interests abroad.

(c) Prestige: Imperialism could be seen as an extension of chauvinistic nationalism. Colonies provided:

   (i) prestige for the country which possessed them,

   (ii) popularity for the politicians who acquired them.

3. The powers which dominated international relations at the beginning of the twentieth century were referred to as the **Great Powers***: Great Britain, France, Germany, Austria-Hungary and Russia. After the Second World War, the world was supposedly dominated by only two **superpowers***: the United States of America and the Soviet Union.

4. During this latter period of Cold War, new forms of domination and exploitation were devised to avoid accusations of imperialism.

5. The pattern for this had already been established in the Western hemisphere. Since the beginning of the century the USA had exercised hegemony over most of the continent, but it had usually done so without installing a US governor, or marking the territory as under foreign control in the traditional fashion. Instead, the fiction that the occupied country was independent of outside control was carefully maintained.

US Military Interventions in the Americas, the Pacific and the Far East before 1939

CHILE 1891 Marines clash with nationalist rebels.

HAITI 1891 Black workers revolt on US-claimed Navassa Island defeated.

HAWAII 1893 (-?) Independent kingdom overthrown, annexed.

NICARAGUA 1894 Month-long occupation of Bluefields.

CHINA 1894-95 Marines land in Sino-Japanese War.

KOREA 1894-96 Marines occupy Seoul during war.

PANAMA 1895 Marines land in what was then a Colombian province.

NICARAGUA 1896 Marines land in port of Corinto.

CHINA 1898-1900 Boxer Rebellion fought by foreign armies.

PHILIPPINES 1898-1910(-?) Seized from Spain, 600,000 Filipinos killed.

CUBA 1898-1902(-?) Seized from Spain, Guantanamo Navy Base still held.

PUERTO RICO 1898(-?) Seized from Spain, occupation continues.

GUAM 1898(-?) Seized from Spain, still use as base.

NICARAGUA 1898 Marines land at port of San Juan del Sur.

SAMOA 1899(-?) US intervention in battle over succession to throne.

NICARAGUA 1899 Marines land at port of Bluefields.

PANAMA 1901-14 detached from Colombia 1903, annexed Canal Zone 1914-99.

HONDURAS 1903 Marines intervene in revolution.

DOMINICAN REP. 1903-04 US interests protected in revolution.

KOREA 1904-05 Marines land in Russo-Japanese War.

CUBA 1906-09 Marines land during democratic elections.

NICARAGUA 1907 "Dollar Diplomacy" protectorate set up.

HONDURAS 1907 Marines land during war with Nicaragua.

PANAMA 1908 Marines intervene in elections.

NICARAGUA Marines land in Bluefields and Corinto.
HONDURAS U.S. Interests protected in civil war.
CHINA 1911-41 Continuous occupation with flare-ups.
CUBA 1912 US interests protected in Havana.
PANAMA 1912 Marines land during elections.
HONDURAS 1912 Marines protect US economic interests.
NICARAGUA 1912-33 20-year occupation, US fought guerrillas.
DOMINICAN REPUBLIC 1914 Fight with rebels over Santo Domingo.
MEXICO 1914-18 Series of interventions against nationalists.
HAITI 1914-34 19-year occupation after revolts.
DOMINICAN REPUBLIC 1916-24 8-year Marine occupation.
CUBA 1917-33 Military occupation, economic protectorate.
PANAMA 1918-20 "Police duty" during unrest after elections.
HONDURAS 1919 Marines land during election campaign.
GUATEMALA 1920 2-week intervention against unions.
HONDURAS 1924-25 Landed twice during elections.
PANAMA 1925 Marines suppress general strike.
CHINA 1927-34 Marines stationed throughout the country.
EL SALVADOR 1932 Warships sent during Faribundo Marti revolt.

Compared with these, the foreign adventures of the European "imperialists", especially the three eastern empires of Germany, Austria-Hungary and Russia, were almost insignificant.

6. There were several advantages to this "imperialism by stealth," or informal imperialism, favoured by US President Theodore Roosevelt and others:
   (a) Imperialism was unpopular in the Third World "Imperialism by stealth" enabled the imperial power to pose as "righteous," as unlike the grasping "imperialist powers," while at the same time exploiting its dependencies in exactly the same ways as imperialist powers.
   (b) The old-fashioned "up-front" imperialism made it clear where responsibility for the state of colonies lay, so that the imperial powers could be held responsible by world opinion for their actions. The USA could claim that its colonies were independent states, entirely responsible for their own sorry condition, and that the USA did not bear any responsibility for the mess it had created.
7. After the end of the Second World War many of the states of eastern and central Europe were subjected to a policy of enforced **sovietization**,* of being forced to adopt forms of government and social and economic systems modelled upon that of the USSR, effectively losing their independence. Yet Stalin wished them to be thought of as independent states, so that they also preserved all the outward marks of sovereign states: such as heads of state, national anthems, etc. However, their dependence upon the USSR was commonly indicated by referring to them as **satellite states**.*
8. Many states in the Western hemisphere had long had a similar relationship to the USA, and in the interests of clarity and balance they might appropriately have been called, and might still be called, "US satellites."
9. A less intrusive form of dominance was exemplified by the relations between the USSR and

Finland, which could survive only as an independent state with the tolerance of its giant neighbour. It was accorded complete independence, contingent upon never creating a significant problem for Soviet governments, and never opposing Soviet foreign policy. This form of dominance was known in the West as **finlandization**.* Such a dependent state is frequently known as a "**client state**."*

10. In Western literature this term is used contemptuously, and never of "allies" of the USA. Yet it is clear that the degree of independence accorded to many of *them* was similarly dependent upon never creating a problem for, or opposing the policies or interests of, US governments.

In understanding the Cold War, it is essential to keep these forms of hidden dominance and dependency in mind.

Glossary

client state: a state which is nominally independent, but the independence of which is limited by its being politically, economically or militarily dependent upon another

colonies: states openly under the governance of another

finlandization: a process by which an independent state deliberately conforms its policies, especially its foreign policies, in line with the interests of a superpower in order to preserve a measure of internal independence

Great Powers: the dominant world powers

imperialism: the practice of acquiring colonies to create an empire

imperial powers: powers which have acquired colonies

satellite states: states which were dependent upon a superpower, usually used in a derogatory fashion only of states under the hegemony of the USSR, in order to draw attention away from the existence of US satellite states

sovietization: the process of conforming the institutions of a state to those of the USSR

superpowers: the remaining Great Powers following the end of the Second Word War. i.e. the USA and USSR.

Harry Truman

2. The Roots of the Cold War

"The Grand Alliance was an artificial short-term expedient." (Stephen J. Lee)

"We have fifty percent of the world's wealth, but only 6.3 percent of its population. . . In this situation we cannot fail to be the object of envy and resentment. Our real task in the coming period is to devise a pattern of relationships which will allow us to maintain this position of disparity. We should cease to talk about the raising of living standards, human rights, and democratization. The day is not far off when we are going to have to deal in straight power concepts. The less we are then hampered by idealistic slogans, the better." (George Kennan, Director of Policy Planning, US State Department)

Origins

1. There are two main related questions about the origins of the Cold War:
    (a) When did it begin?
    (b) Who was responsible for it?
2. Since there was a gradual breakdown of relations between former allies, no *precise* date can appropriately be given for the beginning of the Cold War.

The Grand Alliance

1. Before the outbreak of the Second World War the USA and USSR had rival ideologies in:
    (a) Liberal Capitalism,
    (b) Revolutionary Marxist-Leninist Socialism.
2. Stalin had reason to be suspicious of the USA because:
    (a) The USA had intervened in the Russian Civil War against the Bolsheviks.
    (b) The Western Allies had appeased the growing power of Hitler during the 1930s, probably in the hope that he would destroy the Soviet state for them, forcing Stalin to make his own arrangements (the Molotov-Ribbentrop Pact) to keep the inevitable German invasion of the Soviet Union at bay until he was ready to deal with it.
3. The **Grand Alliance*** against Hitler was an alliance of convenience.
    (a) Only Britain had declared war on Germany voluntarily.

(b) The USSR had been invaded by German forces in *Operation Barbarossa,* in violation of its alliance with Hitler. Before that, the USSR had been supplying the *Luftwaffe* with the aircraft fuel with which to fight the Battle of Britain and to bomb British cities in the Blitz.

(c) The USA was bombed into the war by the Japanese at Pearl Harbour, at which time Hitler also gratuitously declared war on the USA.

The members of the Grand Alliance were only allies in the sense that they were all fighting a common enemy. They were allies on the basis of the principle that "the enemy of my enemy must be my friend." Churchill had remarked: " If Hitler invaded Hell, I would make at least a favourable reference to the Devil in the House of Commons." Stephen J. Lee writes: "The Grand Alliance was an artificial short-term expedient."

4. There were differences and mutual suspicions of bad faith between the Allies **during the war.**

(a) Stalin repeatedly asked for the opening of a second front in Western Europe to take some of the pressure off the Red Army, which was fighting to drive the invader from the Soviet homeland. Churchill argued for the option least helpful to Stalin, the invasion of Italy, in the hope that Germany and the USSR would fight to exhaustion before the West stepped in. The Western leaders promised to open a significant Second Front in 1942 and 1943, but only delivered in mid-1944, leaving the Red Army to bear the main brunt of the war against Hitler. Stalin said: "They want to bleed us white in order to dictate their terms to us later."

(b) Perhaps not surprisingly, under those circumstances, the Soviet Union, in its turn, delayed in declaring war on Japan until almost the last moment.

Differences at the Approach to the War's End

As the end of the war approached, differences began to appear over the future peace settlement, especially as regards Eastern Europe. Those countries which lay close to the USSR had inherited a traditional enmity with Russia as the nearby power which threatened their existence. Thus the US and UK demanded the holding of free elections in Eastern Europe, knowing well that these would result in anti-Soviet, and therefore pro-Western regimes. This demand irritated Stalin, who was being kept out of the restored states of Western European, such as Italy and France.

Poland

1. The future of **Poland** was the most controversial of these issues:

(a) Because of its position adjacent to the much larger Soviet Union, in a bipolar world* an independent Poland would necessarily be an ally of the USA, for its own protection.

(b) The independence of Poland had been the cause for which, at least officially, Britain and France had gone to war in 1939.

(c) Proportionally, Poland had suffered greater losses during the war than any other country. Many places had been fought over three times. The officer corps of the army had been butchered by the Soviets in the forest of Katyn - a crime discovered by, and gleefully publicised by, the Germans during the war.

For all these reasons, but especially the first, the US pressed for an independent, democratic Poland

2. Russia had been invaded once by the French, twice by the Germans and once by the Poles, since 1800. Stalin, determined that if the USSR were invaded again from the West, then next time it would not have to fight on Soviet soil. He wished to create a glacis* in which to meet any new invasion beyond the western frontier of the USSR. This would involve the control of Poland.

3. When the Red Army invaded Poland, they halted at Warsaw to allow the Germans to defeat a rising by the Polish Home Army (partisans).

4. The Soviets then installed a Polish Communist government. These Polish Communists (known as the Lublin Poles) had been retained during the war in Moscow precisely for this day. In doing this, the Soviets ignored the Polish Government-in-exile which had been set up in London.
5. When the Western Allies protested at Yalta, it was agreed that:
    (a) Some of the London Poles would be allowed to join the Polish Government set up by Stalin in Warsaw, and there would be free elections.
    (b) The USSR would retain the Polish territory it had conquered in 1939 in accordance with the secret protocol of the Molotov-Ribbentrop Pact, its eastern boundary being the Curzon Line.
    (c) Stalin wished Poland to receive, in compensation, all German territory east of the rivers Oder and Neisse. This contained five million Germans. The Western Allies would not agree, as they claimed it would create a minority problem like that of the Sudetenland. No decision was reached.
6. By the time the Allies met at Potsdam, Germany east of the Oder and Neisse had already been handed over to the Polish provincial government, and five million German inhabitants had been expelled, in what was a *fait accompli.**

Germany

1. The Allies were faced with the problem of administering Germany after the unconditional surrender of the Nazis.
2. The USSR favoured keeping Germany united, so that all the Allies would have access to all of Germany, since the wealthier industrial region lay in the West. The USA preferred to divide it into spheres of influence, since the richer areas would fall into the US sphere of influence, and the poorer in the east, would lie in the Soviet sphere.
3. At Yalta it was decided:
    (a) to divide Germany into three **zones** of occupation: Soviet, American and British, to be administered by the several military commanders of the Allied Occupation Forces.
    (b) To divide Berlin into **sectors**, to be administered by the several military commanders of the Allied Occupation Forces in Berlin.
    (c) Germany would, in principle, pay for the damage inflicted by the war, and the bulk of the **reparations** would go to the USSR.
4. The final decision of the Potsdam Conference concerning the future of Germany was that:
    (a) The **borders** of Germany would be adjusted:
        (i) Austria to be separated from Germany;
        (ii) Alsace-Lorraine to be returned to France;
        (iii) Northern East Prussia to go to the USSR;
        (iv) Southern East Prussia and all land east of the R. Neisse to Poland;
        (v) The Saar to France for 15 years after which its future to be decided by a plebiscite.*
    (b) Germany was to be to be divided into four **zones** of occupation: British, Soviet, American and French.
        (i) Each zone was to be governed by the Commander of Allied Forces in that zone, taking orders from his national government.
        (ii) The four Allied Commanders-in-Chief were to meet in the **Allied Control Council (ACC)** to co-ordinate their economic policies for the entire country.
    (c) Germany was to be governed as a unity in economic matters with decisions subject to the rule of **unanimity*** in the Allied Control Council.
    (d) Berlin was excluded from the zonal system. It was to be governed as a unity by the

four allied Commanders in Berlin in the **Kommandatura**, but actually administered by the several Allied commanders in four **sectors**. Access to the western sectors from the respective western zones was by air corridors, road and rail routes. The right to use these routes was only vaguely defined.

(e) In due course a peace conference would be convened to set up an independent democratic government of Germany.

(f) The USSR would take reparations

    (i) from its own zone

    (ii) 25% of all industrial plant and machinery not required for the peacetime German economy from the Western zones

    (iii) In return, food, coal and raw materials would be sent from the Soviet zones to the Western zones equal in value to 60% of the industrial plant and machinery taken from them.

5. The arrangements made, intended to be only temporary, involved a degree of close cooperation, especially over:

    (i) economic policy

    (b) control of Berlin

In reality, both sides wanted to secure control over the whole of Germany, or failing that, to ensure that they retained what they had, so that cooperation became impossible.

Harry Truman

1. When Roosevelt died on 12th April, 1945, he was replaced as US president by **Harry Truman**, a new vice-president suddenly called upon to assume power.

2. He was an inadequate leader:

(a) He lacked any experience of foreign policy and diplomacy.

(b) He had not been taken into Roosevelt's confidence about his aims and plans.

(c) He received contradictory advice from advisors: Avril Harriman (US Ambassador in Moscow) and George Kennan (Soviet expert at the State Department) being hard-liners, and Henry Morgenthau, George Marshall and Henry Stimson being in favour of post-war co-operation with the USSR. Given his lack of background in foreign affairs, Truman was incapable of adequately evaluating the arguments they advanced.

(d) He was a religious provincial, inclined to see the world in Manichaean* terms, in which the USA represented righteousness, and in which any other power which had interests which conflicted with those of the USA was *ipso facto* * evil.

(e) He felt the need to "prove himself" on the world stage by adopting a hard-line stance. Thus Truman said in 1946: "Unless Russia is faced with an iron fist and strong language, another war is in the making. Only one language do they understand - how many divisions have you?" He was the first of many US Presidents to use East-West relations as a stage upon which to seek to prove his "political *machismo.*"*

3. At Potsdam he offended Stalin by his attitude, which was determined by:

(a) his personal limitations and prejudices (as above);

(b) the knowledge that the USA had the atom bomb.

Ian Gray writes: "This change in the attitude of the Americans and the British at Potsdam gave dramatic confirmation of Stalin's worst fears and suspicions. Moreover, it offended him deeply as an act of ingratitude and rejection."

4. Truman subsequently followed a policy calculated to cause US-Soviet relations to deteriorate:

    (i) keeping the Soviets out of Japan as much as possible;

(ii) challenging Soviet control of Eastern Europe, and in particular seeking to ensure the establishment of an anti-Soviet and pro-Western Poland;

(iii) expanding US military power by setting up bases across the world, particularly in the areas around the borders of the USSR and China;

(iv) developing nuclear weapons to preserve US military dominance of the world.

5. He fired advisors who became alarmed at the deteriorating relations between the USA and the USSR, e.g. Henry Wallace, Secretary of Commerce.

The End of the Second World War

[For a fuller treatment of the results of the war see the companion volume "Wars and Warfare"]

1. Europe had suffered massive devastation as a result of the war.
2. The USSR, in particular, had suffered incredible destruction, compared with the USA:

(a) The USSR had lost 10 million soldiers in battle or POW camps. By contrast, the USA had lost 3% of that number. Soviet deaths, including civilian, totalled 27 million.

(b) Many of the major population centres in the USSR were in ruins, while the US homeland was untouched by war.

(c) In the USSR, the survivors were threatened with famine. The USA had increased its wealth as a result of the war.

(d) Some non-Russian areas of the USSR resisted the reimposition of Soviet rule by guerilla warfare, threatening the integrity of the country.

3. The **United Nations Relief and Rehabilitation Administration (UNRRA)** provided aid contributed by USA, UK and Canada during the last year of the war. The aid went to the poorest countries: Italy, Greece, Poland, Yugoslavia, Albania, Czechoslovakia, Austria and China. None was given to the richer Benelux countries and France. In Germany aid was only given to refugees.
4. Immediately the war in Europe ended, **Lease lend** was abruptly terminated in Sept. 1945.
5. In most Occupied countries, the **Communist Party** emerged as the most popular party, after having been the most effective anti-fascist partisans. This threatened US hegemony in many places, especially in France, Italy and Greece; and later in China and south-east Asia.

The Immediate Aftermath of War

1. Despite joining the war against Japan, Stalin found himself excluded from virtually any input in the settlement of that country.
2. Nevertheless, during 1945-6 Stalin followed a policy of accommodation towards the USA. He believed that the capitalist powers would inevitably fall out among themselves, and that he need only wait to pick up the pieces afterwards.
3. The State Department Soviet expert "Mr. X" (George Kennan) argued that due to the peculiarities of their history, the Russians only understood force and could not co-operate with their neighbours. Early in 1946, he formulated the **containment** policy which Washington adopted. He saw Russia as

(i) a backward, barbarous society and the most brutal of the great powers;

(ii) whose rulers were chronically insecure;

(iii) which cut itself off from the outside world;

(iv) whose people preferred strong autocrats who made security their priority;

(v) whose leaders sought the total destruction of rival powers, rather than making compromises with them, and responded only to "the logic of force," never to reason.

The USSR was to be treated a an enemy power, not an ally.

The Nuclear War

1. The **nuclear arms race** began during the Second World War when the USA and Germany each began research to build an atomic bomb.
2. The U.S program, called the **Manhattan Project**, was successful. The first nuclear weapon was tested on the Alamogordo Bombing Range in New Mexico on July 16, 1945.
3. During 1945 the USA became the first and only country in the world to engage in **nuclear war** when the Americans dropped atomic bombs:
   (a) on Hiroshima (6th August, 1945) killing 80,000 people immediately, and injured another 100,000. Many died a lingering death. Others were to die later of the effects of radiation;
   (b) on Nagasaki (9th August, 1945) killing 60,000 almost immediately.
   The pretext for dropping the bomb was that it would save lives in the invasion of Japan which would have otherwise been necessary. Churchill claimed it would save a million American lives, Truman that it saved "millions of lives." But:
   (a) Japan was about to surrender.
      (i) Before the bomb was dropped, the US Joint Chiefs of Staff advised that it was highly likely that Japan could be forced to surrender unconditionally without either the use of the bomb or an invasion.
      (ii) Admiral Leahy said: "It is my opinion that the use of this barbarous weapon at Hiroshima and Nagasaki was of no material assistance in our war against Japan. The Japanese were already defeated and ready to surrender."
      (iii) The Unites States Strategic Bombing Survey reported that the Japanese would have surrendered without either an invasion or the atomic bomb.
      (iv) Despite his public statement above, Churchill is on record as expressing the belief that the entry of the Russians into the war would force Japanese capitulation.
      (v) General Marshall said on June 18th: "The impact of Russian entry on the already hopeless Japanese may well be the decisive action in levering them into capitulation."
      (vi) Eisenhower argued that the bomb was completely unnecessary" to save lives.
   (b) The entire force projected for the invasion of Japan was, in any case, considerably less than a million men (800,000).
   (c) A controlled explosion in open country, or in the sea off Tokyo harbour, would have served the purpose of informing the Japanese of US power just as well.
4. The US Strategic Bombing Survey said in its official report: "Hiroshima and Nagasaki were chosen as targets because of their concentration of activities and population." Yet military considerations were not primary in the use of the bomb, for Truman did not even ask the opinion of General MacArthur, his military commander in the region. Thus we must look elsewhere for the real reason for the use of the bomb.
5. It is clear that the explosion of the nuclear bombs over Hiroshima and Nagasaki were at least as much concerned with intimidating the USSR and the rest of the world as with bringing about the surrender of Japan. The main purposes were as follows:
   (a) Liddel-Hart argued that the purpose of the bombing was to bring the war to an end quickly before a Soviet invasion of Japan could take place and justify substantial Soviet claims to a share in the settlement of that country.
   (b) To intimidate* the Soviets with American power.
      (i) Even before the bomb was tested Truman said, in reference to the USSR, "If it explodes ... I'll have a hammer on those boys!"
      (ii) US Secretary of State James Byrnes explained that the atomic bomb would "make Russia more manageable."

(iii) Vannebar Bush, Chairman of the US National Defence Research Committee said it was: "so that there was no necessity for any concessions to Russia at the end of the war."

(c) To demonstrate US might before the entire world. Thus Truman stated that the bomb not only ended the war, it gave the world "a chance to face the facts" i.e. of American power.

(d) To justify the huge cost of the research programme: Admiral Leahy, the president's chief of staff, said: "I know F. D. R. would have used it in a minute to prove that he had not wasted $2 billion."

6. Only this can explain why:

(a) the US Government did not quickly take up Japan's attempts to negotiate a surrender;

(b) the US Government did not did not wait to see what the effect of a Soviet declaration of war would be on Japan.

7. In consequence of:

(a) US possession of nuclear weapons,

(b) the doubly demonstrated preparedness of the US government to use them:

Stalin was afraid of nuclear blackmail, or worse, from the west. President Gorbachev learned of this from older colleagues who had worked in the Kremlin under Stalin.

Summary of Causal Factors

There are many factors which can be cited as possible reasons for the deterioration of relationships between the USA and its allies and the USSR and its allies:

1. Because it was a communist state, the USSR was without allies before the war.
2. The USA, USSR and UK only became allies out of necessity.
3. The Western Allies had proved unreliable during the late 1930s, appeasing Hitler at every turn.
4. Mutual suspicions arose during the war e.g. The western delay in opening a second front in Europe, were held in check by the war. When the war ended they came out into the open.
5. With the destruction of Germany and Japan as Great Powers, and the serious weakening of Britain and France, the USA and USSR were left as rival super-powers. The victorious allied armies met face to face in Central Europe, making this obvious.
6. Roosevelt's policy of avoiding divisive issues during the war, while wise in the short run, enhanced the potential for conflict after the war.
7. Co-operation between the USA, which regarded its own form of government as the only one acceptable, and a totalitarian Soviet Union imbued with Marxist-Leninist ideology would be difficult, as they had rival ideologies.
8. After its experience of repeated invasions from the west, and in view of US nuclear power, Stalin felt the need for a glacis* in Eastern Europe. The manner in which Stalin established control over Eastern Europe, through the communist party and by means of election fraud, was portrayed in the West:

(a) as Soviet expansionism,

(b) as Communist world subversion and revolution.

9. Because of the very significant imbalance of power between the USA and USSR, the Soviets feared the dominance of US power and influence.
10. Soviet fear of US nuclear weapons was paramount. The US had used nuclear weapons on Japan. Stalin was afraid of nuclear blackmail or worse from the west.
11. The popularity of the Communist Party around the world, as the Communists had been the most effective partisans during the war, threatened US/British dominance in many countries, e.g. France, Italy, Greece, China and S. E. Asia.
12. The Soviet leadership may have felt its own position to be threatened by contact with the more

open societies of the West, and sought to demonize them to keep them at a distance.

13. The US leadership felt threatened by the more egalitarian* societies of the East, with their programmes for social justice, and sought to demonize them to prevent the US population demanding similar rights. Certainly Western European governments introduced massive social reforms as soon as possible, e.g. the British Welfare State.

14. Mutually hostile propaganda resumed immediately after the war.

Later Developments

1. The inability of the allies to work together in **Germany** after the war led to their breaking off practical co-operation.

2. The western sectors of **Berlin** constituted a threat to the security of Eastern Europe, from the Soviet viewpoint.

3. Soviet pressure on **Iran, Turkey and Greece** appeared aggressive.

4. The **CIA** was founded in 1947 to wage the Cold War behind the scenes.

5. The policy of "**containment**"* appeared to the Soviets to be an attempt to strangle the USSR.

6. The interpretation of all perceived threats from Communism anywhere in the world as part of a single master-plan organised from the Kremlin contributed to the growth of **paranoia** and anti-Communist hysteria in the USA whipped up by US propaganda.

7. The Soviets perceived the US **"open door" policy** and the **Marshall Plan** as an instrument of US economic imperialism.

8. Western leaders held the belief, or claimed to, that appeasement should on no account be followed again, resulting in an aggressive stance towards the USSR, e.g. in the **Truman Doctrine.**

9. The **US** set up **military bases** across the world, in the UK, Germany, Spain, Italy, Greece, Turkey, Pakistan, Iran, Okinawa, Taiwan, etc., establishing a worldwide military dominance.

10. The **Organisation of American States** (OAS) was founded as an alliance:
    (a) to assist in US control of the Americas;
    (b) to minimise future possible Soviet influence there.

11. The various m**isunderstandings** and **misinterpretations** resulting from these factors led to a vicious circle of increasing hostility, fear and paranoia.*

12. The **USSR** had a vast but damaged sphere of influence. It was under violent rhetorical attack from the much more powerful USA. In attempting to defend themselves, the Soviet leadership adopted a policy of "No compromise." Moscow would make no concessions, since it would not take much to turn the Soviet bloc into another client region of the US economy.

13. The requirements of elections in the **USA** led presidents and others to demonize and provoke the Soviets. Public hysteria was useful for US leaders because:
    (a) It made it easier for presidents to raise taxes from a people notoriously reluctant to pay them, to support the expenditure required for exercising hegemony abroad.
    (b) It enforced some national unity on a very diverse and fractured nation which lacks a genuine common culture.
    (c) It was electorally popular:
       (i) Apparently, US citizens *like* to have an enemy whom they can characterise as evil, it appears to place them on the side of the godly. This is probably due to the US tradition of Calvinism* and its belief in election: "We are special people, chosen by God."
       (ii) Strongly anti-Communist immigrants from Eastern Europe supported it.
       (iii) The arms race was profitable for the powerful military-industrial complex.*

Causal Analyses (Historiography)

1. In the West the **orthodox*** position was that the Cold War was caused by Stalin. This was supported by:

   (a) attributing expansionist motives to Soviet policies and actions, especially in Easter Europe;

   (b) ignoring US policies and actions which demonstrated equally or greater expansionist motives, or explaining them away as purely defensive.

2. During the Vietnam War many Western historians began to see the US and USSR as equally morally culpable empires. These **revisionist*** scholars argued that both sides were guilty of expansionist policies and actions, which generated justifiable mistrust in the other side. Both sides had conflicting political and economic interests. Both sides were therefore equally responsible. This sort of view always sounds fair, and people are inclined to adopt it for this reason alone, but it may not necessarily correspond with the facts.

3. During the later years of the Cold War, some post-revisionist historians, such as J. L. Gaddis, focused upon mutual misperceptions, and the reactions they generated. Thy argued that the cold war was brought about by mutual distrust. Thus post-revisionist historians also blame both of the superpowers.

4. A new view has arisen since the end of the Cold War has enabled a clearer assessment of the situation. This takes due note of the great imbalance of power between the USA and USSR in 1945. Erik Hobsbawm points out that: "On any rational assessment, the USSR presented no immediate danger to anyone outside the reach of the Red Army's occupation forces. It emerged from war in ruins, drained and exhausted, its peacetime economy in shreds, its government distrustful of a population, much of which, outside Great Russia, had shown a distinct and understandable lack of commitment to the regime." He:

   (a) attributes expansionist motives to US policies and actions;

   (b) explains Soviet policies and actions as largely defensive.

On this view, the USA was mainly responsible for the outbreak of the Cold War. This is strongly supported by an examination of US policies since the end of the Cold War.

Glossary

ACC: Allied Control Council, the governing body of Occupied Germany, comprising the four Commanders of each of the victorious Allied Forces in Germany

bipolar world: a world dominated by two superpowers

Calvinism: a narrow form of Protestantism which is characterised by a sense of self-righteousness among believers, who hold themselves to be "saved", and who tend to look down upon outsiders and are inclined to characterise them as evil.

containment: the policy of surrounding the Soviet Union and the rest of the Communist bloc with hostile alliances, US military bases and offensive nuclear weapons.

demobilization: the process of returning troops and industrial production to civilian life

egalitarian: equal

fait accompli: something already done

glacis: a buffer area under one's control lying beyond one's own frontiers, in which foreign invaders can be met and defeated before entering one's own territory

Grand Alliance: The alliance of the UK, USSR and USA against the Axis Powers.

intimidate: overawe, threaten

ipso facto: simply in virtue of that

machismo: manliness

Manichaean: a view of the world in which there are two opposing forces, ours which is good (naturally), and any forces which do not share our ideology or interests, which is evil.

military-industrial complex: those making a living from preparations for war: the military and the arms manufacturers, and those dependant upon them

orthodox: in different contexts, this means many things. Here it refers to historians who hold to a well-established and generally received view of a particular historical subject.

State Department: the US Foreign Ministry

revisionist: in different contexts, this means many things. Here it refers to historians who have departed from a generally received orthodox view of a particular historical subject.

rule of unanimity: everyone has to agree for a decision to be made

Bibliography

Alperovitz, Gar, *Atomic Diplomacy: Hiroshima and Potsdam: The Use of the Atomic Bomb and the American Confrontation with Soviet Power*, rev. ed., Pluto Press (London, 1985)

Douglas, Roy. *From War to Cold War, 1942-48*, St. Martin's Press (New York, 1981)

Gaddis, John Lewis, *The United States and the Origins of the Cold War, 1941–1947*, Columbia University Press (New York, 1972)

Kolko, Gabriel, *The Roots of American Foreign Policy: An Analysis of Power and Purpose*, Beacon Press (1969)

Maddox, Robert J., *The New Left and the Origins of the Cold War*, Princeton University Press (Princeton, 1973)

McCauley, Martin, *The Origins of the Cold War*, Seminar Studies in History, Longman (London & New York, 1995)

Paterson, Thomas G., *Cold War Critics: Alternatives to American Foreign Policy in the Truman Years*, Quadrangle Books (Chicago, 1971)

Sherwin, Martin J., *A World Destroyed: The Atomic Bomb and the Grand Alliance*, Alfred A. Knopf (New York, 1975)

The Origins of the Cold War, ed. Thomas G. Paterson, Heath (Lexington, MA, 1974)

The Specter: Original Essays on the Cold War and the Origins of McCarthyism, eds. Robert Griffith & Athan Theoharis, New Viewpoints (New York, 1974)

Thomas, Hugh, *Armed Truce: The Beginnings of the Cold War, 1945–46*, Hamish Hamilton (London, 1986)

Joseph Stalin

3. The Cold War 1945-1953

"It is part of the general pattern of misguided policy that our country is now geared to an arms economy which was bred in an artificially induced psychosis of war hysteria and nurtured upon an incessant propaganda of fear." (US General Douglas MacArthur)

The release of atom power has changed everything except our way of thinking... the solution to this problem lies in the heart of mankind. If only I had known, I should have become a watchmaker. (Albert Einstein)

Overview

1. Overt* US–Soviet hostility began in 1945 over:
   (a) the treatment of occupied Germany;
   (b) the future of Poland.
2. It grew during 1946 as:
   (a) Differences began to appear in their treatment of Germany.
   (b) The Sovietisation of Eastern Europe began.
   (c) The US began setting up military bases around the world to establish its world-wide military hegemony.*
   (d) The superpowers failed to agree on a plan for the control of atomic energy.
3. During 1947, both superpowers solidified their control over the areas over which they exercised control or influence:
   (a) The USSR in Eastern Europe with continued Sovietisation;
   (b) The USA in the rest of Europe with the Truman Doctrine and the Marshal Plan.
4. The Cold War reached its peak during 1948–53 with:
   (a) the Berlin blockade;
   (b) the formation of NATO;
   (c) the beginning of the nuclear confrontation;

(d) the victory of the Chinese Communists;

(e) the Korean War.

5. The perceived threats to each side from the other froze the provisional post-war division of Europe, and much of the world outside, into two rival blocs, institutionalizing the Cold War.

Developments

The Propaganda War

1. In March 1946, Churchill made his famous "Iron Curtain" speech at Fulton, Missouri, in the USA: "From Stettin in the Baltic to Trieste in the Adriatic, an iron curtain has descended across the continent. Behind that line lie all the capitals of the ancient states of central and Eastern Europe. Warsaw, Berlin, Prague, Vienna, Budapest, Belgrade, Bucharest and Sofia: all these famous cities and the populations around them lie in the Soviet sphere, and all are subject, in one form or another, not only to Soviet influence, but to a very high and increasing measure of control from Moscow. Athens alone, with its immortal glories, is free to decide its future at an election under British, American and French observation."

In reading this it should be noted that:

(a) The reason that the Red Army had occupied so much of Eastern Europe was that Churchill had himself persuaded the US to delay the opening of a Second Front in Europe as long as possible, so that the USSR and Germany could inflict as much damage on each other as possible, allowing the USA and UK to come in later and "pick up the pieces." Then they panicked that they had left it too late, and that the Red Army would occupy much of Eastern and central Europe.

(b) Churchill himself had secretly, in Moscow in 1944, explicitly recognised and accepted the *fait accompli*, that Soviet influence would dominate in many of those capitals by proposing the Percentages Agreement.

(c) At Yalta and Potsdam, he had himself been party to the agreement by which Berlin and Vienna would fall under Soviet control.

(d) He was deliberately exaggerating the situation, in including Belgrade within the Soviet sphere of influence.

Thus there is hardly a shred of truth in the words quoted above.

2. In response, Stalin called Churchill a "warmonger."

3. In May, in a deliberate counterpoint to Churchill's "Iron Curtain" speech, Molotov deplored the setting up of US military bases across the world.

4. In July, George Kennan, under the pseudonym "X," published an influential article on "The Sources of Soviet Conduct" and outlined the strategy of containment in the journal *Foreign Affairs*.

The Iranian Problem

1. Because Iran was a vital:

    (i) source of oil

    (ii) supply line to the USSR

    (iii) and the Shah was pro-German

the Soviets and the British occupied the country during the Second World War:

    (a) dividing it into three zones:

        (i) a northern zone under Soviet protection

        (ii) a central, neutral, autonomous zone around Teheran

(iii) a southern zone under British protection

    (b) forcing the shah* of Persia to abdicate* and go into exile

    (c) The occupation troops were to be withdrawn within six months of the end of the war.

2. In September 1944 the British set up the Anglo-Iranian Oil Company, which received the concession to operate most of the oilfields, which were partly owned by the British government. (American Standard Oil was associated with the deal).

3. The Soviets tried to obtain a similar deal, but it was blocked.

4. In March 1946, British troops withdrew.

5. In the northern provinces, the Soviets:

    (a) refused entry to Iranian troops,

    (b) encouraged a movement for local autonomy in the area near Azerbaijan, which set up an independent government,

    (c) insisted on the inclusion of members of the Tudeh party, which was friendly to them, in the Iranian Government,

    (d) again requested a deal to receive Iranian oil.

6. After the Iranians had taken the problem to the UN Security Council, Soviet forces left Iran.

7. When the Iranians moved their forces to attack the northern separatists, the USSR massed its own forces on the border.

8. The British moved troops to Basra, and the Soviets withdrew their forces.

9. The Iranians then suppressed the separatists.

The Turkish Problem

1. The Straits at Constantinople (Istanbul) are an important waterway which provides the sole access from the Black Sea into the Mediterranean for the Russian fleet. For that reason, the occupation ad garrisoning of the Straits had for centuries been a goal of Russian foreign policy. In 1936 the Straits had come under Turkish sovereignty.

2. The USSR wished to revert to an earlier situation, when they had been under international supervision. Stalin raised the issue during the wartime conferences, and Roosevelt and Churchill had agreed that his request was a reasonable one.

3. In March 1945 Stalin demanded the revision of the 1936 treaty.

4. Three months later he added requests for:

    (a) a Soviet naval base in the Dardanelles

    (b) The provinces of Kars, Ardahan and Artvin, which had been part of the Tsarist empire.

5. At Potsdam Stalin added that he might be satisfied with a naval base at Alexandroupolis, or perhaps Rhodes.

6. In summer 1946, the USSR delivered a strong note on control of the Straits to the Allies.

7. Truman sent an aircraft carrier to Istanbul as a threatening gesture.

8. Over time the matter was dropped.

The Baruch Plan

1. In 1946 the US offered the **Baruch Plan**, allegedly to preserve nuclear science for peaceful development in the future:

    (a) a UN authority would be set up to:

        (i) survey and control all uranium deposits,

        (ii) ensure that atomic research was conducted for peaceful purposes only.

    (b) The USA would then place all its nuclear weapons under the control of the UNO.

2. An alternative plan was presented by Andrey Gromyko, on behalf of the USSR. This called for:

(a) Immediate prohibition of all manufacture and use of atomic weapons.

(b) Measures to ensure compliance would be developed, but the Soviet refusal to allow immediate on-site inspection.

3. The USSR refused to accept the Baruch Plan as:

(a) the USA virtually controlled the UN at this time with the votes of its satellites.

(b) The United States was in effect asking all other countries to reveal the state of their own research *before* the USA gave up its own arsenal.

(c) The Soviets did not want UN officials (who would probably be US spies) freely searching about all over the territory of the USSR.

(d) US scientists already possessed the know-how to develop nuclear weapons. A ban on research would freeze this advantage, which could always be employed at a later date.

Stalin's Peace Moves

1. Stalin believed that the capitalist countries were, by their very nature, destined to quarrel with each other, and in the end destroy each other. Therefore there was no need for him to exert pressure on them, only to be patient. In September 1946, Stalin made a number of conciliatory moves. He:

(a) pulled Soviet troops out of N.E.China;

(b) pulled Soviet troops out of Iran;

(c) pulled Soviet troops out of Finland;

(d) surrendered Soviet trusteeship of Tripolitania (Libya);

(e) declared that cooperation between people of different ideologies should be possible.

2. The US Government chose not to reduce tension by responding to these moves.

The Finlandization of Finland

1. Finland was of great concern to the USSR:

(a) It was of geo-strategic* importance.

(b) It had been an ally of the Germans.

2. The Finns agreed to:

(a) Finnish neutrality in the Cold War, including membership of no alliances;

(b) a foreign policy which would not work against that of the USSR;

(c) the hosting of Soviet military bases;

in return for:

(d) Soviet non-interference in Finland's internal affairs.

3. This arrangement, known as **finlandization**, was repeatedly denigrated in western propaganda, so that the word became a synonym for a dishonourable form of nominal* independence and real subordination. Yet, with the exception of the right to neutrality, finlandization represented the reality of the relationship between the USA and many of its own "allies".

The Truman Doctrine

[For fuller treatment of the Greek Civil War, see Chapter 5, "Eastern Europe (1)"]

1. Civil war had broken out in Greece for a third time in 1946. A royalist government was fighting Communist-led insurgents. According to the Percentages Agreement drawn up by Churchill and Stalin in Moscow in 1944, the British were responsible for oversight of this country.

2. Due to the winter crisis of 1946-7, the British government shed foreign policy problems. This one was offered to the US, and Truman hastened to take over Britain's influence over Greece.

3. On 12th March the **Truman Doctrine** was announced, in lurid Manichaean terms.* In this manner, the US policy of **containment** was publicly revealed.

   "At the present moment in world history, nearly every nation must choose alternative ways of life. The choice is too often not a free one. One way of life is based upon the will of the majority, and is distinguished by free institutions, representative government, free elections, guarantees of individual liberty, freedom of speech and religion, and freedom from political oppression. The second way of life is based upon the will of a minority forcibly imposed upon the majority. It relies upon terror and oppression, a controlled press and radio, fixed elections, and the suppression of personal freedoms. I believe that it must be the policy of the United States to support free peoples who are resisting attempted subjugation by armed minorities or by outside pressures. I believe that we must assist free peoples to work out their own destinies in their own way."

   Greece was granted 250 million dollars, and Turkey 150 million. This was almost entirely for arms.
4. Stalin's deputy, A. A. Zhdanov commented: "The United States proclaimed a new, frankly predatory and expansionist course. The purpose of this new, frankly expansionist course is to establish the world supremacy of American imperialism."
5. At the same time, the US forced the coalition governments of France and Italy to dismiss all their Communist ministers.

The Marshall Plan

1. The US feared that the poverty, unemployment, and dislocation of the post-war period were reinforcing the appeal of communist parties to voters in western Europe.
2. On June 5, 1947, in an address at Harvard University, Secretary of State George C. Marshall advanced the idea of a European self-help program, to be financed by the United States. The US Congress authorised, and US Secretary of State, General George C. Marshall, launched, the **European Recovery Program (the Marshall Plan)** on 5th June 1947. This was a three year grant of food, fertilisers, raw materials, machinery and investment aid.
3. Aid was originally offered to almost all the European countries, including those under military occupation by the USSR.
4. Stalin did not reject the plan out of hand, but sent a delegation to Paris. When Soviet intelligence in London warned Stalin of Anglo-American discussions taking place on how to employ the plan against Soviet interests, the USSR withdrew from participation, and was soon followed by the other states of the Eastern bloc.
5. This left the following countries to participate in the plan: Austria, Belgium, Denmark, France, Greece, Iceland, Ireland, Italy, Luxembourg, The Netherlands, Norway, Portugal, Sweden, Switzerland, Turkey, the United Kingdom, and western Germany.
6. Under Paul G. Hoffman the **Economic Co-operation Administration (ECA)** distributed over the next four years some $13 billion worth of economic aid. Direct grants accounted for most of the aid, with the remainder in the form of loans. To co-ordinate the European participation, the Committee of European Economic Co-operation, and later the permanent Organisation for European Economic Co-operation (OEEC) were set up.
7. The Marshall Plan was very successful:

   (a) It helped to restore industrial and agricultural production. The western European countries experienced a rise in their gross national products (GNP) of 15% - 25%.

   (b) The plan contributed greatly to the rapid renewal of the Western European chemical, engineering, and steel industries.

      (c) It established financial stability;

      (d) and expanded trade.

8.   The motives behind the Marshall Plan were probably:

      (a) to remove economic distress, and so reduce the attractiveness of communism;

      (b) to bind western states economically, and therefore politically, to the USA;

      (c) to provide leverage (threat of withdrawal of aid) to consolidate US influence and dominance over the countries of Western Europe;

      (d) to pre-empt the rise of socialist and government controlled economic systems in Western Europe, whose benefits might appeal to the American people, and so threaten capitalism and the interests of the wealthy elite in the USA;

      (e) to generate markets for future US trade.

9.   Stalin's refusal to accept aid, and his denunciation of the Plan, ensured that there would be no economic co-operation between East and West, and separate economic development would take place. The **Molotov Plan** was set up by the USSR, supposedly provide aid for the countries of Eastern Europe.

10. On 5th October the European Communist parties were placed more firmly under Soviet control by the formation of the **Communist Information Bureau (Cominform)**.

11. On 25th January 1949 the **Council for Mutual Economic Assistance (Comecon)** was founded to integrate the economies of the Soviet bloc.

12. Zhdanov and Molotov accused the USA of:

      (a) seeking to isolate and strangle the USSR;

      (b) seeking to solve its economic problems by economic penetration of Western Europe, Japan and the colonies of the imperial powers,

      (c) seeking world domination.

The Secret War

1.   **The Central Intelligence Agency (CIA)** was created by the US National Security Act of 1947, effectively to:

      (a) conduct espionage;

      (b) conduct sabotage;

      (c) ensure the obedience of client governments;

      (d) maintain and spread US power throughout the world;

2.   Elections were interfered with to ensure the election of governments favourable to US policies.

Some Elections Subject to US Interference

Australia 1974-5; Bolivia 1966; Brazil 1962; Chile 1964-70; Dominican Republic 1962; Greece 1950-61; Guatemala 1963; Guyana 1953-64; Haiti 1987-8; Indonesia 1955; Italy 1948-70s; Jamaica 1976; Japan 1958-70s; Laos 1960; Lebanon 1950s; Nepal 1959; Nicaragua 1984,90; Panama 1984,89; Portugal 1974-5; Vietnam 1955.

---

e.g. When Italy seemed likely to elect a leftist government in the elections of 1948, pressure was put on the electorate:

      (a) by recruiting and paying former blackshirts from the Fascist Party, and collaborators with the Nazis, to intimidate the voters;

      (b) by making it clear that food aid would be cut off if the results were not what the US wanted.

(c) by bankrolling, or bribing, politicians and others:

"[In 1948] ...millions were delivered to Italian politicians . . The CIA's practice of purchasing elections and politicians with bags of cash was repeated in Italy -- and in many other countries -- for the next twenty-five years." (*Legacy of Ashes: The History of the CIA* by Tim Weiner (Doubleday, p. 27.)

3. In 1951, so-called "stay behind" units were set up across Western Europe. In the UK, France, Holland, Belgium, Italy, Spain, Portugal, Germany, Norway, Denmark, Austria, Greece and Turkey units of local military commanders whose primary loyalty lay with the Americans were secretly established. In some countries, they were directed by former officers of the *Werhmacht* and *SS*. Later they were associated with the NATO command. Officially, they were created to fight a guerilla war behind the lines in the event of an invasion by the Soviet Union. Unofficially, they existed to ensure the loyalty of Western governments to the USA. They:

(a) compiled blacklists of leftists.

(b) engaged in terrorist provocation: e.g. They infiltrated left wing organisations and carried out acts of terrorism, such as bombings and assassinations. These were usually blamed on the left, so as to create a backlash and prevent the rise of an elected Communist government.

(c) carried out coups: In Greece a military junta, took over the state in 1967, using a NATO plan supposedly designed to "prevent the country from falling into Communist hands".

[See Chapter 12 "The Junta of the Greek Colonels"]

(d) engaged in organised crime: The Belgian government investigated links between its own parastate network and a number of particularly deadly robberies of supermarkets in and near Brussels during the mid 1980's, in which twenty-eight people died. The investigations were mysteriously never completed.

(e) It is likely that many otherwise inexplicable incidents, such as the murder of Swedish prime minister Olaf Palme, were due to actions either by these "parastate" organisations or by the CIA directly.

The problem only clearly came to light in 1990. Since that time these organisations have been dissolved in some Western countries.

4. Hundreds of Russian and other Eastern Europeans in the West were organized, trained and equipped by the CIA, then sent back into Eastern Europe:

(a) to set up spy rings,

(b) to stir up armed political struggle,

(c) to carry out acts of assassination and sabotage, such as damaging arms factories and power plants, derailing trains, wrecking bridges, etc.

5. Soviet and other East European agents bribed and compromised Western politicians and trades union leaders.

6. Both sides engaged in a propaganda war:

(a) The USSR used *Radio Moscow* as its chief propaganda channel.

(b) The United States government funded *Radio Free Europe, Radio Liberty* and the *Voice of America* to broadcast US propaganda to the rest of the world.

The German Problem (1948-53) *[See Chapter 4, "The German Problem"]*

The Yugoslav Problem

[For fuller treatment of this subject, see Chapter 5, "Eastern Europe 1945-50"]

1. According to the **Percentages Agreement**, the share out of influence in Yugoslavia had been 50% for the USSR and 50% for the USA.

2. When the Germans evacuated the country, the Communist-led partisans under Joseph Broz Tito took over.
3. As a Communist leader Stalin expected Tito to conform to Soviet directives and incorporate his country into Soviet-dominated Eastern Europe, but Tito valued Yugoslav independence more than the Leninist dogma which required conformity to central directives.
4. Stalin orchestrated a **propaganda campaign** to unseat him, but refrained from even covert* direct action.
5. This campaign was unsuccessful.

The Fall of China to the Communists

[For fuller treatment of the Chinese Civil War, see the companion volume: "War and Warfare"]
1. After a break during the Sino-Japanese War, the Civil War broke out again in late 1946.
2. After some initial setbacks, the Peoples Liberation Army (PLA), with the support of the vast majority of the people, swept the nationalists of the Guomindang (GMD) out of mainland China. They took refuge on the island of Formosa (Taiwan).
3. On 1st October, the **People's Republic of China** officially came into existence.

The Korean War

[For fuller treatment, see Chapter 6, "The Korean War"]
1. On 25th June 1950 the Korean War began, when North Korea invaded the South.
2. The US assembled a UN force to recover the South.
3. In October, under US direction, UN forces crossed the 38th Parallel and invaded North Korea.
4. On 15th October the People's Republic of China intervened in the Korean War by sending thousands of "volunteers."
5. On 11th April, 1951 General MacArthur was dismissed for insubordination after he argued publicly against the policy of fighting a "limited war."
6. On 10th July inconclusive armistice talks began.
7. An armistice was finally signed at Panmunjom on July 27, 1953.

The Nuclear Arms Race

1. In the USA, contingency planning for the next war began immediately. Within ten weeks of the end of the Second World War, US joint chiefs of staff produced a plan to drop atomic bombs on twenty of the chief cities of the USSR.
2. In May 1948 the "Half Moon" war plan was drawn up. This projected an air offensive against the enemy "designed to exploit the destructive and psychological power of atomic weapons."
3. However, the US nuclear force was of only limited value at this time:
    (a) Even a nuclear attack, with the resources available at the time, could not have prevented the Soviet conventional army from overrunning Western Europe, if Stalin wished to do so.
    (b) The nuclear threat was of no use in cases of insurgency, civil war, or small-scale conflicts.
4. In September 1949, the US discovered the existence of the Soviet atom bomb.
5. At the end of that year the US began research to develop a much more powerful hydrogen bomb.
6. In January 1950 Claus Fuchs was accused of spying on the US nuclear programme for the USSR.
7. In 1952 The British exploded their first atomic bomb on Christmas Island.

8. On 1st Nov. 1952 the US exploded the first hydrogen bomb at Enewetak atoll in the Marshall Islands. At 65 tons, it was too heavy to be used as a weapon.
9. In March 1953 the US exploded a hydrogen bomb in the Pacific, which was small enough to be used as a weapon.
10. On 12 Aug. 1953 the Soviets exploded their first hydrogen bomb.
11. In that year Julius and Ethel Rosenberg were executed for passing on atomic secrets from the Americans to the Soviets.
12. Many scientists opposed this escalation of the nuclear arms race. The dispute polarized the political and scientific communities. The **Stockholm Appeal** (1950), initiated by a French physicist gathered petitions signed by over 250 million people. Similar movements organized marches and protests.
13. The formation of NATO faced Stalin with encirclement in Europe by a hostile line of capitalist states with US bases from Norway to Turkey from which a nuclear attack could be launched.

The US "Red Scare"

1. Anti-Communist paranoia* was carefully built up in the USA. A Manichaean* world view was encouraged, in which Communism was portrayed as "evil". Americans began to regard any form of sympathy with communism, or any form of socialism, or desire for social justice, as treasonous. The identification of social justice with Communism and Communism with evil suited the purposes of the capitalist élite.
2. Under J. Edgar Hoover, the **Federal Bureau of Investigation (FBI)** began to forego hunting organised crime and the Ku Klux Klan, in favour of seeking out alleged Communists and "un-American activities".
3. Members of the US Communist Party (CPUSA) were systematically harassed. Many leading members received long-term prison sentences for working for the Party. The CPUSA was in time destroyed as an effective political organisation.
4. A **Commission on Employee Loyalty** combed through the records of state employees looking for traces of communism.
5. The **Internal Security Act** (1950) restricted the rights of Communists to be employed at all in the USA.
6. The self-appointed "witchunter", **Senator Joseph McCarthy,** claimed that there were fifty-seven secret Communists working in the US State Department,* but failed to find any. In 1953 he was himself censured for conduct "contrary to senate traditions" when he made the mistake of attacking people in the powerful US Army.
7. Hollywood films provided a major stimulus to the Red Scare during this era. e.g. US secret service agencies financed a cartoon adaptation of George Orwell's *Animal Farm.*
8. Popular paranoia could reach a frenzy. e.g. In 1949, James Forrestal, Truman's Secretary of State for the Navy, committed suicide because he thought he saw the Communists "coming to get him," from his window in the hospital where he was being detained.
9. The document *NSC 68*, composed by Paul Nitze, stated the classical Manichaean* American view of the Cold War, as an apocalyptic struggle between good (the USA) and evil (the USSR).

Stalin's Position

1. The USSR had:
   (a) restricted itself to the areas of Soviet influence agreed in conference;
   (b) withdrawn from many other areas, e.g. NE. Iran, N.E. China, Finland;

(c) acquiesced in being barred from Japan;

(d) refrained from the chance of imposing puppet governments in Finland and Austria;

(e) accepted the declaration on liberated Europe;

(f) discouraged the Greek resistance;

(g) kept the French and Italian Communists operating within a democratic framework.

Despite this, he:

(h) found the USA, in concert with Britain and France, acting unilaterally in Germany;

(i) was confronted by a US government seeking to preserve and extend the US nuclear monopoly;

(j) was confronted by a US government which consistently overestimated Soviet military strength in order to gain popular support for an arms race;

(k) was confronted by a US government which augmented to its own resources those of industrial Germany and Japan;

(l) was confronted by a US government which had systematically sought to undermine Soviet control of Eastern Europe.

2. It is clear that Stalin then decided to adopt a similar tough stance when he realised that US intentions were going to remain hostile and expansionist.

Subsequently, in response to US pressure, Stalin adopted a more active policy. He:

(a) denounced the American drive to world domination;

(b) pulled the European communist parties under tighter control through Cominform;

(c) halted demobilisation;

(d) engineered a coup in Czechoslovakia;

(e) purged the nationalist communist leadership of Eastern Europe;

(f) blockaded Berlin.

3. Both sides engaged in the polarization of Europe

(a) The USA:

(i) falsified elections in Greece;

(ii) made preparations for military intervention in Italy in 1948, if the Communists won the election;

(iii) set up one-party systems in Italy and Japan:

In Italy under the Christian Democrats;

In Japan under the Liberal-democrats.

This led to institutionalizing the Communists in Italy and socialists in Japan as the main opposition party,

(iv) supported very corrupt regimes in many parts of the world because they were anti-Communist;

(v) set up NATO.

(b) The USSR:

(i) falsified elections in Eastern Europe;

(ii) sovietized* the Eastern European regimes;

(iii) sought to blockade Berlin.

(iv) set up the Warsaw Pact.

Glossary

abdicate: give up the throne

covert: secret, undercover

CPUSA: the Communist Party of the United States of America

demobilization: the process of returning troops and industrial production to civilian life

ipso facto: simply in virtue of that

Manichaean: a view of the world in which there are two opposing forces, ours which is good (naturally), and any forces which do not share our ideology or interests, which is evil.

nominal: in name only, not in reality

overt: open, not secret

paranoia: the irrational belief that one is surrounded by enemies, overt and covert

para-state: secret organisations supported by the most powerful in the country, which act beyond the confines of the law, in order to maintain the power of the elite groups and their US overlords.

Shah: Iranian (Persian) title for an emperor of that country

sovietize: making the institutions and the political and cultural life of a country conform to the pattern of those in the USSR

State Department: US Foreign ministry

Bibliography

Andrew, Christopher & Gordievsky, Oleg, *KGB: The Inside Story of its Foreign Operations from Lenin to Gorbachev, Hodder & Stoughton* (London, 1991)

Ashton, S. R., *The Politics of East-West Relations since 1945*, Macmillan (London, 1989)

Bernhard, Nancy E. *U.S. Television News and Cold War Propaganda, 1947-1960*, Cambridge University Press, (Cambridge & New York, 1999)

Blum, William, *Killing Hope: U.S. Military and CIA Interventions Since WWII,* Common Courage Press (Monrie ME., 1995)

Brown, Colin & Mooney, Peter J., *Cold War to Détente*, Studies in Modern History, Heinemann (London, 1984)

Calvocoressi, Peter, *World Politics since 1945, 4th ed.*, Longman (London, 1982)

Chomsky, Noam, *Terrorizing the Neighborhood: American Foreign Policy in the Post-Cold War Era,* Pressure Drop Press, (San Francisco, 1991)

Chomsky, Noam, *What Uncle Sam Really Wants,* Odonian Press, (Berkeley, CA., 1992)

Cold War Statesmen Confront the Bomb: Nuclear Diplomacy Since 1945, ed. J. L. Gaddis, Oxford University Press (Oxford & New York, 1999)

Cowie, L. W., *The Super Powers*, Nelson (London, 1971)

Fowkes, Ben, *The Rise and Fall of Communism in Eastern Europe*, 2nd ed Macmillan, (London, 1995)

Gaddis, J. L., *Russia, the Soviet Union and the United States*, 2nd ed. McGraw- Hill, (New York, 1990)

Gaddis, J. L., *Strategies of Containment: A Critical Appraisal of Post-War American National Security Policy*, Oxford University Press (Oxford & New York, 1982)

Gaddis, J. L., *The Long Peace: Inquiries into the History of the Cold War*, Oxford University Press, (Oxford & New York, 1987)

Hartley, L., *Superpower Relations Since 1945,* Unwin Hyman (London, 1987)

Heater, D., *The Cold War*, Oxford University Press (Oxford & New York, 1970)

Higgins, Hugh, *The Cold War, 2nd ed.,* Studies in Modern History, Heinemann (London, 1984)

Horowitz, David, *The Free World Colossus: A Critique of American Foreign Policy in the Cold War*, rev. ed. Hill & Wang (New York, 1971)

Knapp, W., *A History of War and Peace 1939-1965*, Oxford University Press (Oxford & New York, 1967)

Kraft, Joseph, *The Grand Design*, Harper & Bros., (New York, 1962)

La Feber, W., *America, Russia and the Cold War*, 7th ed., McGraw (New York, 1992)

Laquer, W. Z., *Europe Since Hitler, rev. ed.*, Penguin (London, 1982)

Lukacs, John A., *A History of the Cold War,* Anchor Books (Garden City NY., 1961)

Lucas, Scott. Freedom's War: The American Crusade Against the Soviet Union, New York University Press (New York, 1999)

Mazower, Mark, *Dark Continent*, Penguin (London, 1998)

McDougall, Walter A., *The Heavens and the Earth: A Political History of the Space Age* Basic (New York, 1985)

McGehee, Ralph W., *Deadly Deceits: My 25 years in the CIA,* Ocean Press (Melbourne, 2000)

Mitrovich, Gregory, *Undermining the Kremlin: America's Strategy to Subvert the Soviet Bloc,* Cornell Univ. Press (Ithaca, NY, 2000)

Nogee, J. L., & Donaldson, R. H., *Soviet Foreign Policy since World War II*, 4th ed. Pergamon, (New York, 1992)

Quester, George H., Nuclear Diplomacy: The First Twenty-five Years, Dunellen Co., (New York, 1970)

Rostow, W. W., *The Diffusion of Power: An Essay in Recent History* Macmillan (London & New York, 1972)

Sayer, J., *Superpower Rivalry*, Arnold (London, 1987)

Ulam, Adam Bruno, *The Rivals: America and Russia Since World War II*, Viking Press, (New York, 1971)

Walker, Martin, *The Cold War: And the Making of the Modern World,* (London, 1993)

Watson, Hugh Seton, *Neither War nor Peace,* Methuen (London, 1960)

Young, J. W., *Cold War Europe 1945-89: A Political History*, Edward Arnold, (London, 1991)

Zinn, Howard, *A People's History of the United States: 1492 — Present*, Harper Collins (New York, 2000)

Chancellor Konrad Adenauer

4. The German Problem

[Berlin is a] smouldering fuse that has been connected to a powder keg. Incidents arising here ... may, in an atmosphere of heated passions, , suspicions and mutual apprehensions, , cause a conflagration which will be difficult to extinguish." (Soviet Note on Berlin, 27th November, 1958)

The Occupation

1. Fighting in Berlin ended on May 2nd 1945. The Soviets occupied Berlin and began to set up a local government structure, placing Communists in key positions in the police, education, etc. This was organised by Communists, led by Walter Ulbricht, who had been retained in the Hotel Luxe in Moscow for this purpose.

2. Marshall Zhukov, Commander of Soviet forces in Germany, authorised four political parties:
   - (i) Communists (KPD),
   - (ii) Socialists (SPD),
   - (iii) Liberal Democrats (LDP)
   - (iv) Christian democrats (CDU).

3. The Americans arrived in the city on 1st July and authorised the same parties. They were followed by the other Western Allies.

4. Problems arose with Allied patrols straying into each others' sectors of Berlin. This did not matter between the Western Allies, but the Russians held straying soldiers for a while.

5. A policy of denazification was followed. Certificates of denazification had to be obtained to hold certain jobs. The leading Nazis faced trial at Nuremberg.

6. Refugees flooded into the Western Zones from:
   - (a) areas which had become part of the USSR or Poland,
   - (b) the Czech Sudetenland,
   - (c) the Soviet Zone of Germany.

7. The Soviets conscripted the Germans to forced labour. As had been agreed at Potsdam, they took reparations in the form of property, industrial plant, livestock and art treasures. They also demanded that reparations be taken from the other zones for the USSR. When the infrastructure was removed from western zones for this purpose, aid had to be given to prevent starvation by

the Western Allies. Thus the Western Allies found themselves indirectly subsidising the Soviet Union.

8. In Spring 1946, US General Cassius Clay arbitrarily stopped the handing over of reparations to the Russians, who protested in the Allied Control Council (ACC).

The Breakdown of Co-operation

The Sovietization of East Germany

1. The KPD performed disappointingly in the elections of winter 1945-6 in the Soviet zone.
2. The SPD was harassed, its leaders arrested, while rank and file members lost their jobs and ration cards. Their officers and workers were "spontaneously" attacked by "angry workers".
3. In Feb. 1946, Schumacher recommended the dissolution of all SPD organisations in the Soviet zone since their activities had been made impossible.
4. The eastern SPD leader, Otto Grotewohl, sought to save the party by co-operation with the communists. A merger was proposed between the KPD and SPD. Only 12% of Berlin's Social Democrats voted in favour, but in the Soviet zone the vote was carried. The **Socialist Unity**

Party (SED) was formed out of the union of the two, Its joint leaders were Otto Grotewohl of the SPD and Wilhelm Pieck of the KPD, but it was under communist control.

5. In the eastern zone elections of 1946 the bourgeois parties received half the vote but the leaders who were unwilling to follow the lead of the SED were forced to resign. The parties became independent only in name.

6. In Berlin the soviets also tried to unite the SPD and KPD. Instead the Berliners formed an anti-Soviet coalition which, in Oct. 1946, thwarted an attempt to get control of the new city administration for the Communists.

7. In 1947 Ernst Reuter, an anti-Russian ex-communist socialist, was elected as mayor.

8. The effect of the attempt to gain power through a united socialist party was used as a pretext by the western Allies to co-ordinate their policies without reference to the Soviets in breach of the Potsdam agreement.

The Birth of the Two Germanies

1. The Americans and British began to co-ordinate their economic policies in their zones without reference to the Soviets, and in Jan. 1947 these were merged into the single **BiZone.**

2. Two conferences of Foreign Ministers in Moscow in March and November 1947 failed to produce a peace treaty to deal with the German question.

3. The French were initially against any form of German re-unification, but they began to co-ordinate their policies with the British and Americans during summer 1947.

4. When the US decided arbitrarily to introduce a new currency in the Western zones,in breach of the Potsdam Agreement, which required unanimity in the Allied Control Council (ACC). The Soviet commander, Marshall Sokolovsky, walked out of the (ACC), so that it fell into abeyance. This marked the end of formal Allied co-operation in Germany.

5. The Americans and British introduced a second chamber into the Economic Council for the BiZone, as a means of transforming their zones into a parliamentary democracies.

6. In June 1948, the currency reform was introduced. Ten old *Reichmarks* were replaced by one new *Deutschmark*.

7. Price controls and rationing were ended.

8. At first prices rose and unemployment increased, but these stabilised, and gave way to full employment. Production rose by 50% in six months.

9. Denazification* was ended in the Western zones. Many ex-Nazis quickly returned to positions of responsibility in government, etc.

10. The Soviets had been offended by the independent actions of the US and its Allies in governing the economy of their zones without reference to the Soviets in the ACC.

11. The Western Allies were offended by the sovietization of the Eastern zone.

12. Both had found it impossible to co-operate in a detailed day-to-day fashion. Thus by 1947, East and West Germany were already set on different paths of development.

The Berlin Blockade

The Reasons for the Blockade

Stalin decided to move against the Western Allies in Berlin.

1. Stalin's attempt to take over the whole of Germany by stealth through the KPD and the SED had failed, due to the hostility of Germans to the Russians, brought about by:
    (a) Fear of reprisals because of the history of:
        (i) Nazi racist propaganda, which portrayed the Russians as sub-humans;

        (ii) awareness of the behaviour of German forces in the USSR during the war;

        (b) The behaviour of the Red Army during the first years of the occupation (numerous rapes of women);

        (c) Soviet insistence upon recovering reparations from Germany for war damage had been obstructed by the Americans.

2. Stalin was angered by the decision of the Western Allies to govern their zones in matters of the economy independently, instead of by unanimity in the ACC, as previously agreed at Potsdam. He was particularly angered by their decision to introduce a new currency in the western zones.

3. West Berlin had become an embarrassment to Stalin because:

        (a) It was a reason for soldiers of the Western Allies to travel through the Soviet Zone.

        (b) Due to the influx of Western aid, its well-being soon contrasted sharply with that of the Soviet Sector. This was the result of a deliberate policy of the Americans.

4. Thus he wished to get the Western Powers out of Berlin.

5. The cause he cited as justification for action was the violation of the Potsdam agreement by the USA over the unanimity rule in the ACC on matters of the German economy, particularly the introduction of a new currency.

6. The Western powers had never negotiated a pact with the USSR guaranteeing rights of access to Berlin, since the post-war division of Germany had been thought to have been a temporary measure..

7. Stalin did not wish to risk war by an attack. But by blockading access to the city, he could force the onus on to the Western Allies. They could either:

        (a) Force their way in and so appear aggressors and risk war, or

        (b) Allow the Berliners to be taken over by the Soviets as an alternative to starvation. This would be the likely outcome, as:

        (i) The leaders of the Western democracies would be unwilling to initiate war,

        (ii) particularly for the Berliners, who were so recently "the enemy".

The First Berlin Crisis

1. The expected Peace Conference which was to settle the fate of a united Germany did not materialise. The continued access of the Western Allies Western sectors of Berlin was along routes under ill-defined conditions.

2. In March 1948 the Soviets began to harass Allied communications between their zones of Germany and their sectors of Berlin. They demanded to inspect passes, even on trains. A train full of US soldiers which refused access to the inspectors was shunted into a sidings until they got hungry and withdrew.

3. On 24th June, all road, rail and canal links between the Western zones of Germany and the Western sectors of Berlin were closed.

4. At the same time, the Western sectors of Berlin were cut off from the city power grid, depriving the inhabitants of industrial and domestic electricity.

The Berlin Airlift

1. The Western Allies claimed that appeasement of Stalin over Berlin would lead to his attacking West Germany, but:

        (a) the French refused to agree to the use of force;

        (b) The 6,000 western troops in Berlin, surrounded by Soviet troops, were effectively hostages.

2. It was decided to supply West Berlin indefinitely by air using the air corridors* from the Western zones of Germany to Berlin. This would place the onus of starting a war upon Stalin if he chose to have Western planes shot down.
3. Over 10 months, two million tons of supplies were flown into Berlin, keeping 2.5 million West Berliners fed and supplied throughout the winter.
4. There were many accidents, with 79 pilots and groundsmen killed.
5. From summer 1948 the Allies imposed a counter-blockade of goods going from the Western zones to the Eastern zone. This was very damaging to the economy of the East.
6. Part of the US long-range bomber force was moved to England.
7. In May 1949 the Soviets admitted defeat by lifting the blockade.
8. The Western Allies then lifted their counter-blockade.

The Consequences of the Berlin Blockade and Airlift

1. It was a psychological blow for the USSR, which had brought pressure upon the Western Allies which had in turn called Stalin's bluff.
2. The USSR could hardly pose as champion of the workers when they had tried to starve 2.5 million Berliners. It did not harmonise well with Marxist doctrine.
3. It made the West Germans and West Berliners firmly anti-Communist and pro-western, if they had not been already.
4. It was used by the US Government to justify the reversal of the post-war decline in US defence budgets, and to trigger a new arms race between the USA and USSR.
5. It gave a pretext for the USA to construct a strong European alliance directed against the USSR. In March 1948 Britain, France Belgium Holland and Luxembourg had signed the **Brussels Defence Treaty,** by which they would link their defences in case of war. But this had been directed against a future reunified Germany. In May 1949 they were joined by the USA, Canada, Portugal, Denmark, Ireland and Italy in forming the **North Atlantic Treaty Organisation (NATO)**. The Americans pledged themselves in advance to military action if any of the NATO countries was invaded. A joint NATO command structure was created to co-ordinate the defence of the West.
NATO was to become a major instrument whereby the USA would exercise control over the other countries in the "alliance".
6. It further provided a pretext for the permanent Western appropriation of Western Germany.
(a) In September 1948 a **German Parliamentary Council** was convened in Bonn, representing all the districts of the zones of the Western Allies. Konrad Adenauer was elected its president.
(b) In May 1949, the Council agreed on a constitution.
(c) In August 1949, the Western Allies created the **Federal Republic of Germany (FDR)** or "West Germany", under Allied control. Elections were held, and Konrad Adenauer of the CDU became the first Chancellor. This government of West Germany claimed to be the legitimate government of the entire country.
7. The Soviets responded by setting up the **Peoples' Republic of Germany (DDR)** or "East Germany", in Oct. 1949 in the Soviet Zone.
8. Thus Germany was officially divided. Along the 800 miles of frontier, the East German authorities began to erect barriers to movement.
9. In June 1950 West Germany began contributing to the West's military strategy.
10. In 1951, the three Western Allies formally ended the state of war with Germany.
11. In 1952 the Soviets proposed a plan for the **reunification** of Germany:

(a) All occupying forces to be withdrawn one year after the signing of the treaty.

(b) A guarantee of all civic and religious rights to all German citizens.

(c) Germany could maintain forces necessary for her own defence.

(d) All organisations and parties hostile to democracy e.g. neo-Nazi parties, would be banned.

(e) Germany would not be allowed to join any alliance directed against any state which had fought against her in the Second World War.

(f) The new government would be a coalition of the two existing governments.

The West turned the plan down.

13. The division of Germany worsened East-West relations.

Glossary

air corridors: recognised flight paths

Bizone: the joint Anglo-American zone of Germany created by merging the American and British zones

Chancellor: the German Prime Minister

CDU: Christian Democrat Union

DDR: Peoples' Republic of Germany (East Germany)

denazification: the process of screening applicants for sensitive jobs to exclude and punish former Nazis

FDR: Federal Republic of Germany (West Germany)

Federal Republic of Germany (FDR): West Germany

Kommandatura: the Commanders of Allied Forces in Berlin

KPD: German Communist Party

LDP: Liberal Democratic Party

NATO: North Atlantic Treaty Organisation

North Atlantic Treaty Organisation (NATO): Western (US dominated) anti-Soviet alliance

Peoples' Republic of Germany (DDR): East Germany

plebiscite: a vote on a particular subject

sectors: the post-war divisions of Berlin

SED: Socialist Unity Party

zones: the post-war divisions of Germany

Bibliography

Grosser, A., *Germany in Our Time: A Political History of the Post-War Years,* Praeger (New York, 1971)

McCauley, Martin, *The German Democratic Republic since 1945*, Studies in Russia and East Europe, Macmillan (London, 1983)

Vyachyslav Molotov

5. Eastern Europe 1945-50

"On our part we should recognize that we have no more business in the political affairs of Eastern Europe than Russia has in the political affairs of Latin America, Western Europe or the United States... Whether we like it or not, the Russians will try to socialize their sphere of influence just as we try to democratize our sphere of influence. The Russians have no more business stirring up our native Communists to political activity in Western Europe, Latin America or the United States than we have in interfering with the politics of Eastern Europe and Russia." (Henry A. Wallace, US Secretary of Commerce in the Madison Square Gardens speech of September 1946, which led to his dismissal by President Truman)

The Percentages Agreement

1. In October 1944, Churchill visited Stalin in Moscow.

    The moment was apt for business, so I said [to Stalin], "Let us settle about our affairs in the Balkans. Your armies are in Roumania and Bulgaria. We have interests, missions, and agents there. Don't let us get at cross-purposes in small ways. So far as Britain and Russia are concerned, how would it do for you to have ninety percent predominance in Roumania, for us to have ninety per cent of the say in Greece, and go fifty-fifty about Yugoslavia?" While this was being translated I wrote out on a half-sheet of paper:

    > Rumania: Russia 90%, The others 10%;
    > Greece: Great Britain (in accord with USA) 90%, Russia 10%;
    > Yugoslavia: 50-50%;
    > Hungary: 50-50%;
    > Bulgaria: Russia 75%, The others 25%.

    I pushed this across to Stalin, who had by then heard the translation. There was a slight pause. Then he took his blue pencil and made a large tick upon it, and passed it back to us. It was all settled in no more time than it takes to set down … After this there was a long silence. The pencilled paper lay in the centre of the table. At length I said, "Might it not be thought rather cynical if it seemed we had disposed of these issues, so fateful to millions of people, in such an offhand manner? Let us burn the paper". "No, you keep it", Stalin said. (Churchill, W. S., *History of the Second World War,* v.6 *Triumph and Tragedy).*

Eastern Europe in 1945

2. In a message to London on October 12th, Churchill claimed that the arrangement "is not intended to be more than a guide ... nor does it attempt to set up a rigid system of spheres of influence ..." In his memoirs, he said: "of course we were only dealing with immediate war-time arrangements."

3. The percentages for Hungary were later modified after the Red Army occupied the country.
4. Churchill did not publicly reveal the affair until he was out of office and published his memoirs, when again he claimed: "It is absolutely necessary that we should try to get a common mind about the Balkans ... nothing will be settled except preliminary agreements between Britain and Russia, subject to further discussion and melting down with [Roosevelt]."
5. Despite Churchill's protestations, the Percentages Agreement became the basis for the division of the Balkans into spheres of influence after the war, perhaps by default.

The Greek Civil War

Background

1. Before the outbreak of war, Greece had been governed by a dictator, Ioannis Metaxas, installed by King George II. He had arrested, tortured, imprisoned in island camps thousands of those associated with left-wing parties or critical of the monarchy or dictatorship.
2. National unity had been restored only after the Italian invasion.
3. After the German invasion, Greek political forces divided into three:
    (a) Collaborators with the Axis Powers in Greece;
    (b) A Government in exile (in London, then Cairo);
    (c) The Resistance in Greece:
        (i) ELAS, related to EAM and dominated by the KKE;
        (ii) EDES, largely based in Epirus.
4. In June 1943, ELAS proposed the creation of a unified resistance, EDES refused.
5. In July 1943, the republicans demanded that the king agree to return to Greece only in the event of gaining majority support in a plebiscite. He refused to agree.
6. In August resistance leaders arrived in Cairo, and demanded
    (a) key posts in the government;
    (b) the King's commitment to refrain from entering Greece unless and until a referendum had voted in his favour.
    The Resistance delegates went back to Greece with their demands unfulfilled.

The First Stage of the War

1. During October-February 1943-4 ELAS sought to monopolise resistance. EDES attempted to establish groups in areas under ELAS control, and fighting broke out between them.
2. In March 1944 a Political Committee of National Liberation (PEEA) was founded as a government of Free Greece in the mountains. It was dominated by the Communists.
3. In April 1944 there was a mutiny by Greek forces in Middle East:
    (a) in protest at the King's refusal to rule out entering Greece before a plebiscite,
    (b) to force the Government-in-exile to deal with PEEA.
    After several weeks, the mutiny was crushed. Prime Minister George Papandreou replaced republican officers with royalists.
4. A Greek government in exile, headed by George Papandreou, held a conference in the Lebanon to form a government of national unity. Representatives of PEEA, EAM, ELAS and the KKE all attended.
    (a) EAM agreed to disarm ELAS, integrating it into a regular national army.
    (b) The main Centre and Left parties insisted that King George must not enter Greece until a plebiscite had been held. The king reluctantly agreed.
    (c) PEEA demanded:

     (i) fascists and ultranationalists be removed from the national army;

     (ii) there must be an amnesty for the mutineers;

     (iii) seven of fifteen cabinet positions were to go to PEEA representatives.

     Papandreou rejected those demands, deferring to British hegemony.

5. During 1944, low intensity fighting broke out in Athens and elsewhere between ELAS and the collaborationiist Security Battalions in advance of the German evacuation.

6. When the German Army left Greece, British forces under General Scobie arrived, together with the Greek government-in-exile, headed by George Papandreou.

7. In November, EAM demanded disarmament of collaborationist Security Brigades. Papandreou agreed, and then reversed his decision.

8. When General Scobie ordered the disbanding of partisan groups the EAM ministers refused on behalf of ELAS and left the government.

The Second Stage of the Civil War

1. Fighting broke out in Athens on 3rd Dec. 1944, when a Communist-organised demonstration was fired upon. ELAS forces occupied police stations.

2. Churchill and Eden arrived in Athens on Christmas Day and held an all-party conference under the chairmanship of Archbishop Damaskinos. Damaskinos became Regent,* while General Plastiras became prime minister. It was agreed finally that the monarchy would not be restored until after a plebiscite.

3. A truce followed with a peace settlement at the Varkiza Conference.

     (a) ELAS agreed to surrender its weapons.

     (b) The Greek government promised to control right-wing extremists.

4. Aris Veloukhiotis and some other ELAS partisans refused to accept the peace, and died fighting in the hills.

5. A period of disorder followed during which several governments took office, inflation soared out of control.

6. There took place a "White Terror" with 80,000 arrests, overwhelmingly of EAM and ELAS supporters. Far-right gangs established a parastate, or shadow state, which used state organs to terrorize the population. There were mass arrests, deportations and executions of left-wingers.

7. Despite Soviet advice to the contrary, the KKE boycotted general elections in March 1946. Constantine Tsaldaris became prime minister.

8. He held a plebiscite* on the monarchy, which very surprisingly, considering the overwhelming opposition to the monarchy in most parts of the country, resulted in a victory for the monarchists, after which King George II returned to Greece.

The Third Stage of the Civil War

1. Leftists fleeing the White Terror in the cities and in some rural regions, regrouped in the mountains. There the KKE formed the 'Democratic Army'.

2. Fighting broke out in northern Greece in May and in the Peloponnese (southern mainland Greece) in November 1946. The British supported the Government and right-wing irregular forces. This Civil War was seen by the partians as a continuation of their struggle against the foreign Occupation of their country.

3. In December Greek Prime Minister Tsaldaris complained to the UN of interference from the communist countries to the north (Albania, Yugoslavia and Bulgaria). He claimed that they were supplying the rebels and offering them refuge from security forces.

The Truman Doctrine

1. During winter 1947 the British faced great hardships in what was the hardest winter of the century. The British Government decided to withdraw from her commitments in India, Palestine and Greece, and on 21st Feb. 1947 signalled its decision to the US Government..
2. The USA rushed to replace the British as the hegemonic power in Grece. On 12th March Truman issued the **Truman Doctrine**.
3. The US granted aid to Greece and Turkey totalling $250,000,000 and $150,000,000 respectively. Most of it was spent on infrastructure repairs of military use and weapons.
4. The Americans took over oversight of the war from the British. They supplied the Royalist Air Force with napalm with which to bomb the Democratic Army.

The Final Stage of the Civil War

1. The US sponsored state persecution of the left:
    (a) Leftist newspapers were suppressed;
    (b) The right to strike was abolished;
    (c) Leftist trade union leaders were forcibly replaced;
    (d) There was a purge of government employees suspected of leftist sympathies.
2. Many villagers were forcibly resettled in Athens and other big cities in order to place them under more efficient police supervision.
3. CBS correspondent George Polk, a critic of the Greek government was found murdered in the sea off Thessaloniki. His death presented a public relations problem. The Greek Government, with the cooperation of the US government and US media, pinned the killing on the Communists Several were forced to "confess" that it had been done it to "discredit" the Greek rebels. A stalinist-style show trial was held. The *New York Times* reporter in Greece, A. C. Sedgwick, who had married into the Greek royal family, described the trial as "honestly and fairly conducted". Later it became clear that the whole thing had been set up to discredit the communists.
4. In Jan 1949 the Democratic Army began to collapse.
5. After his quarrel with Stalin, Tito closed his frontier to the Greek communists.
6. In 1952, Greece became part of NATO.

The Significance of the Greek Civil War

1. Greece became the first proxy* battleground of the Cold War.
2. It was an indication of how what was originally a local dispute (between the partisand fighting the German Occupation and the right-wing collborationists) could get tangled up with super-power politics.
3. Stalin's non-intervention and failure to aid the rebels signalled his preparedness to stand by the Percentages Agreement.
4. Many aspects of US control of Greece during the Civil War and afterwards directly parallel the Sovietization,* under Stalin, of the Eastern European satellite states.
    (a) The subversion of the desire of most of the Greeks for genuine independence by falsified elections and plebiscites;
    (b) The systematic repression of opposition using:
        (i) police supervision,
        (ii) enforced loyalty declarations,
        (iii) torture,
        (iii) a network of prison camps.

The Sovietization* of Eastern Europe

The General Pattern

The incorporation of the countries of Eastern Europe into the Soviet sphere of influence followed a single general pattern, with minor local variations:

1. The **Red Army** would establish military control.
2. Local armies and police forces were reconstituted under soviet control.
3. In many areas, local German populations were expelled,
    (a) partly by popular action, taking revenge for German wartime atrocities;
    (b) partly due to the authorities' wish to see ethnic cleansing take place, so as to prevent the "minority problems" which had been used in the pre-war years to justify German aggression.
4. A process of "denazification" was instituted to detect and punish prominent Nazis or Nazi collaborators. However, "class enemies" were also purged, in what became in each country a social revolution.
5. Communists loyal to Stalin, nationals who had taken refuge in the USSR during the war, were imported from Moscow to lead local communist parties. These parties were usually very small, except in Czechoslovakia, as they had:
    (a) usually been persecuted by the right-wing inter-war regimes,
    (b) lost members during Stalin's purges.
6. Membership of Communist parties quickly grew, due to:
    (a) the prestige acquired by Stalin and the Red Army during the war;
    (b) continuing fear of German power;
    (c) the desire among many for revolutionary change among a profoundly radicalized population;
    (d) the patronage they could exercise over vacated properties of expelled Germans;
    (e) general opportunism* and the tendency of some people always to support the most powerful authorities.
7. Left wing parties were a majority everywhere after the war as a reaction from Nazism. They were pressured to join the Communist parties in "**Popular Fronts**."
8. These, being a majority, would form the **provisional government** of the country. Although the Communists would be a minority in the provisional governments, they would dominate them:
    (a) because of the prestige of the Communists and the USSR;
    (b) by taking key posts in the government, such as Minister of Defence, Minister of the Interior and Minister of Justice;
    (c) because land reform was popular.
9. These Popular Front governments would organise future elections.
10. The elections would be held under circumstances which ensured a victory for the communist led popular fronts, e.g. by intimidation of the opposition and vote rigging.
11. Communist ministers frequently became popular because of their efficiency in reconstruction, e.g. "Gerö the bridge-builder," the Hungarian Minister of Transport, who quickly reconstructed the bridges over the Danube.
12. In time, the coalition parties would become independent only in name. Genuine opposition parties would be suppressed.

13. The economies of the satellite states would be incorporated into the Eastern bloc.

In Jan. 1949 the Council for Mutual Economic Assistance (Comecon) was set up as a Soviet-dominated common market to co-ordinate economic policies. It supervised the integration of national economies with those of the USSR to the benefit of the USSR:

(a) Soviet raw materials had to be purchased at well above world market prices;

(b) Peoples' democracies sold their goods to the USSR at well below world market prices.

The satellites were not allowed to make independent arrangements with each other.

14. The countries would undergo political and cultural "**sovietization**";

(a) the local military and police would be infiltrated by Soviet Military Intelligence (GRU).

(b) education and culture would be remodelled on the soviet pattern.

(c) censorship would be imposed.

Note that sovietization was not Russification.

15. The countries of Eastern Europe were not simply incorporated into the USSR, probably because:

(a) If fully absorbed these areas would cease to be a buffer-zone.

(b) Stalin was naturally a cautions man. If, like the Americans, he could get the substance of empire without the title, and without alienating the West entirely, he was content to do that.

(c) The war-ravaged USSR could not absorb the new territories.

(d) Many of the states of Eastern Europe were accustomed to a much higher standard of living than the USSR. If absorbed, they would lose this, and so might become difficult to control.

(e) Stalin was imitating the American policy of "disguised control" of satellites employed so successfully in Latin America.

Poland

1. Since they were unequal neighbours, the USSR and Poland generally had bad relations with each other. The Russians had three times participated in the partition of Poland, and had ruled over most of it for several centuries. The Poles had unsuccessfully invaded Russia immediately following independence.

2. In negotiations with the Allies during the War, Stalin insisted on keeping Eastern Poland, seized by the Soviets in 1939.

3. During the War, the Germans uncovered the bodies of some 14,000 Polish officers who had been prisoners of the Russians and who had been executed in the forest of Katyn in 1940. Stalin denied responsibility and blamed the Germans. The Soviet government cut off relations with the Polish government in exile in London.

4. During July 1944, the Red Army halted its advance to allow the Germans to massacre the Polish resistance, which had risen against them in Warsaw.

5. In view of their traditional enmity, Stalin insisted that he wanted a friendly government in Poland after the war. Two rival governments-in-exile emerged, the London Poles and the Lublin Poles. The latter were Communists held by Stalin in Moscow. After the liberation, Stalin installed the Lublin Poles in Warsaw as a government.

6. At Yalta it was determined that:

(a) The new Eastern frontier of Poland should be the Curzon Line, meeting Stalin's demand.

(b) No agreement could be reached about the western border. A decision was postponed.

(c) The Polish Government was to be enlarged, and free elections held. The West interpreted this to mean a democratic Poland, while Stalin held it to mean that a few non-communists would be allowed into the Polish Government.

7. Marshall Zhukov invited sixteen leaders of the Polish Home Army to Moscow to discuss co-operation against Germany. While there, they were arrested for sabotage.
8. At Potsdam Stalin got his way over the western boundary of Poland, effectively moving the border of the country westwards, leading to the flight and expulsion of millions of Germans.
9. The Communist Boleslaw Bierut was made President, with a cabinet almost entirely of Communists. As a sop to the West, the head of the London Poles, Stanislaw Mikolayczyk became deputy prime minister.
10. The elections held in January 1947 were accompanied by various abuses. Afterwards Mikolayczyk fled to the West and denounced the elections.
11. His Peasants' Party was merged with others under the leadership of Communist Party first secretary Wladislaw Gomulka.
12. The dispute over Poland was the most bitter between the Allies during the last year of the war.

Hungary

1. Hungary was treated by the invading Red Army as a defeated enemy.
2. Its fate had been an issue in the Percentages Agreement concluded by Churchill and Stalin in Moscow in 1944. At that time it was to be 50% under the influence of the USSR and 50% under the USA. Later, it was accepted that it would fall within the Soviet sphere of influence.
3. A coalition government was formed led by the Smallholders party. Zoltan Tildy was president and Ferenc Nagy prime minister.
4. In Jan. 1946 the monarchy was officially abolished, thirty years after the King had left.
5. During winter 1946-7 rumours were circulated of a plot against the state by the Smallholders. The Secretary-General of the Smallholders Party, Bela Kovacs, was abducted by the Russians.
6. In May 1947 the prime minister, Ferenc Nagy went to Switzerland to see a medical specialist. While away he was asked to resign; his family in Hungary being used as hostages.
7. Rigged elections were held in August 1947. Leaders of non-communist parties fled, and their parties were incorporated into a communist led coalition, the National Independence Front.

Rumania

1. Rumania was a defeated enemy.
2. Its fate had been settled by Churchill and Stalin in the **Percentages Agreement** (1944). It was to fall within the Soviet sphere of influence.
3. In 1947, Peasant party leader Ion Maniu was accused of being an agent of the US and Britain. He and other leaders were arrested.
4. The King went on strike, refusing to sign parliamentary bills into law, and then abdicated.
5. In February 1948 the Peasant party was merged with the communists.
6. The coalition of parties won rigged elections.

Bulgaria

1. Bulgaria had been an enemy, but was treated as a liberated ally.
2. Its fate had been settled by Churchill and Stalin in the **Percentages Agreement** (1944). It was to fall within the Soviet sphere of influence.
3. In June 1947 the leader of the Agrarian Party, Nicola Petkov, was arrested.
4. The Agrarian Party was merged with the Communists in the Fatherland Front.
5. During 1948, the coalition won rigged elections.

Czechoslovakia

1. The most industrially advanced and culturally westernised part of Soviet-occupied Eastern Europe, the Communist Party already had a mass following of workers and students.
2. Czechoslovakia was a liberated ally.
3. Edward Benes returned as president. The prime minister, Klement Gottwald, presided over a coalition of many parties.
4. In Feb. 1948, the communist Minister of the Interior, Vaclav Nosek, replaced the eight police commissioners in Prague with communists. The cabinet voted to reverse this, but the minister refused to agree and the prime minister supported him. The non-communist members of the cabinet all resigned in protest.
5. Anti-Communist demonstrations took place in Prague.
6. Two ministers, including Foreign Minister Jan Masaryk, son of the first president of the country, died after falling through windows. (Defenestration* had been a custom in medieval Bohemia).
7. In June president Benes resigned, and was replaced by Gottwald.
8. The political parties were merged into a single communist dominated National Front.
9. When Benes died later that year, the silent funeral procession attended by millions was a last protest at the suppression of the democracy.
10. Because of the failure of appeasement to save Czechoslovakia from Hitler, public opinion was very much affected by the events in Czechoslovakia.

Significance

1. Stalin was securing:
    (a) compensation for the suffering of the Russians during the war;
    (b) the prize for the Red Army's winning of the war;
    (c) a glacis* against further aggression from the West;
    (d) a buffer zone against the spread of US economic and military dominance.
2. The model for the establishment of Soviet influence in eastern Europe was not the seizure of power by a Leninist elite, but the gradual coming-together of progressive forces in a coalition of parliamentary parties.
3. In the manipulation of elections and the suppression of opposition in order to maintain their spheres of influence, both the USSR (from Poland to Bulgaria) and the British and Americans (in Greece) behaved absolutely identically.
4. In Western propaganda, the manner in which the communists took control, in defiance of promises of free elections and democracy, was used to create revulsion in Western Europe.
    Western propaganda portrayed the process as:
    (a) an ominous extension of the reach an aggressive Soviet superpower, which threatened its neighbours in Western Europe;
    (b) a threatening extension of Communism with its ambitions of spreading world-wide revolution (even though this ambition had been long been dropped in the USSR with the fall of Trotsky).
    For historical reasons, much was made of the treatment of Poland and Czechoslovakia:
        (i) Czechoslovakia had been surrendered to Nazi totalitarianism without a fight at Munich, and remained a potent symbol of appeasement;
        (ii) Poland had been the ostensible* reason for the Allies going to war in 1939.
5. Historians differ as to whether the pattern of sovietization, set out above, was the result of:
    (a) a deliberate plot hatched by Stalin to take over Eastern Europe by stealth,

    (b) a much less planned process.
6. Hugh Seton Watson saw a threefold pattern:
    (a) a genuine coalition;
    (b) a bogus coalition;
    (c) a monolithic* regime.
7. Mark Mazower notes that:
    (a) Many of the coalitions were genuine, and hardly Communist dominated, for some time, e.g. Hungary and Czechoslovakia.
    (b) The only states in which the Communists seized power, or tried to seize power, were those in which the Red Army was **not** in control: Yugoslavia, Albania and Greece!
    (c) In Finland, Stalin was content to allow autonomy.
    (d) Many countries had:
        (i) no tradition of democracy, only of pre-war authoritarian governments;
        (ii) educated elites tainted with collaboration (or wiped out in the case of Poland).
    (e) The bourgeois of Soviet occupied Eastern Europe nourished hopes of a Third World War, when they would be "liberated" - hopes which only faded in 1956 with the crushing of the Hungarian uprising.
8. It is clear that the principle of spheres of influence had been accepted by both sides, as early as the Percentages Agreement, and that Western "astonishment" at Soviet domination of the East was disingenuous,* to say the least.

The Yugoslav Crisis

1. Yugoslavia was not occupied by the Red Army. When the Germans withdrew the communist partisans led by Joseph Broz Tito took over the country. Tito had great prestige as a guerrilla leader against the Italians and Germans.
2. Tito wished to form a South Slav Federation with Bulgaria and a Balkan Customs Union.
3. There were problems between the USSR and Yugoslavia:
    (a) Soviet advisers in Yugoslavia behaved in an arrogant manner, like an imperial power in a colony, and they were better paid than the Yugoslavs. This was resented by the Yugoslavs.
    (b) Stalin offered Yugoslavia no support in its claim upon Trieste.
4. Stalin wished to gain control over Yugoslavia, but was restrained by the terms of the Percentages agreement. He tried to put pressure on Tito to conform by correspondence and propaganda during March-May 1948.
    (a) He complained of Yugoslavia's laxity in eliminating capitalism;
    (b) He argued that the Yugoslav Foreign Minister, Vladimir Velebit, was a British agent.
    (c) He argued that the Yugoslav economy should be integrated into the East European economic system.
5. Tito resisted Soviet pressure, since:
    (a) He wanted to maintain Yugoslavian independence;
    (b) He wanted to be free to trade with the west.
6. Stalin tried to overthrow Tito by non-military means:
    (a) He expelled Yugoslavia from Cominform;
    (b) Cut off economic aid;
    (c) Withdrew Soviet advisors;
    (d) Made all the satellites break their agreements with Yugoslavia and ostracise it;
    (e) Launched an unprecedented propaganda campaign against Tito.

7. He did not invade as:
   (a) Tito had been a successful resistance leader against the Italians and Germans;
   (b) The West might not remain neutral since the Percentages Agreement gave both the USSR and the USA a 50% interest in the country.
8. Tito was not overthrown since:
   (a) He was a popular war leader;
   (b) Standing up to Stalin was popular in the country;
   (c) Yugoslavia did not have a common frontier with the USSR;
   (d) Tito received western economic aid.

The effects of the Yugoslav Crisis

1. The failure of South Slav unity talks and plans.
2. The closing of the border with Greece to the communist partisans in the Civil War cut off supplies and retreat, and helped bring that war to an end.
3. Witch hunts and mass trials were held in other satellite states in order to remove nationalist communists from positions of authority and make those states subservient to Stalin.
   (a) In Poland Wladyslaw Gomulka was expelled from the party and arrested.
   (b) In Hungary Laszlo Rajk and others were accused of spying for Horthy, the Nazis, Americans, British and Tito.
   (c) In Czechoslovakia First secretary Rudolf Slansky and Foreign Minister Vladislav Clementis were purged. The purges there took on an anti-Semitic character.
4. Yugoslavia settled its dispute with Italy over Trieste peacefully in 1954 by partition.
5. The creation of a non-aligned communist state not subservient to or modelled upon the USSR showed that a non-Stalinist Communism was possible.
6. In time, Yugoslavia was to exhibit a type of neutralism never envisaged in the Percentages Agreement. It would provide a model for Third World states to follow.

Glossary

anti-Semitic: hostile towards Jews

Axis Powers: Nazi Germany and Fascist Italy

defenestration: execution by being thrown out of upper storey windows

disingenuous: having ulterior motives, insincere

EAM: The National Liberation Front

EDES: The National Republican Greek League

ELAS: The National Popular Liberation Army

glacis: an area beyond one's own territory in which to meet and fight invaders

GRU: Soviet Military Intelligence

KKE: The Greek Communist Party

monolithic: of one piece

opportunism: seeking immediate advantage from circumstances

ostensible: outward

partisans: irregular fighters resisting the occupation of their country by an enemy

PEEA: Political Committee of National Liberation

plebiscite: a popular vote on a particular issue

proxy: acting on behalf of another agency

regent: one who officially acts on behalf of an absent monarch

Sovietization: assimilating a society to the Soviet model

Bibliography

Alexander, George E. *The Prelude to the Truman Doctrine: British Policy on Greece, 1944-1947,* Oxford University Press (Oxford & New York, 1982)

Clogg, Richard, *Greece 1940-1949, Occupation, Resistance, Civil War, A Documentary History*, Palgrave (London, 2002)

Close, David H., *Greece Since 1945: Politics, Economy and Society*, Longman (London & New York, 2002)

Close, David H., *The Origins of the Greek Civil War*, Pearson. (London & New York, 1995)

Communist Power in Europe, 1944-1949, ed. Martin McCauley, Studies in Russia and East Europe, Macmillan (London, 1977)

Foreign Interference in Greek Politics: An Historical Perspective, eds. Theodore A. Couloumbis, John A. Petropulos & Harry J. Psomiades, (New York, 1976)

Greece: From Resistance to Civil War, ed. M. Sarafis, (Nottingham, 1980)

Iatrides, John, *Greece at the Crossroads: The Civil War and its Legacy*, Penn State University Press (University Park, 1995)

Kuniholm, Bruce. *The Origins of the Cold War in the Near East: Great Power Conflict and Diplomacy in Iran, Turkey, and Greece,* Princeton University Press, (Princeton, 1980)

Newsinger, John, *British Intervention and the Greek Revolution*, Socialist Historians Society (London, 2002)

Roubatis, Yannis P., *Tangled Webs: The United States in Greece 1947-1967*, Pella (New York, 1987)

The Greek Civil War 1943-1950. Studies of Polarization, David H. Close, ed., Routledge (London & New York, 1993)

Wittner, Lawrence, *American Intervention in Greece, 1943-9*, Contemporary American History Series, Columbia University Press (New York, 1982)

Woodhouse, C. M., *The Struggle for Greece 1941-1949* Hart-Davis (London, 1976).

General Douglas MacArthur

6. The Korean War

"After I looked at that wreckage and those thousands of women and children and everything, I vomited." (US General Douglas MacArthur)

Background

1. In 1895 Korea had been taken from China by Japan, but at the Cairo Conference 1943 the Allies agreed that when liberated, it would become independent.
2. On 12th Aug. 1945 the Soviet Army entered Korea as far south as latitude 38 degrees north before the Japanese surrendered. By the end of Aug. the Americans had occupied the south of the country. This division was intended as a temporary measure, merely to organise the surrender of the Japanese occupying forces.
3. In South Korea General John R. Hodge began as early as the autumn of 1945 to establish an army and police force under US supervision, and to set up a separate government for the South. He also permitted the return of the nationalist leader Syngman Rhee.
4. The United Nations Organisation requested elections throughout the country. The USA supported this, since two-thirds of Koreans lived in the south.
    (a) In the south elections were held for a National Assembly in May 1948. The anti-Communist Dr. Syngman Rhee was elected president.
    (b) No elections were allowed in the north, which was taken over by the Communist leader, Kim Il Sung.
5. In the South, the Republic of Korea was set up in August 1948.
    In the North, the People's Democratic Republic of Korea was set up one month later.
6. Thus the *de facto** partition of the country had become a permanent division. However both governments claimed authority over the whole country, and each government threatened to unify Korea by force. .
7. This externally imposed division of their country was bitterly resented by most Koreans,
8. Soviet forces withdrew from North Korea in Dec. 1948, and Americans from the South in June 1949. Both powers armed their own client state* with weapons.

The Causes of the Korean War

1. Between October 1949 and June 1950 several thousand soldiers were killed in border incidents and incursions from the north into the south and from the south into the north along the 38th parallel.
2. On Jan. 12, 1950, US Secretary of State Dean Acheson outlined his Asian policy in a speech before the Press Club in Washington. He specifically included Japan, Okinawa, and the Philippines within the American sphere of influence (i.e. control), but failed to mention Taiwan and South Korea.
3. The orthodox* view is that five months later, on June 25, 1950, the North Koreans invaded the South across the 38th parallel.
4. Since the Soviets had absented themselves from the UN Security Council, (over the refusal of the Americans to allow the Chinese Communist Government to take the seat of the deposed Jiang Kaishek (Chiang Kai-Shek) on the Security Council) they were not able to use their veto to prevent a UN force being created to defend South Korea. The forces would be, according to Dean Acheson: "solely for the purpose of restoring the Republic of Korea to it status prior to the invasion from the North."
5. The orthodox view of the reasons for the invasion from the north is that Kim was acting on Stalin's orders and that Acheson's omission had "invited" such an attack. It has been argued that Stalin may have encouraged North Korea to attack:
    (a) in order to keep Kim dependent on the USSR;
    (b) to create a diversion for the Americans.
6. However, there has been some suspicion that the "invasion" was not as simple and unambiguous an action as it has usually been portrayed:
    (a) There was for some time a considerable amount of activity in the form of cross-border raids on either side of the 38th parallel;
    (b) The timing of the "invasion" of which the Americans complained coincided suspiciously with the absence of the Soviet delegates from the UN, allowing the formation of a nominally UN Force.
    Thus it has been suggested that a particularly deep cross-border raid was "designated" an invasion by the Americans, at a time when they could take advantage of the absence of the Soviet veto in the UN, and that the formation of a UN Force forced Kim's hand.
7. According to Khrushchev's memoirs, Kim Il Sung then decided to invade, and Stalin approved, although possibly without considering fully the consequences.
    However:
    (a) this would not have been in line with the usual caution with which Stalin behaved. It is much more likely that Kim acted independently in pursuit of the goal of uniting Korea as a Communist state.
    (b) It is hardly likely that Stalin would arrange for Kim to attack South Korea when the Soviet delegates were missing from the UN and unable to exercise their veto.

The Course of the War

1. As well as the USA, fourteen countries sent troops: Australia, Belgium, Canada, Colombia, France, Greece, Netherlands, Panama, Thailand, Turkey and the UK. Most troops were from the USA, and the UN forces were under the command of the US General MacArthur.

2. Initially, the South Korean army and four American divisions were driven steadily southward across the Korean Peninsula, and by Sept. 1950 they held only a small area around Pusan, on the south-eastern tip of the peninsula.

3. General MacArthur transferred US forces from Japan to Korea for the defence of Pusan.

4. On September 15, US and South Korean troops commanded by General Douglas MacArthur made amphibious landings in the rear of the enemy lines just south of the 38th parallel on both coasts.

5. The North Korean army found itself in danger of being caught between the two forces, one to the north and one to the south. They were forced to retreat.

6. By the end of Sept. Allied forces had entered Seoul, and the South had been recaptured.

7. Chinese Prime Minister Zhou Enlai (Chou En-lai) warned that if US forces went on to invade the North, China would go to its aid.

8. Truman ordered US forces to invade North Korea. He wished to establish a united US dominated Korea as a foothold on the Asian landmass. Thus the USA had changed the supposed goal of the war from containment to a **rollback** strategy. This was in breach of the terms by which the United Nations Force had been set up.

9. By the end of Oct. US forces had captured Pyongyang, and in some places reached the Yalu River, the border with China.

10. The Chinese became concerned:

    (a) They feared a US-backed attempt by Chinese Nationalists to attack China.

    (b) General MacArthur had expressed his desire to invade China.

    (c) The Chinese wished to keep North Korea as a buffer between themselves and US forces. Over 300,000 Chinese "volunteers" from the Peoples' Liberation Army (PLA) crossed the border and drove the US army back beyond the 38th parallel. Pyongyang and then Seoul was captured by the Chinese.

11. Truman abandoned his plans to take the whole of Korea, and decided to settle for "containment" when allied troops once more fought their way back to the 38th parallel.

12. General MacArthur criticised Truman's "**limited war**"* and called for an all-out attack upon Red China. He demanded the authority to blockade China and bomb Manchuria with atomic weapons. British Prime Minister Clement Atlee went to Washington to express disquiet over this proposal. Truman refused to give him MacArthur permission to widen the theatre of war, afraid that this would lead to a new world war.

    In his retirement MacArthur explained that he merely wished to drop thirty to fifty atomic bombs on North Korea, and sow a fifty mile wide stretch of cobalt (with a radio-active life of sixty years) along the Chinese-North Korean border.

13. When MacArthur tried to bypass Truman and appeal to the public, going so far as to issue his own ultimatum to China, Truman dismissed him, and sent out General Matthew B. Ridgway.

14. MacArthur was accorded a hysterically rapturous reception when he returned to the USA. The Senate held hearings on the "limited war" strategy. MacArthur argued that limited war was just a form of appeasement. Other generals testified that an extended war in Asia would expose Europe to attack.

15. A strong Chinese offensive failed with great losses and the Chinese sought an armistice in June 1951. Talks began on July 10, 1951 and dragged on for many months.

16. In the South, Sygman Rhee:

    (a) imposed martial law*;

    (b) arrested opposition deputies in the National Assembly;

    (c) imposed a right-wing dictatorship.

17. Truce negotiations continued while each side sought to improve its position. They focused on:
    (a) the exact demarcation line between North and South Korea;
    (b) the repatriation of prisoners of war.
18. After himself threatening to use the atomic bomb, newly elected US president Dwight D. Eisenhower signed an armistice signed at Panmunjom on July 27, 1953.
    (a) The armies would be separated by a demilitarised zone;
    (b) otherwise restored the *status quo ante bellum* would be restored at the 38th parallel.
    (c) Prisoners of war would be exchanged.

The Consequences of the War

1. The Korean War resulted in the deaths of about:
    1,300,000 South Koreans
    1,000,000 Chinese
    500,000 North Koreans
    54,000 Americans
    4,500 of their allies.
    Many of the Korean casualties were civilians.
    About 5 million Koreans were homeless.
    Much of South Korea's industrial infrastructure was damaged, while North Korea was devastated by heavy American bombing.
2. The war had failed to resolve the division of the country.
3. It increased Sino-American hostility. The subsequent conclusion of a defence treaty with Nationalist China (Taiwan), ensured continued hostility between the USA and China.
4. It has been argued that the UN had been saved the loss of face the League had suffered after the seizure of Manchuria by the Japanese in 1931, although the anti-Communist forces were a UN force only in name. Most non-US military contributions were small, and designed to cover US actions with a facade of respectability as the leader of a "coalition of the willing."
5. A precedent had been established for United States intervention on the other side of the world "to contain Communist expansion".
6. It increased anti-Communist paranoia* in the USA, Americans began to regard any form of sympathy with communism, or indeed any form of socialism, as treasonous - a prejudice which remains today:
    (a) Under J. Edgar Hoover, the Federal Bureau of Investigation (FBI) began to forego hunting gangsters and the Ku Klux Klan, in favour of seeking out alleged communists and so-called "un-American activities."
    (b) A Commission on Employee Loyalty combed through the records of state employees looking for traces of "Communism."
    (c) The Internal Security Act (1950) restricted the rights of Communists to be employed in the USA.
    (d) Senator Joseph McCarthy claimed that there were 57 secret Communists working in the US State Department,* but failed to find any. He led a witch-hunt, until in 1953 he was himself censured for conduct "contrary to senate traditions" when he began to attack important figures in the US Army.
7. Since economic factors pressured Eisenhower to adopt defence cuts, he announced the policy that any future Communist (i.e. supposed Soviet) aggression would invite "massive retaliation" by the USA with nuclear weapons. i.e. The USA would not again fight a limited conventional

war, but would treat any future war as a nuclear war.

8. The Korean War hastened atomic and conventional rearmament by the USA.

9. Both Korea's armed themselves, taking up valuable resources for what were poor third-world countries.

10. Scarce Chinese resources were diverted to the war, and to paying off the USSR for supplies.

11. The niggardliness of Stalin's aid to China during the war poisoned Sino-Soviet relations.

12. The war production generated by the Korean War stimulated the US economy.

13. The post-war Japanese economy was "jump started" by the Korean War.

14. North Korea turned in upon itself, and became a defensive totalitarian state.

15. In the south, corrupt, repressive right-wing dictatorships held the country for the Americans.

16. The Chinese gained considerable prestige, as they had forced the USA into a stalemate.

17. The USA formed the South East Asia Treaty Organisation (SEATO) to "contain" China and North Korea, consisting of the USA, Britain, France, Australia, New Zealand, Pakistan, the Philippines and Thailand. Since only two genuinely South East Asian nations joined it. It was a failure.

18. Incidents have recurred ever since along the demilitarized zone (DMZ), and the uneasy truce remains until this day.

The Significance of the War

1. Despite many threats by US leaders Truman, Eisenhower and MacArthur, to use nuclear weapons, they were not used. However, this was a "nasty" war.
    (a) Both sides tortured prisoners.
        (i) The US claimed its prisoners were "brainwashed" by the Chinese and North Koreans
        (ii) The US military employed POWs as human guinea pigs to test the effectiveness of germ warfare (*United Press* 18th May 1951).
    (b) The US practised the indiscriminate bombing of civilians.
    (c) There were many massacres, e.g. 18th October 1950, "US forces arrested more than 900 innocent civilians and herded them into the air-raid shelter of the Sinchon County Committee of the Workers' Party of Korea and set them on fire after pouring gasoline over them, killing every one."
    Since September 1999, evidence of more than 160 instances of US-led military attacks on more than 2.5 million Korean non-combatants (*Washington Post*, June 13, 2000). Such attacks were clearly a matter of policy, and came from a high level of command. In 2006 a letter emerged from the US Ambassador to the military ordering them to fire upon refugees fleeing south in order to prevent infiltration of the south by Communist northerners.
    (d) For a time, the US engaged in **biological warfare**.* Stephen Endicott and Edward Hagerman, two Canadian historians who researched archives in China, Canada and the US, and conducted interviews with eyewitnesses, came to the conclusion that the US used biological weapons* by bombing parts of North Korea and nearby areas of China with anthrax, encephalitis cholera, the plague, and other diseases during January-March 1952.
    This is the first example of the waging of biological warfare in modern times.

2. Since the Allies had agreed during the war that Korea should become a single independent country, and since the division along the 38th parallel and the administration by the USA and USSR had been understood as temporary, the Korean War may be considered as a civil war.

3. Since both client states on the peninsula were ideologically opposed to each other, and represented the opposing superpowers, the Korean War was a proxy war, and an integral part of the Cold War.

4. This was the first example of the preparedness of the USA to use any means, even if that meant largely destroying a country, in order to "save" it, or keep it within the US sphere of influence.
5. Although it was largely a conventional war, the use of biological weapons provides a second example of the use by the USA of non-conventional weapons (weapons of mass destruction) under the condition that the enemy did not also possess them.
6. The Korean War marks the drawing of the Third World into the Cold War. Great pressure would be put on developing nations to align themselves with one or other of the superpowers.
7. The subsequent isolation and victimization of North Korea by the USA, (to be followed by other states, such as Cuba) demonstrates the constancy and vindictiveness of the US policy of never allowing a state which has successfully defied US hegemony to enjoy normal relations with the rest of the world.

Glossary

biological warfare: the use of biological agents, e.g. agents of infectious diseases, in warfare

biological weapons: the means used deliberately to infect the enemy with infectious diseases

client state: a state which is firmly under the hegemony of a ruling power

de facto: in fact

DMZ: demilitarized zone

limited war: war restricted to certain theatres or regions

martial law: military rule, during which civic rights and freedoms are suspended

paranoia: the irrational belief that one is surrounded by enemies, overt and covert

SEATO: the South East Asia Treaty Organisation

State Department: US Foreign Ministry

status quo ante bellum: the situation as it was before the war began

Bibliography

Cumings, Bruce, *The Origins of the Korean War*, Princeton University Press (Princeton, 1981)

Halliday, Jon & Cumings, Bruce, *Korea: The Unknown War, Pantheon Books* (London, 1988)

Hastings, Max, *The Korean War,* Pan (London, 1988)

Kaufman, Burton I., *The Korean War: Challenges in Crisis, Credibility, and Command,* Temple University Press, (Philadelphia,1986)

Lowe, P., *The Origins of the Korean War*, Longman (London, 1986)

The Korean War, A 25-Year Perspective, ed. Francis W. Heller,. Regents Press (Lawrence, Kan.. 1977)

John Foster Dulles

7. THE THAW (1953-55)

"The War economy provides comfortable niches for thousands of bureaucrats in and out of military uniform who go to the office every day to build nuclear weapons or plan nuclear war; millions of workers whose jobs depend on the system of nuclear terrorism; scientists and engineers hired to look for that final 'technological breakthrough' that can provide total security; contractors unwilling to give up easy profits; warrior intellectuals who sell threats and bless wars." (Richard Barnet)

The Soviet Peace Offensive

1. The Soviet leadership which succeeded Stalin wanted a more peaceful climate in foreign relations, known as "**peaceful coexistence**":

    (a) to secure their regime and their control over eastern Europe after Stalin's death;

    (b) because they were changing from a system of defence based upon a large conventional army and a glacis* in Europe to one of airborne nuclear deterrence, and were temporarily vulnerable.

    (c) In 1953 the USSR had acquired the hydrogen bomb.

    (i) Both sides now had hydrogen bombs, so that confrontation was more dangerous.

    (ii) For this reason, the USSR felt less threatened by the USA.

    The Soviet leadership thus came to regard peaceful coexistence as the only possible policy to follow.

2. The USSR stopped taking reparations from Eastern Germany.

3. The USSR granted diplomatic recognition to Greece and Israel, two US satellites.

4. In order to demonstrate that Stalin's policy was a thing of the past, Khrushchev visited Tito and healed the rift between the USSR and Tito and the Yugoslav Communists (against the opposition of some on the Soviet Politburo, such as Vyacheslav Molotov). An agreement with Yugoslavia in June 1956 recognised that "the conditions of Socialist development are different in different countries" and stated that no Socialist country should impose its views on another. This was recognition by the Soviet leadership that a country could be Socialist without being obliged to follow the path of the Soviet Union.

5. Soviet claims on Turkish territory were dropped.

6. Relations between the USSR and Iran were normalised.
7. An armistice was reached in Korea in 1953.
8. An armistice was reached in Indo-China in 1954.
9. Foreign Minister meetings were held in Geneva, followed later in 1955 by a meeting between Bulganin and Eisenhower.
10. The USSR unilaterally* withdrew from its naval base at Porkkala in Finland.
11. Agreement was reached between the USSR and the Western Allies over the future of Austria. By the **Austrian State Treaty** (1955) Austria would become independent and neutral, within its pre-1938 boundaries. Possible reasons for the Soviets agreeing to surrender their influence in Austria include:

    (a) It would inconvenience western defences, since the Allied forces stationed in West Germany would be separated from the Allied forces stationed in northern Italy by a deep neutral belt created by Switzerland and Austria.

    (b) The Soviet government may have feared that the Western Allies might seek to incorporate Western Austria into Western Germany.

    (c) It may simply have been part of their "peace offensive," another gesture of friendship and reconciliation.

12. Comintern was abolished, suggesting the recognition by the Soviets of a new freedom for non-Soviet Communist Parties.
13. The size of Soviet conventional forces was substantially and unilaterally* reduced.

The US Rejection

1. The British tried to build on this consistent peace offensive:

    (a) Churchill also wished to take advantage of the death of Stalin to defuse international tensions. When he suffered from a stroke, Sir Anthony Eden continued his policy.
2. Proposals for the demilitarization of Central Europe were put forward by:

    (a) the British,

    (b) the USSR,

    (c) the Poles.

    All were rejected by the USA.
3. The USA announced a policy of **massive retaliation:** If any state which they considered to be under their "protection" was attacked with conventional weapons,* they would use their nuclear weapons in response.
4. At this time the CIA was given additional duties, to:

    (a) destabilize regimes unhelpful to the USA;

    (b) murder leaders who were not compliant;

    (c) falsify the results of elections to ensure compliant regimes in "democratic" countries, e.g. Greece, Italy;

    (d) in the last resort, to sponsor or organise local military coups to impose repressive regimes upon peoples insufficiently passive.
5. The Americans propounded the **Domino Theory** in order to justify the policy of **Containment**. If a single country was "allowed" to become Communist, the others would inevitably follow until the entire world would fall under the dominance of Communism. (This implied a striking lack of faith in capitalism and the Western way of life on the part of the Americans.)

    (i) On 8th September the signing of the Manila Pact created the **South-East Asia Treaty Organisation (SEATO)**.

(ii) The Baghdad Pact **Central Treaty Organisation (CENTO)** was founded to keep the Soviets out of the Middle East (joining NATO and SEATO).

(iii) The **US nuclear umbrella** was extended to include Jiang Kai-shek (Chiang Kai-shek) on Formosa (Taiwan).

6. The Federal Republic of Germany (FDR) West Germany was integrated into the Western defence system in a way which hardened the division of Germany:

(a) West Germany was invited to join NATO. This was a calculated insult to their former Soviet allies, who had suffered so much from the Germans during the Second World War.

(b) The Chancellor of the FDR, Konrad Adenauer, visited Moscow and established diplomatic relations with the USSR in return for the repatriation of 10,000 POWs.

(c) Adenauer proclaimed the **Hallstein Doctrine**, that the FDR would not have diplomatic relations with any country which recognised the DDR.

7. In response, on 14th May 1955, the USSR founded the **Eastern European Mutual Assistance Treaty**, usually known as the **Warsaw Pact**, a military alliance of Soviet satellites to balance NATO, initially comprising the USSR, Poland, Czechoslovakia, Hungary, Rumania, Bulgaria and Albania.

Reasons for the US Rejection of the Peace Offensive

1. An atmosphere of anti-Communist paranoia had been whipped up in the USA. Eisenhower had just won an election on the grounds that the Truman administration was "soft on communism"; thus he had left himself little room for manoeuvre.

2. At the end of 1955 President Eisenhower had a heart attack, and may have been unable to control his hawkish* Secretary of State, John Foster Dulles. A Presbyterian lawyer, he brought to the conduct of international affairs typical right-wing American qualities:

(a) a simplistic, Manichaean, or "black and white" view of the world,

(b) a strong sense of self-righteousness,

(c) an eagerness to use, force against weaker parties,

(d) identifying goals dictated by reasons of power and economics as morally worthy.

He became known for his "**brinkmanship**."*

The Race for Delivery Systems

1. In January 1954, US Secretary of State John Foster Dulles announced that the US had adopted the policy of "**massive retaliation**." Any conventional attack on the US or an ally would result in massive nuclear retaliation. The reasons for this were:

(a) NATO had planned to build up conventional forces to match Soviet ground forces in Europe. They had planned on 96 divisions, but by 1954 had managed to create only 15. Instead it was decided to deploy enough conventional forces to slow down a Soviet advance long enough to threaten a nuclear attack.

Large conventional forces were:

(i) expensive,

(ii) unpopular with the voters.

(b) The USA had a clear superiority over the USSR in long-range bombers. Thus the USA could threaten the USSR, but the USSR could not threaten the USA, only Europe.

2. From 1954 there was a race to:

(a) stockpile bombs;

(b) develop new delivery systems. The United States had an advantage in the development of long-range rocketry, in that the German V-2 rocket team, led by Wernher von Braun, had surrendered to the US Army, and was employed by the US against its former allies.

3. US President Eisenhower:

    (a) increased the production of warheads;

    (b) the development of long-range bombers;

    (c) the construction of air bases on the territory of "allies" encircling the USSR

4. In January 1954 the United States launched the *Nautilus*, the first nuclear-propelled submarine.

5. In 1954 the US **Killian Report:**

    (a) forecast increasing American superiority in nuclear weapons until 1958–60 at least.

    (b) warned that the USSR

        (i) was ahead in long-range rocketry,

        (ii) would soon achieve its own secure nuclear deterrent.

    The report recommended:

    (a) rapid development of **intercontinental ballistic missiles (ICBMs);***

    (b) construction of a distant early warning (DEW) radar system in the Canadian Arctic;

    (c) strengthening air defences;

    (d) measures to increase intelligence-gathering capabilities.

6. At the Geneva summit (1955) Eisenhower advanced his "**open skies**" proposal. The USA and the USSR should:

    (a) exchange blueprints of all military installations;

    (b) each side would allow the other side to conduct unhindered aerial reconnaissance.

    After some hesitation, Khrushchev refused the offer as a crude espionage trick.

Glossary

brinkmanship: pushing hostility and aggressiveness almost to the point of war

conventional weapons: weapons other than nuclear or biological weapons. Usually it refers to non-nuclear weapons

DDR: German Democratic Republic (East Germany)

FDR: Federal Republic of Germany (West Germany)

glacis: a buffer area under one's control lying beyond one's own frontiers, in which foreign invaders can be met and defeated before entering one's own territory

hawkish: belligerent, warlike; politicians were sometimes divided into hawks, favouring an aggressive approach to the other side, and doves, favouring a non-aggressive approach

intercontinental ballistic missiles (ICBMs): strategic missiles, capable of reaching targets on the other side of the world

modus vivendi: a compromise allowing the two hostile parties to coexist

unilaterally: without reference to the other side

Nikita Khrushchev

8. The Cold War 1956-63

" ... [We have been compelled to create a permanent armaments industry of vast proportions. Added to this, three and a half million men and women are directly engaged in the defence establishment. We annually spend on military security more than the net income of all United States corporations.
This conjunction of an immense military establishment and a large arms industry is new in the American experience. The total influence -- economic, political, even spiritual -- is felt in every city, every State house, every office of the Federal government. We recognize the imperative need for this development. Yet we must not fail to comprehend its grave implications. Our toil, resources and livelihood are all involved; so is the very structure of our society.
"In the councils of government, we must guard against the acquisition of unwarranted influence, whether sought or unsought, by the military industrial complex. The potential for the disastrous rise of misplaced power exists and will persist." (US President Eisenhower)

Eastern Europe

The Polish Leadership Crisis

Before the Crisis

1. After the breach between Stalin and Tito there was a purge of communists with nationalist tendencies. Wladislaw Gomulka lost power then was imprisoned. Other prominent Communists were imprisoned and 300,000 expelled from the party.
2. During 1949 the cultural life of Poland was reorganised following the Soviet model. e.g. All writers' and artists' unions were taken over by the party. History was rewritten in the interests of Soviet Russia.
3. After Stalin's death some dissidents began to raise their voices:
   Adam Wajyk with his poem on life in the new "socialist paradise" of Nova Huta.
   Jan Kot attacked socialist realism.
   The philosopher Leszek Kolakowski criticised Marxist-Leninism.
   Historians began to acknowledge the role of a "home army" resisting the Germans during the occupation.
4. There was open talk about the shortcomings of the party and the need for change.

The Crisis

1. During summer 1956 First Secretary Boleslaw Bierut died, leading to a succession crisis. The party was divided, even at the top, between:

(a) The Diehards, the "Natolin Group," were opposed to change and willing to call in Soviet troops to enforce order;

(b) The Liberals, who wanted drastic reforms, were a minority at the top but had the overwhelming support of the rank and file;

(c) The "Moderates" were prepared to ally with the liberals.

Moscow favoured Eduard Ochab, a moderate.

2. Public protest began to be apparent on the streets:

(a) Mass demonstrations in favour of liberal reform were held in Warsaw and other towns;

(b) In June 1956 there were strikes and riots in Poznan in support of higher wages and shorter working hours;

(c) In August 1956 Roman Catholic pilgrims demonstrated in Czestochowa.

3. The party politburo refused to re-elect Marshall Rokossowski, a Soviet citizen naturalised as a Pole, as Defence minister. Instead, they decided to elect Wladislaw Gomulka, released from prison in 1954 but not yet officially rehabilitated, to some government position. Offered a minor post, he refused it. He held out for a major post with mass support.

4. The Soviet leaders arrived unexpectedly at a meeting of the Polish Communist Party Central Committee, and were refused admission. Seen later, they accused the Poles of anti-Soviet propaganda and threatened a Soviet invasion of their country. The Poles stood their ground, supported by mass demonstrations in the streets.

5. Gomulka privately assured Soviet leaders that under his control:

(a) Poland would remain in the Soviet bloc;

(b) He would preserve the supremacy of the Party;

(c) Poland would support Soviet policies.

The Soviets then accepted the appointment of Gomulka as First Secretary.

The Outcome of the Crisis

1. On appointment, Wladislaw Gomulka:

(a) opposed calls for a withdrawal of Soviet troops;

(b) persuaded the Soviet leadership to cancel Poland's debts to the USSR;

(c) ended the attempts to collectivise agriculture. 80% of the collective farms already created were subsequently split up;

(d) sought a *modus vivendi** (compromise) with the Roman Catholic Church.

2. However, he also:

(a) gradually reimposed censorship of artistic and literary culture;

(b) followed a pro-Soviet line in international relations;

(c) Most Jewish communities had identified with the liberals in the crisis. They were accused of wartime collaboration with the Nazis. A Commission for supervision of the Jews and to propagate anti-Jewish propaganda was set up.

3. The public felt betrayed. Their attitude became cynical and apathetic.

The Hungarian Uprising

Before the Rising

1. First Secretary Rakosi ran a Stalinist regime. This was intensified after the breach between

Stalin and Tito. Laszlo Rajk, the leading anti-Stalinist communist, was executed, as were 2,000 others. 200,000 were imprisoned and 200,000 expelled from the party.

2. The regime was very unpopular, since:
   (a) It was imposed upon Hungary by conquerors;
   (b) It was tyrannical and harsh;
   (c) it followed a policy of sovietization of Hungarian life, and Hungarians were traditionally anti-Russian;
   (d) living standards dropped.

3. After Stalin's death Rakosi was ousted by the more liberal Imre Nagy, and there was a relaxation of state and party controls.

4. In 1955 Rakosi regained control and ousted Nagy. This led to a build-up of resentment. This was expressed most openly by intellectuals led by the Petofi Circle, and by the party newspaper, *Szabad Nep*. This was intensified by news of Khrushchev's secret speech to the Twentieth Congress of the CPSU.

5. The Soviets engineered Rakosi's removal in favour of the more liberal Ernö Gerö.

The Uprising

1. Meetings were held by students in the University of Budapest and other universities in order to work out how they might gain greater independence, as they believed the Poles had done. They decided to hold a mass demonstration in front of the Polish Embassy in Budapest on 23rd October. Over 50,000 people turned up.

2. When Ernö Gerö broadcast to the nation, the people expected him to offer concessions, but instead he made a Stalinist speech.

3. Public demonstrations against the government took place. A massive statue of Stalin was demolished.

4. When students tried to take the radio station, the Hungarian secret police (AVO) fired on the crowd. More crowds gathered, calling for Imre Nagy to take power. Troops sent to disperse them joined them instead. The riots turned into a revolution against the Soviets, the Communists and the government.

5. The Hungarian politburo panicked. They:
   (a) appealed for Soviet aid;
   (b) appointed Imre Nagy as prime minister, while retaining Gerö as first secretary.

6. On that evening, two members of the Soviet politburo arrived in Budapest: Anastas Mikoyan and Mikhail Suslov. They agreed to the dismissal of Gerö in favour of János Kádár.

7. A revolutionary fervour swept Hungary, as people took revenge against the the Hungarian secret police (AVO). American broadcasts encouraged the revolt and promised US aid against any attempts to suppress it.

8. On 27th October, Imre Nagy formed a coalition of Communists and Smallholders, with Zoltan Tildy and Bella Kovaks.

9. 28th October Soviet forces began to withdraw from Hungary.

10. On 31st October Mikoyan and Suslov were informed that:
    (a) Hungary would become a multi-party democracy.
    (b) It would leave the Warsaw Pact and become a neutral country.

11. The Soviet Government:
    (a) did not wish to see a country leave the Warsaw Pact, as the Pact might collapse, and the glacis be lost.
    (b) Czech, Roumanian, Bulgarian and Chinese leaders were calling for repression of the revolt.

(c) The world's attention was diverted by the Anglo-French expedition to occupy the Suez Canal and topple Nasser *(see below)*.

They decided to act.

12. On 1st November, an alternative and pro-Soviet government was formed under János Kádár, who had left Budapest and denounced Nagy as a counter-revolutionary.

13. On 3rd November, General Pal Maleter, Hungarian Minister of Defence, was seized and arrested by the Red Army while negotiating the final withdrawal of Soviet forces from Hungary.

14. On 4th November, Soviet forces began their advance upon Budapest. In the fighting there 20,000 were killed. Nagy was executed. 180,000 fled across the border into Austria.

15. Martial Law was imposed. Many writers were arrested and given long prison sentences. Later anti-Soviet strikes were suppressed by mass arrests.

The Outcome of the Uprising

1. International indignation was diverted by the Suez Crisis. However, the Hungarian crisis led to:
    (a) a drop in support for the USSR throughout the world;
    (b) a sharp drop in support for communist parties in much of western Europe.

2. The Soviets allowed Kádár to provide more consumer goods to Hungarian citizens to maintain a higher standard of living than elsewhere in the Soviet bloc. There was gradual decentralisation of control of industry after 1966, and a very gradual easing of restrictions generally.

3. Inside the other Communist states, the suppression of the Hungarian Revolution had a restraining effect. There was, nevertheless, no return to the Stalinist type of domination and exploitation; a slow evolution followed toward a degree of internal autonomy.

4. The events of 1956 also had profound effects upon Communists outside the Soviet bloc. There were many resignations after the Hungarian Revolution, and those who remained in the fold began to question both Soviet leadership and the nature of a system that had made the ascendancy of Stalin possible.

The Italian Communist Party leader, Palmiro Togliatti, concluded that the Soviet pattern could no longer be the model for Communism in all other countries, and argued for the decentralisation of the Communist movement, a view that became known as "**polycentrism**."

The Significance of the Uprising

Although the USA was prepared to incite revolt in Hungary, and promised aid to the insurgents, it was also clear that they were not prepared to risk war to intervene, in violation of the terms of the final version of the Percentages Agreement.

The Suez Crisis

[For a more detailed treatment of the Suez Crisis, see the companion volume "Wars and Warfare"]

1. The Suez Crisis had many dimensions:
    (a) It was part of the struggle of the Arab nationalists against British and French colonialism.
    (b) It was part of the struggle between Israel and the Arab states.
    (c) It was part of the Cold War.

2. In 1954 King Farouk of Egypt was overthrown by an army coup. Gamel Abdel Nasser gradually emerged as the new ruler of Egypt. He was in favour of:
    (a) ending British colonial influence in Egypt;
    (b) ending the existence of the state of Israel;
    (c) creating a more just society in Egypt to the benefit of Egyptians.

3. He:
    (a) blockaded the Gulf of Aquaba leading to the Israeli Red Sea port of Eilat.
    (b) insisted that the British evacuate the Suez Canal (an agreement made in 1936 would expire in 1956)
4. In Sept. 1955 he concluded an arms deal with Czechoslovakia, while Soviet experts went to train the Egyptian army.
5. In 1956 Nasser recognised the government of Communist China.
6. The US then cancelled a promised grant of $56,000,000 towards the building of the Aswan High Dam. This was to force Nasser to break with the Communists.
7. Nasser retaliated by nationalising the Suez Canal, and using the revenues to finance the dam.
8. British Prime Minister, Sir Anthony Eden, decided that Nasser:
    (a) was out to build a united Arab nation under communist influence,
    (b) threatening the West's oil supply.
9. In secret negotiations, the British, French and Israelis conspired to attack Egypt. The Israelis sought to expand their territory at the expense of the Egyptians, and destroy Egyptian forces.
10. On 29th Oct. the Israelis invaded Egypt, and within a week had captured the Sinai Peninsula. The British and French bombed Egyptian airfields and landed troops at Port Said, at the northern end of the Suez Canal.
11. The attacks caused an outcry in the rest of the world. The Americans became afraid that the Arabs would move towards the Communists, and refused to support Britain, France and Israel:
    (a) At the UN they joined with the Russians in demanding withdrawal.
    (b) They also generated a run on the British and French currencies.
12. The British, French and Israelis agreed upon withdrawal, while the UN moved in to police the Israeli-Egyptian border.
13. The Soviets were preoccupied with the suppression of the Hungarian revolt, but Khrushchev threatened Britain and France with inter-continental ballistic missiles (ICBMs).
14. As a result of the incident:
    (a) Since the British and French had been seen to fail to topple Nasser, his prestige was increased among the Arabs. He became a focus of Arab nationalism throughout the Middle East.
    (b) The Egyptians blocked the Canal with sunken ships, causing a disruption of international trade.
    (c) The Arabs reduced oil exports to the West, causing petrol rationing for a while.
    (d) British and French influence in the middle East waned.
15. Nasser took Soviet money and experts to build the Aswan high dam, and became an opponent of the West in the Middle East
16. On 5th January, 1957 Eisenhower announced his determination to "contain Communism" in the Middle East. This was known as the **Eisenhower Doctrine**.
17. On 14th July the US intervened in Lebanon and the U.K. in Jordan to prop up pro-Western regimes.

The Nuclear Arms Race

1. In 1956 American U-2 spy planes began illegally overflying the USSR above the range of Soviet air defence taking photographs. This rendered Soviet sites very vulnerable to attack. These planes could fly at altitudes of above fourteen miles. The U-2 could photograph and read a newspaper headline from a height of 12 miles. In minutes they could take several thousand

photographs covering an area 125 miles wide by 3,000 miles long. It was thus possible for the USA to work out the size and location of Soviet forces.

2. A research program was set up in the USA to develop reconnaissance satellites to observe the USSR from outer space.

3. During 1957 the British exploded their first hydrogen bomb.

4. By 1957 both the USSR and the USA had developed inter-continental ballistic missiles (IBMs). The United States had the Atlas missile that could travel 6,000 miles. Preparation for launching took over an hour.

5. However, on October 4th, 1957 the Soviet program won the first space race with the launch of *Sputnik 1*, the first orbiting space satellite. This achievement caused panic in the USA. Colleges were suddenly pressured to open courses in Russian.

6. In February 1958 the US launched *Explorer*, its first satellite.

7. By the end of the 1950s the United States had developed the Minuteman missile, which stored its fuel in its own engines. It was now possible to fire such a missile within a minute. Being small, they were stored in underground silos, protected from an attack.

8. In July 1960 the first test of the firing of a Polaris missile from a US nuclear submarine took place. Deeply submerged, these **Polaris submarines** could move close to the Soviet Union under the ice sheet covering the North Pole carrying nuclear missiles. They therefore increased the range and accuracy of the missiles. A single Polaris submarine could carry more destructive power than all the bombs dropped during the whole of the Second World War.

9. The Soviet Union was extremely concerned by these developments as they were a long way behind the United States in nuclear technology. They had concentrated on producing large missiles that could travel long distances. However, these missiles were inaccurate and their size made them difficult to conceal.

10. In January 1961 retiring President Eisenhower warned that the growing power of the US military-industrial complex threatened democracy.

11. The USSR became concerned when, in 1961, President Kennedy announced:
    (a) a program to build nuclear shelters in the USA.
    (b) Pamphlets were distributed throughout the country on how to survive a nuclear war.
    (c) When in March 1962, Kennedy told a journalist that in some circumstances the USA might start a nuclear war.
    It seemed as though the USA was preparing for a first strike.
    Declassified documents relating to America's first **Single Integrated Operational Plan (SIOP)**, developed in 1960, shows that the US military high command had prepared, and US civilian leadership had approved, a plan for the possible launching of a first strike against the Eastern bloc, delivering over 3,200 nuclear weapons to 1,060 targets. At least 130 cities would have been annihilated. Official estimates of casualties from such an attack were 285 million dead and 40 million injured. But some military men feared that the lethal effects of fallout on the USA itself might be devastating. (The US has had a SIOP ever since.)

12. On 4th May 1962 the US put forward a new **Flexible Response Doctrine**, by which a US response to perceived aggression would not necessarily result in a massive nuclear attack. Due to the unacceptable consequences of such a policy, the previous position had by this time lacked credibility.

13. During 1963 the French acquired nuclear weapons. Unlike the British nuclear force, the French was not placed under NATO control. The *Force de Frappe* included:
    (a) Missiles in silos on the Plateau d'Albion, north of Marseilles
    (b) Mirage jets which could each deliver a warhead

(c) Nuclear submarines

14. The British and French deterrents were based upon the theory of "**proportional deterrence**". Although they would not be able to destroy a superpower, they could inflict enough damage upon it to deter an attack. The development of these deterrent systems demonstrated:

(a) fear of the USSR;

(b) lack of trust by Britain and France in the willingness of the USA to deter attacks upon their territory. De Gaulle said that to give up her deterrent would be "to entrust France's defence to a foreign, and therefore unreliable, protector." Even a representative of the British Government said: "We wouldn't allow ourselves to be wholly in their hands."

(c) the desire of the old imperial powers to preserve their status as "Great Powers."

15. From 1963 camera carrying spy satellites were launched.

16. In 1964, the Chinese exploded an atomic bomb.

US-Soviet Relations

1. In 1956 Khrushchev and Bulganin visited the UK.
2. In Sept. 1959, Khrushchev visited the USA. A summit was arranged for May 1960 in Paris.
3. In a counterpoint to the Truman Doctrine, in January 1961, Khrushchev gave notice of the USSR's general support for national liberation movements in under-developed countries.

The U-2 Spy Plane Incident

1. On 5th May 1960 an American U-2 spy plane* was shot down while illegally flying over the Ural Mountains in the USSR.
2. When the USSR announced the incident and complained about the illegality of the practice, the USA denied both the practice and the loss of a plane.
3. Then the USSR released photographs of the wreckage with its US markings.
4. The US admitted that it was an American plane, but claimed that it was a meteorological research plane which had strayed over the USSR by mistake.
5. The USSR then displayed the pilot, Gary Powers. He explained that he was performing illegal espionage for the US government, and that on landing he had not swallowed the cyanide capsule with which the US authorities has equipped him, preferring to take his mother's advice instead.
6. The USA refused to apologise or to promise to obey international law in the future.
7. This incident displayed the continuing intention of the US government to act in breach of international law whenever it could get away with it.
8. There was a sharp deterioration of relations afterwards:

(a) On 16th May, the Paris peace summit broke up in disarray.

(b) An invitation to Eisenhower to visit the USSR was cancelled.

(c) The Soviet delegate walked out of the Disarmament Conference.

(d) Khruschev made an angry speech at the UN.

The Berlin Crises

1. The Soviets regarded Germany as a defeated enemy, and treated it as such. In 1953 disorders in East Berlin were suppressed by force.
2. The US poured money into West Berlin to make the contrast with the unrewarded East as a "shop window" for demonstrating the superiority of Capitalism over Communism.
3. East Germany experienced a problem in that its best trained and educated citizens, particularly doctors and engineers, educated at the expense of the state, could earn much better money in the

West, where wage differentials were higher, than in the more egalitarian East. After 1952 it was made difficult for Germans in the Russian sector to emigrate to the West by crossing from the Soviet sector of Berlin to the Western sectors. Yet some 200,000 a year still managed to cross from East to West, causing a significant "**brain drain**" which hurt the economy of the DDR.

4. Between 1958 and 1960 Khrushchev several times threatened to hand over responsibility for the control of Berlin, and access routes to the Western sectors of Berlin, to the DDR, which the West did not recognise.

5. Hopes were built up that an agreement might be reached over Berlin at the Paris Summuit between Eisenhower and Khrushchev in may 1960, but it broke up after the U-2 spy plane incident, and Eisenhower's refusal to apologise.

6. On 3rd June 1961, Khrushchev met Kennedy in Vienna. He once more gave an ultimatum about Berlin.

7. During 13-19th August the **Berlin Wall** was erected surrounding the 30 mile perimeter of the Western sectors of Berlin. The number of crossing points was reduced to four. The division of Berlin became as fixed as the division of the rest of Germany.

8. The wall stopped the haemorrhaging of educated people from East Germany and the undermining of its economy.

[For "The Cuban Missile Crisis" See Chapter 9]

Glossary

ABMs: anti-ballistic missile systems

AVO: Hungarian secret police

ICBMs: inter-continental ballistic missiles

inter-continental ballistic missiles (ICBMs): long-range nuclear missiles

INF: Intermediate Nuclear Force

Intermediate Nuclear Force (INF): medium and short range nuclear missiles

IRBMs: intermediate range ballistic missiles

MAD: Mutually Assured Destruction

MIRVs: Multiple independent re-entry vehicles

Multiple independent re-entry vehicles (MIRVs): rockets with multiple independently targeted warheads

Mutually Assured Destruction (MAD): both sides would be totally destroyed

neutron bomb: a "small" nuclear bomb which had enhanced radiation to kill people without destroying property.

NUTs: Nuclear Use Theorists

proliferation: spreading

Single Integrated Operational Plan (SIOP): US plan for launching a nuclear war

SIOP: Single Integrated Operational Plan

U-2 spy plane: high-flying American aeroplanes equipped with sophisticated cameras for illegally overflying the territory of other countries and spying on them

Che Guevara

9. Cuba and the Cuban Missile Crisis

The amount of poverty and suffering required for the emergence of a Rockefeller, and the amount of depravity that the accumulation of a fortune of such magnitude entails, are left out of the picture, and it is not always possible to make the people in general see this. (Ernesto Che Guevara)

Background

1. By 1898 Cuba had liberated itself from Spanish imperial control after a long struggle
2. The US promptly invaded, to ensure that the Cuban people would be "free and independent." Cuba was quickly turned into a US colony in all but name:

    (a) President McKinley declared that Cuba must "needs be tied to us by ties of singular intimacy and strength."

    (b) The Cuban government was forced to include in its constitution the right of the USA to intervene on the island "to preserve independence (!) and maintain law and order."

    (c) Guantanamo Bay was taken as a US naval base to establish a permanent military presence in the region.

    (d) US economic exploitation of the island began immediately;

    (e) The US ambassador came to be recognised as the real governor of the country, US diplomats adopting an attitude of racial superiority;

    (f) The US military intervened many times, governing directly 1906-9. It intervened militarily again in Cuba in 1912. From 1917-33 the country was under continuous military occupation.
3. By the 1950s, the USA controlled the Cuban economy: US companies owned half of the land, four fifths of the island's utilities, including all the electricity and telephones, most of the railways and control of all Cuban industries, including the production of the dominant sugar industry, tobacco, mining and rum. US organised crime (the Mafia) controlled tourism. The profits of these industries were all exported to benefit chiefly the US owners.
4. Outside the months of the sugar harvest, unemployment was over 30%, with no social security. Fewer than 50% Cuban children received any education at all.

5. Within Cuba wealth was overwhelmingly concentrated in the hands of a privileged few collaborators with the Americans. The government was corrupt.
6. In 1952 Fulgencio Batista seized control, sweeping aside the outward appearances of democracy, and brutally suppressing opposition.

The Cuban Revolution

Castro's Background

1. Fidel Castro Ruz was born in Mayarí in the easternmost part of Cuba. His father, an immigrant from Spain, was a sugar cane farmer in a region dominated by the American-owned United Fruit Company.
2. He attended Roman Catholic boarding schools in Santiago de Cuba, and then in Havana. In 1945 he entered the School of Law of the University of Havana, where his chief interest was politics:
    (a) In 1947 he joined an attempt by Dominican exiles and Cubans to invade the Dominican Republic and overthrow Generalissimo Rafael Trujillo.
    (b) He took part in riots in Bogotá, Colombia, in April 1948.
    After his graduation in 1950, he began to practice law.
3. He became a member of the reformist Cuban People's Party, and their candidate for a seat in the House of Representatives in elections scheduled for June 1952. However, in March of that year, General Fulgencio Batista, overthrew the government of President Carlos Prio Socarras and cancelled the elections.

The National Liberation Struggle

1. When legal means failed to overturn Batista's dictatorship, in 1953 Castro organised a rebel force
2. On July 26, 1953, he led some 160 men in a suicidal attack on the Moncada military barracks in Santiago de Cuba, which was intended to ignite a popular uprising. Most of the men were killed and Castro was arrested and sentenced to 15 years' imprisonment.
3. He and his brother Raul were released in a political amnesty in 1955, and they went to Mexico to continue their campaign against the Batista regime. There Castro organised Cuban exiles into a revolutionary group called **the 26th of July Movement**.
4. On December 2nd 1956, Castro and an armed expedition of 81 men landed on the coast of Oriente province from the yacht *Granma*. All were killed or captured except for Castro, Raul, Ernesto (Che) Guevara, and nine others, who retreated into the Sierra Maestra of Oriente province to wage a guerrilla war against the army of Batista.
5. Volunteers flocked to them from all over the island, as the dictator's forces suffered successive military defeats. On January 1st 1959, Batista fled the country. Castro's (by then) 800 guerrillas had defeated the Cuban government's 30,000-man army.
6. Despite Cuba's theoretical independence before 1959, this was a **war of national liberation** or **decolonization**.

Reasons for Castro's Success

1. Batista's regime was very unpopular.
2. Batista reacted to the revolt by torturing and killing potential sympathisers, so that many even of the middle classes began to support Castro as a preferable alternative.

3. Batista's army was poorly led and badly paid. Morale was low.
4. Batista's wanton cruelty embarrassed even the Americans, and they stopped supplying him with arms.
5. Castro was an effective, charismatic leader.
6. Castro had the enthusiastic support of most of the people.

The Establishment of the Castro Regime

1. As the revolutionary leader, Castro became commander in chief of the armed forces in Cuba's new provisional government, which had Manuel Urrutia, a moderate liberal, as its president.
2. Castro retained real power, and in February 1959, he became the head of the government.
3. Castro immediately began to remove sources of social distress and foreign domination.
   (a) Cuba's private commerce and industry were nationalised;
   (b) the large estates of the US companies were confiscated.

US Hostility and Aggression

1. In March 1959 the US National Security Council decided to install a regime "more devoted to the true interests of the Cuban people and more acceptable to the US" in Cuba. Eisenhower's plan was for the overthrow of Castro by a military operation, to be carried out "in such a manner as to avoid any appearance of US intervention."
2. In May, the CIA began to arm terrorists inside Cuba to destabilise the new regime. "During the Winter of 1959-1960, there was an increase in CIA-supervised bombing and incendiary raids piloted by exiled Cubans" based in the US.
3. US congressmen and senators began to denounce Castro; and in June the Congress passed legislation enabling President Dwight D. Eisenhower to take "retaliatory steps":
4. Castro accused the United States of trying to undermine his government. In July Cuba called on the UN for help, providing the Security Council with records of some twenty bombings, including specific details.
5. In a bid to wreck the Cuban economy, the United States, which normally purchased the entire sugar crop, suddenly cut off all sugar purchases from Cuba and soon afterwards placed an embargo on all exports to Cuba except food and medicine.
6. In February 1960, he concluded a trade agreement with the USSR.
7. The CIA then initiated the first of many plots to murder President Castro.
8. CIA chief Allen Dulles urged Britain not to provide arms to Cuba since "this might lead the Cubans to ask for Soviet or Soviet bloc arms," a move that "would have a tremendous effect," allowing the USA to portray Cuba as a threat to the hemisphere; an approach which had worked in the past with Guatemala.
9. Castro sent agents to initiate revolutions in several Latin-American countries, and established diplomatic and economic ties with leading socialist powers, including a trade agreement he made the Soviet Union in February. The United States objected to these policies.
10. In January 1961 Eisenhower broke diplomatic ties with Cuba.
11. In response to the threat from the USA, Castro then created a one-party government to exercise dictatorial control over all aspects of Cuba's political, economic, and cultural life. All political dissent and opposition were suppressed.
12. Many members of the Cuban upper and middle classes emigrated to the United States, especially Florida, from where they conducted a terrorist campaign against the Castro regime with the active support of the CIA.

The Bay of Pigs Invasion

1. In April 1961 an invasion force of Cuban exiles trained in the USA by the CIA invaded Cuba. They landed at the Bay of Pigs. Castro, whose agents had successfully infiltrated the CIA, had been informed of the details. With only two planes, the Cubans quickly defeated the invaders.

2. An invasion of Cuba was planned by the US Central Intelligence Agency (CIA) by May 1960. On April 15, 1961, three US-made aeroplanes piloted by Cubans bombed Cuban air bases. Two days later the Cubans from US bases in Guatemala, trained by the United States and using US equipment, landed at several sites, the principal one being the Bay of Pigs on the southern coast. Castro's troops were waiting for them, since his agents had penetrated the CIA. By April 19th they had been defeated, and more than 1,100 men had been captured and imprisoned.

3. The Tractors for Freedom Committee, headed by Eleanor Roosevelt, failed to raise the $28,000,000 needed for heavy-construction equipment demanded by Castro as reparations. After negotiations by James B. Donovan, Castro finally agreed to the repatriation* of the prisoners in exchange for $53,000,000 worth of food and medicine. It was only between December 1962 and July 1965 that the survivors were returned to the USA.

4. Castro announced that, on the basis of his experience as a Cuban of successive US governments, he had been converted to Marxism, and that Cuba would become a socialist country. Cuba began acquiring weapons from the USSR, which soon became the island's chief supporter and trade partner.

5. The attempt by the USA to overthrow Castro's government by force highlighted the fact that *realpolitik** and not the much vaunted ideological commitment to "freedom" and international law and peace were the determinants of US foreign policy in the region.

6. Castro became even more popular throughout Latin America as a symbol of resistance to US hegemony.

7. This failure of US military might threatened to teach other American states that they also might successfully win their freedom from US dominance and exploitation. To prevent this, Castro's regime had to be destroyed. Robert Kennedy informed the CIA that the Cuban problem carried "the top priority in the United States Government — all else is secondary — no time, no effort, or manpower is to be spared" in the effort to overthrow the Castro regime.

8. In November 1961 Kennedy asked his brother, Attorney-General Robert Kennedy, to oversee Operation Mongoose, a program of economic warfare, sabotage and terrorism designed to topple Castro."

9. In January 1962 the USA secured the expulsion of Cuba from the Organisation of American States (OAS).

10. In 1962, the Joint Chiefs of Staff approved a plan to:
    (a) use "covert means . . . to lure or provoke Castro ... into an overt hostile reaction against the United States; a reaction which would in turn create the justification for the US to not only retaliate but destroy Castro with speed, force and determination." Incidents included:
       (i) speedboat strafing attacks on a Cuban seaside hotel,
       (ii) attacks on British and Cuban cargo ships;
       (iii) the contamination of Cuban sugar shipments;
       They were to be carried out by Cuban exile organizations in Florida.
    (b) Committing terrorist attacks on American citizens in Miami and Washington D.C. and blaming Castro. "Operation Northwoods" was intended to provide the basis for a propaganda campaign to generate support among US citizens for an invasion of Cuba.

11. During 1962 plans and preparations for the aerial bombardment and military invasion of Cuba moved forward.

12. A further consequence was that US President Kennedy had been shown up as a failure. He became determined that this must not happen again, and that in the next confrontation, he would not back down. This desire to demonstrate his *machismo** was to have near fatal consequences for all mankind.

Glossary

Central Intelligence Agency (CIA) - US espionage organisation

machismo: manliness

OAS: Organisation of American States

realpolitik: politics determined not by ideals or ideology but only by realistic calculations of national interest

repatriation: being returned to one's homeland

Bibliography

Anderson, Jon Lee, *Che Guevara: A Revolutionary Life*, Bantam Press (New York, 1997)

Geyer, Georgie Anne, *Guerrilla Prince: The Untold Story of Fidel Castro* Andrews Mcmeel Pubs. (1991)

Hansen, Joseph, *Dynamics of the Cuban Revolution*, Pathfinder Press (New York, 1978)

Harnecker, Marta, *Fidel Castro's Polictical Strategy, From Moncada to Victory*, Pathfinder Press (New York, 1987)

Rodríguez Juan Carlos, *The Bay of Pigs and the CIA*, Ocean Press (Melbourne, 1999)

John F. Kennedy

The Cuban Missile Crisis

"The Americans had surrounded our country with military bases and threatened us with nuclear weapons, and now they would learn just what it feels like to have enemy missiles pointing at you; we'd be doing nothing more than giving them a little of their own medicine. ... After all, the United States had no moral or legal quarrel with us. We hadn't given the Cubans anything more than the Americans were giving to their allies. We had the same rights and opportunities as the Americans. Our conduct in the international arena was governed by the same rules and limits as the Americans." (Nikita Khrushchev)

Background

1. Diplomatic, economic and propaganda warfare, a terrorist campaign and an attempted invasion (the Bay of Pigs), had driven Castro to seek Soviet aid, creating a hostile Communist regime in an area the US had been long accustomed to considering under its exclusive control.

2. In 1962, Cuban spies in the CIA warned Castro, and Castro warned Khrushchev, of the determination of the US government to get Castro out of Cuba before the end of that year. Both Castro and Khrushchev assumed this to be by another invasion attempt.

   In fact the USA was actively preparing for a massive aerial attack and ground invasion of Cuba.

3. The USA had ringed the USSR with hostile alliances and nuclear missiles aimed at that country.

   (a) Less than 50 miles from the Soviet border lay Pakistan, a close ally of the United States and member of the South-East Asia Treaty Organization (SEATO), an anti-communist alliance created by the USA.

   (b) On the border of the Soviet Union, in Iran, were electronic listening posts, and bases for aerial surveillance and infiltration into Soviet territory.

   (c) Also bordering the Soviet Union, was Turkey, a member of NATO. The United States had placed Jupiter nuclear missiles and bomber bases in Turkey.

   (d) Other Jupiter nuclear missiles in Western Europe, e.g. in Italy and the UK, were aimed at the Soviet Union, while US military bases were scattered throughout Western Europe.

4. Khrushchev made the decision to install medium-range nuclear missiles in Cuba and bombers:

(a) The USSR was behind the USA in strategic nuclear fire power. Khrushchev was concerned that the imbalance was such that the USA might be tempted to launch a first strike, in the belief that it could win a nuclear war. Khrushchev saw in Cuba an opportunity to redress the balance by placing Soviet missiles closer to US territory, and so compensating for their greater inaccuracy. It would have doubled the number of targets in the USA accessible to Soviet fire-power.

(b) The development of U-2 planes fitted with cameras, which could photograph and read a newspaper headline from a height of 12 miles allowed the USA to work out the position of Soviet missile sites. This again might tempt them to launch a pre-emptive strike.

(c) Khrushchev also became concerned when, in 1961, President Kennedy announced a programme to build nuclear shelters, and pamphlets were distributed to Americans on how to survive a nuclear war.

(d) Further concern was provoked when in March 1962, Kennedy told a journalist that in some circumstances the United States might decide to launch a nuclear war.

(e) The presence of missiles on the island would deter the expected US invasion of Cuba.

(f) He may have hoped for a diplomatic benefit:

(i) He may have hoped that these missiles could be used as a bargaining chip in negotiations leading to a united neutral Germany.

(ii) He may have sought to improve his position as the leading Communist statesman against Chinese leader Mao Zedong.

5. On 5th September the first missiles arrived in Cuba.

6. On the 12th missile transporters were spotted by a CIA agent. Ironically, his report was discounted as the USSR (unlike the USA) never stationed nuclear missiles outside their own borders.

The Missile Crisis

1. In Summer 1962, the US government became aware that missiles were being imported and set up in Cuba.

(a) In July 1962, they learned that the Soviet Union had begun missile shipments to Cuba.

(b) By August 29th, military construction had been spotted by U-2 spy planes over flying the island.

(c) On October 14th a ballistic missile was observed on a launching pad.

(d) On the same day, U-2 spy planes photographed the missile sites.

2. On October 16th, US President Kennedy convened a secret crisis-management committee. They considered:

(a) An air strike to destroy the missile sites

(b) An invasion of Cuba

But these would have invited Soviet retaliation against US forces in Berlin.

(c) Negotiations

(d) The President opted for:

(i) a naval blockade* to prevent Soviet ships bearing missiles from reaching Cuba,

(ii) an ultimatum demanding that the bases be dismantled and the missiles removed.

3. On October 18th Soviet Foreign Minister Andrey Gromyko met with Kennedy and when asked, denied that the USSR had any offensive intentions in connection with Cuba.

4. On October 22nd, in a dramatic television broadcast, Kennedy publicly announced the presence of the missiles in Cuba. He:

(a) warned that US forces would seize "offensive weapons and associated materiel" that Soviet vessels might attempt to deliver to Cuba, sinking their ships if they refused to be searched,

(b) demanded the withdrawal of the missiles within a time limit.

Blockades are regulated by international customary law and international treaty. A blockade must be declared in advance by notification of all neutral powers, and it must be applied impartially against ships of all states. The US blockade was illegal in international law.

5. It was known that two Soviet ships in the North Atlantic were on course for Cuba. During Oct. 22-24th the world waited to see what would happen.

6. Tension arose around the world:
    (a) The USA
        (i) put its nuclear forces on red alert
        (ii) assembled an invasion force in Florida
    (b) Castro mobilised his armed forces
    (c) The USSR made no military preparations, as these would be liable to escalate the situation

7. The USSR did denounce the blockade, pointing out that the sinking of the ships of another nation on the high seas is considered in international law both a crime and a legitimate *casus belli,** or justification for war.

8. Lord Harlech, the British Ambassador to Washington suggested pulling back the blockade closer to Cuba to give Khrushchev and the Soviet leadership more time to react.

9. On Wednesday October 24th, the Soviet ships in transit first slowed down and then changed course away from Cuba and from the quarantined zone. US Secretary of State Dean Rusk boasted: "We're eyeball to eyeball, and I think the other fellow just blinked."

10. On the same day, U Thant, the Secretary General of the UN, called upon the USA to lift the blockade and engage in three weeks negotiations. He was ignored.

11. On Friday Oct. 26th, Kennedy ordered:
    (a) U-2 spy plane flights over Cuba every two hours;
    (b) 5 million leaflets in Spanish giving reasons for invading Cuba;
    (c) discussions between his brother and the Soviet Ambassador

12. On the same day, Khrushchev sent Kennedy a message offering to withdraw the missiles in Cuba in exchange for a US pledge never to invade the island.

13. On 27th October, events threatened to get out of hand:
    (a) A US U-2 spy plane over flying Cuba was shot down.
    (b) Another US U-2 spy plane "accidentally" flying over the sensitive Chokut Peninsula in the USSR opposite Alaska was damaged but returned to base.
    (c) Realising at last some of the dangers of the situation he had created, Kennedy ordered US missiles around the world to be disarmed, and only rearmed on his personal orders.
    (d) Soviet embassy staff in Washington were said to be burning their papers, preparatory to leaving.

14. On the same day, a harsher message arrived, with a new demand that the USA withdraw its own missiles from Turkey. Clearly, a US attack upon Cuba would invite a Soviet attack upon Turkey. It was later claimed that Kennedy "did not know" that US missiles were in Turkey(!) In fact, he had himself ordered them there in 1961, much too recently, surely, to have "forgotten" about them.

15. Attorney General Robert Kennedy, the president's brother, suggested replying to Khrushchev's first note, as if the second had never been sent. But a demand was included for a reply by Sunday

28th October. They then planned for an invasion of Cuba on Monday 29th, if no reply had been received. (Some of the US generals wanted to invade anyway.)

16. On Oct. 28th, Khrushchev informed Kennedy, via Radio Moscow, that work on the missile sites would be halted and that the missiles already in Cuba would be returned to the USSR.

17. In return, Kennedy:

   (a) committed the United States never to invade Cuba

   (b) secretly (so as not to lose face), promised to withdraw the nuclear-armed missiles that the US had stationed on the borders of the USSR in Turkey.

18. US Secretary of State Dean Rusk boasted: "We looked into the mouth of the cannon. The Russians flinched." This is how the result was portrayed in the press, together with a rider that Kennedy was being modest about his "victory," and not crowing.

19. During the following weeks both superpowers began fulfilling their promises.

20. It later became clear that the Soviet military commander in Cuba had nine tactical nuclear weapons* he was authorised to use in self-defence without consulting Moscow. The assumption was that if the USA invaded a nuclear-armed Cuba, they would have already decided on all-out nuclear war, and there would not be time for consultations. The US assumed that if they invaded Cuba, the commander there would have to consult with the Kremlin, and they would have time to make it clear that they were not launching a Third World War. Thus it is likely that a US invasion of Cuba would have resulted in a nuclear response, leading the USA to think that the USSR had decided on war.

On October 28th 1962, the world was within twenty-four hours of the precipitation of a nuclear war, due to a mutual misunderstanding.

The Results of the Crisis

1. The Soviet nuclear missiles were removed from Cuba.

2. The United States had to tolerate a Communist base in the Caribbean; although in breach of the promises made, secretly tried many times to destabilise the regime and murder Castro.

3. The US Jupiter missiles were removed from Turkey.

4. The enormity of the catastrophe avoided led to a decrease in tension, and to détente.*

5. At the same time, however, it had hardened Soviet determination never again to be humiliated by being exposed in a position of military inferiority. Thus Khrushchev and his successors thus began the largest peacetime arms race in Soviet history.

The Nature of the Cuban Missile Crisis

1. The Cuban Missile Crisis marked the climax of the antagonism in US-Soviet relations.

2. It is not useful to consider the causes of, and responsibility for, the Cuban Missile Crisis without being clear about what that crisis actually was. There are two views:

   (a) The orthodox Western view is that Khrushchev created the crisis by placing Soviet missiles in Cuba, thus threatening the USA. On this view, the crisis began in July 1962. This view was assiduously propagated when the crisis became public by Western propaganda.

   (b) However, it makes more sense to argue that Kennedy created the crisis on October 22nd, when he publicly announced in that dramatic television broadcast an immediate naval blockade of the island of Cuba, warning that US forces would sink Soviet vessels if they refused to be searched, and demanded withdrawal of the missiles within a time limit.

   The US had placed nuclear missiles on the Soviet border in Turkey, aimed at the USSR, yet there was no "Turkish Missile Crisis," simply because Khrushchev did not choose to provoke one. Thus merely placing missiles near the other country did not, of itself, create a crisis. Had

Kennedy's response to the Cuban missiles been as cool and level-headed as Khrushchev's was to the Turkish missiles, there would have been no crisis at all.

The Causes of, and responsibility for, the Crisis

1. It is clear that the Cuban Missile Crisis was caused by President Kennedy when he:
    (a) instituted a blockade of Cuba,
    (b) threatened to sink Soviet ships
    (c) demanded the withdrawal of the existing Soviet missiles
    (d) and did so in a dramatic public confrontation.
2. Thus while the actions of Khrushchev in placing the missiles on Cuba was a causal factor, the engineering of the crisis was a conscious choice made by Kennedy. Therefore a causal investigation must concern itself with his motives.
3. By 1962 the USA had recently been humiliated:
    (a) by the U-2 spy-plane* incident
    (b) by the failure of the Bay of Pigs expedition, and the establishment of a pro-Soviet state in a region over which the USA had previously exercised hegemony.*
4. Kennedy was determined not to be seen as a weak president, and felt that he needed to force and win a showdown in order to secure his election for a second term, and was apparently prepared to place all life on the planet on a knife-edge crisis to secure this.
5. There is also some evidence that Kennedy felt so surrounded by aggressive warmongers among the US military that if he did not act aggressively, he would be impeached. Robert Kennedy was of the opinion that the US military would have seized power.

The Significance of the Cuban Missile Crisis

1. The importance of the Cuban Missile Crisis cannot be overestimated. It was the nearest point at which the superpowers came to all-out nuclear war, threatening all life on the planet. It was therefore the most dangerous point in human history.
2. Therefore the deliberate engineering of the crisis was the most criminally insane act of any leader or politician in world history. The crimes of Hitler and Stalin were vast and horrific; but neither of them ever threatened the existence of all mankind, as Kennedy did.
4. The Western media presented Kennedy as a young champion of the Free World who had won a great and unmitigated victory over the sinister forces of Communism. The myth is usually created to disguise an opposite truth: that the US President was a dangerous fool.
5. The crisis was not, in any case, an unqualified victory for Kennedy:
    (a) Kennedy's pledge never to overthrow Castro by force meant that the US would have to tolerate a Communist base in the Caribbean; although the Kennedy administration, in breach of promises made, secretly tried many times to destabilise the Castro regime with a campaign of assassination and terrorism.
    (b) The Cuban missile crisis hardened Soviet determination never again to be humiliated by being exposed in a position of military inferiority. Khrushchev and his successors thus began the largest peacetime arms race in history. By the 1970s the Soviet Union had achieved near-parity with the United States in nuclear forces, and in the ability to project naval power into the oceans of the world.
6. The Soviets' humiliation in Cuba gave ammunition for Khrushchev's enemies and played an important part in securing his fall from power in October 1964. Yet every man, woman and child alive on the planet today owes his/her existence to Khrushchev's humane preparedness to back down in public, with all the personal and political consequences for himself which that would entail.

7. The astounding priority given by the Kennedy administration to managing publicity in their favour in such a dangerous situation, e.g. in insisting that their removal of the missiles in Turkey be secret, just beggars belief. The favourable view of the President's handling of the crisis largely comes, with appropriate nepotism, from his brother Robert in his book *Thirteen Days*, in which President Kennedy calmly and resolutely stood up to "nuclear blackmail."

8. In view of the US superiority in the nuclear arms race, then carefully disguised from the public, it is clear that had Khrushchev made the weapons operational, it would not have significantly altered the existing imbalance of power in Washington's favour.

9. The crisis also made clear outside the heavily propagandized countries of East and West the realities of world power: that appeals by the Secretary General of the UN, the Pope and other world leaders counted for nothing in the games of Washington and the Pentagon. The decision whether or not to end all life on earth in some mad gamble lay with a few individuals on each side, who made their decisions in secret. And this was true whether they controlled Communist or "democratic" states. There lay the true threat to mankind. And on that occasion, the world had been saved by the men in the Kremlin.

Glossary

blockade: an attempt to intercept and block traffic on the high seas from reaching a particular country - a breach of international law

casus belli: justification for waging war

tactical nuclear weapons: medium and short-range nuclear weapons

U-2 spy plane: high-flying spy planes, used by the USA illegally to overfly other countries

Bibliography

Abel, Elie, *The Missile Crisis,* JB Lippincott Company (Philadelphia, 1966)

Allison, Graham T., *Essence of Decision: Explaining the Cuban Missile Crisis,* Little Brown (Boston, 1971)

Beggs, Robert, *Flashpoints : The Cuban Missile Crisis*, Longman (London, 1971)

Dinerstein, Herbert, *The Making of a Missile Crisis,* Johns Hopkins Press (Baltimore, 1976)

Divine, Robert A., *The Cuban Missile Crisis*, M. Wiener Pubs. (New York, 1988)

Ferrell, Robert H., *American Diplomacy: The Twentieth Century,* W. W. Norton, (London & New York, 1988)

Fursenko, Aleksandr and Timothy Naftali, *One Hell of a Gamble : Khrushchev, Castro, and Kennedy, 1958-1964*, W.W. Norton & Co. (New York, 1997)

Pachter, Henry Maximilian, *Collision Course: The Cuban Missile Crisis and Coexistence*, Praeger (New York, 1963)

Wenger, Andreas, *Living With Peril: Eisenhower, Kennedy, and Nuclear Weapons*, Rowman & Littlefield, (Lanham, MD., 1997)

Fidel Castro

Cuba After the Crisis

"There is no similar case of such a sustained assault by one power against another - in this case the greatest superpower against a poor, Third World country - for forty [now read "fifty"] years of terror and economic warfare." (Noam Chomsky)

Building Socialism

1. Agriculture:
    (a) Land was nationalised and collective farms introduced.
    (b) Attempts were made to modernize and increase sugar production.
2. Industry: New industries were founded to reduce Cuba's dependence upon sugar.
3. Human rights: Castro introduced:
    (a) equality for blacks;
    (b) more rights for women;
    (c) Every citizen was guaranteed employment.
4. Social services were founded, and extended to all classes of society on an equal basis.
    (a) Educational was made available to Cubans free of charge. Cuba soon had the best educational system in Latin America.
    (b) Health services were made available to Cubans free of charge Cuba soon had the best health system in Latin America.
    (c) The housing stock was improved.
    (d) Improvements were made in sanitation.
5. Culture was made available to the people by the institution of touring theatres, cinemas, concerts and art exhibitions.
6. Government corruption was severely reduced.
7. The Cuban economy under the Castro regime, however, failed:
    (a) to achieve significant growth;
    (b) to reduce its dependence on the country's chief export, cane sugar:
    This was because:
        (i) economic warfare was waged against the island state by the US. US Allies were

pressured to join the trade embargo;

(ii) Economic decision-making power was concentrated in a centralised bureaucracy headed by Castro.

8. In 1976 a new constitution was passed, which set up a National Assembly. Castro became president of the State Council. He retained the posts of commander in chief of the armed forces and secretary-general of the Communist Party of Cuba and he continued to exercise the major influence in the government.

9. During the 1980s the sugar and tobacco crops were attacked by mysterious fungal infections which only seemed to break out on this particular island in the hemisphere. Covert* biological warfare by the USA is the most likely explanation. Food rationing had to be introduced.

10. Cuban troops fought:

(a) In the Angolan civil war on the side of the Popular Movement for the Liberation of Angola;

(b) In 1978 Cuban troops assisted Ethiopia in defeating an invasion by Somalia.

11. In 1980 a flood of 125,000 immigrants to the USA was released when he opened the port of Mariel for five months.

12. During the 1980s Castro was prominent as one of the leaders of the Third World and the nonaligned nations.

Later US Political/Economic/Terrorist Warfare

1. In 1969 US President Nixon directed the CIA to once more to intensify covert operations against Cuba. Terrorist activities peaked in the mid-1970s, with attacks on fishing boats, embassies, and Cuban offices overseas, and the bombing of a Cubana civil airliner, killing all seventy-three passengers.

2. The tourist industry was particularly targeted, to deprive Cuba of foreign exchange. On the thirtieth anniversary of the missile crisis, a machine-gun attack was launched against a Cuban hotel; responsibility was claimed by a terrorist group in Miami. A bombing in 1997, which killed an Italian tourist, was also traced back to Miami. Cuban offers to cooperate in intelligence-sharing to prevent terrorist attacks were repeatedly rejected by Washington.

3. Through all this, Castro continued to express his willingness to renew diplomatic relations with the USA in return for the end of the trade embargo.

The "Special Period"

1. With the collapse of the Soviet bloc, the price for Cuban sugar declined and the price for Cuba's main import, oil, rose many times. Fidel Castro has called the period from 1989 to the present, the "Special Period." From 1989 to 1993, the Cuban economy went into a free fall, with output and incomes falling far more than it did in the United States during the worst years of the Great Depression. Cuba has survived the difficult years of the Special Period, but it is a society much less equal than the late 1980s with far more economic hardship.

2. The claim that Cuba was a threat to US security lost all credibility after the collapse of the Soviet Union in 1991, but the Bush administration made the terms of the embargo much harsher.

3. The constitution was revised in 1992, defining the Communist Party as the "organized vanguard of the Cuban nation."

4. In 1994, when economic unrest led to anti-government demonstrations, restrictions were lifted on those wanting to leave the country, and thousands left for the USA.

5. Economic warfare was made still more stringent in 1996, causing a furore even among the closest US allies.

6. US economic warfare against Cuba has been strongly condemned in almost every international forum, and declared illegal by the Judicial Commission of the Organization of American States (OAS). In 1997 the European Union brought charges against the United States for flagrant violation of World Trade Organization (WTO) rules by the embargo. The US rejected its jurisdiction on the grounds that Cuba was "a threat to the national security of the USA."

7. In 1999 the Clinton administration eased economic sanctions for all countries on the official US list of "terrorist states" except Cuba.

The Effects of US Aggression

1. It forced the Castro regime on to the defensive, ensuring the development of an illiberal state as a defence mechanism, which could then be denounced as totalitarian. It seems likely that this effect, already observed as a result of foreign attempts to stifle the Revolution in Russia under Lenin, was deliberately intended.

2. It forced Cuba into the Communist camp, and so made possible the Cuban Missile Crisis.

3. It has damaged the development of Cuba. A study by the American Association for World Health concluded that by barring food and medicine, the embargo had severe consequences for the health of the Cubans,; and that only Cuba's socialist health care system, unique in the Americas, had prevented a "humanitarian catastrophe."

4. Even so:

   (a) The level of education in Cuba is high. Literacy is 100% and virtually everyone has a secondary education. Even in the most rural areas, there are secondary schools. This may be compared to Mexico, a much richer country in average income, where secondary schools and even elementary schools are lacking in many rural areas. University education is free and access is far more equal in Cuba than in the United States.

   (b) Life expectancy and infant mortality are similar to the United States, in a country where GDP per person is less than one tenth of the US level. Although hospital care and doctors' visits are free, Cubans must pay for prescriptions. Medicines produced in Cuba are affordable to all, but those that have to be imported are necessarily expensive.

   This compares very favourably with similar countries in the Americas under US dominance.

Reasons for US Aggression

1. Noam Chomsky points out, in *Hegemony or Survival, America's Quest for Global Dominance,* that concern over a Russian threat could not have been a major factor in the US terrorist campaign and embargo against Cuba. "The plans for forceful regime change were drawn up and implemented before there was any significant Russian connection, and punishment was intensified after the Russians disappeared from the scene. True, a Russian threat did develop, but that was more a consequence than a cause of US terrorism and economic warfare."

2. Arthur Schlesinger had warned President Kennedy that "the distribution of land and other forms of national wealth greatly favours the propertied classes" and "the poor and underprivileged, stimulated by the example of the Cuban revolution, are now demanding opportunities for a decent living." Thomas Paterson writes, "Cuba, as symbol and reality, challenged US hegemony in Latin America." Thus the problem was:

   (a) US embarrassment over the example of social justice afforded by the Cuban Revolution to other American states;

   (b) Concern over what this example might encourage other Latin American states to do;

   (c) Outrage over Cuban defiance of US hegemony.

The Wider Consequences of the Success of the Cuban Revolution

1. Kennedy sought to outbid Castro in appealing the American nations by announcing the **Alliance for Progress,** promising US development aid in return for reforms reducing inequality:

    (a) in land ownership

    (b) in taxation

    (c) in legal rights

    (d) in political rights.

2. His real policy, in the meantime, was to strengthen the internal security of the American states by providing aid to governments in the fields of:

    (a) internal intelligence and surveillance of their populations;

    (b) interrogation and torture;

    (c) equipment.

3. In consequence, the security forces of the American states transformed themselves into armies of occupation on behalf of the USA within their own states, managing "death squads" and torturing and "disappearing" hundreds of thousands of citizens, particularly defenders of democracy, social justice and the environment.

4. Where governments did not act in accordance with US wishes, coups were organised, beginning with Brazil in 1964.

5. Under US President Johnson, pressure was put on American governments in the interests of big business to:

    (a) lower tariffs on US exports;

    (b) lower taxes on US companies operating within their countries.

6. US control over the states of the American continent was strengthened to prevent the example of Cuba being followed by other states.

Glossary

covert: secret

détente: a state of permanently reduced tension in relations between the Superpowers

hegemony: domination

OAS - Organisation of American States, a forum for the states of the Western hemisphere

WTO: World Trade Organization, an international organization, which sets the rules for the global trading system and resolves disputes between its member states, which have all signed agreements to facilitate international trade

---

Bibliography

Balfour, Sebastien, *Castro*, Profiles in Power, Longman (London & New York, 1995)
Cannon, Terence, *Revolutionary Cuba*, José Martí Publishing House (Havana, 1982)
Dumont, René, *Cuba: Socialism and Development*, Grove Press (New York, 1970)
Ferrell, Robert H., *American Diplomacy: The Twentieth Century,* W. W. Norton, (London & New York, 1988)
Harnecker, Marta, *Cuba: Dictatorship or Democracy*, Lawrence Hill & Co (Connecticut, 1979)
Morley, M. H., *Imperial State and Revolution: The United States and Cuba, 1952-1986*, Cambridge University Press (Cambridge, 1987)
Quirk, Robert E., *Fidel Castro* W. W. Norton & Company (New York, 1993)
Szulc, Tad, *Fidel: A Critical Portrait,* Perennial (New York, 1986)
Thomas, Hugh, *Cuba or the Pursuit of Freedom*, Macmillan (London & New York, 1971)

Ho Chi-minh

10. THE VIETNAM WARS

"I have never talked or corresponded with a person knowledgeable in Indo-Chinese affairs who did not agree that, had the elections been held [in 1956]... possibly eighty per cent of the population would have voted for the Communist Ho Chi-minh." (US President Dwight D. Eisenhower)

THE INDO-CHINA WAR

Background

1. French Indo-China (Vietnam, Cambodia and Laos) had been part of the French Empire since the late nineteenth century.
2. During the mid-1930s serious disturbances took place under the leadership of Communists. This was part of a general crisis of colonialism generated by the World War and the Depression.
3. During the Second World War the Japanese occupied the country.
4. The League for the Independence of Vietnam, generally known as the **Vietminh**, was organised in 1941 in order to resist occupation. Composed of people of many shades of opinion, it was led by **Ho Chi Minh** and the Communists. They were armed by the Americans to fight the Japanese.
5. In the areas they controlled, the Vietminh:
    (a) relieved a famine by comandeering the supplies hoarded by wealthy profiteers to put the price of food up;
    (b) ending high rents and high interest rates on loans;
    (c) redistributed land
    This made them very popular with the peasants.
6. On the surrender of the Japanese, Chinese troops occupied the north and British the south.
7. At the end of the war Ho Chi Minh declared Vietnam an independent country.

The Causes of the Indo-China War

1. When the French, returned to take control, they initially recognised Ho's government in Hanoi as autonomous, under French hegemony.

2. In November 1946 the French ordered Ho Chi-minh's government to leave Hanoi. When they refused, the French bombarded Hanoi and Haiphong, killing 6,000. Ho and the Vietminh were forced into a war of national liberation.
3. The French, wishing to keep control of the rice and rubber of the south, set up Bo Dai as a puppet.

The Course of the Indo-China War

1. The Viet Minh fought a guerilla war.
2. Increasingly this struggle became seen in the USA as part of the Cold War. Although the Chinese and Vietnamese were traditional enemies, the Communist Chinese began to supply the Vietminh with some arms and equipment from 1950. The Americans began to help the French with money, equipment and advisers.
3. By 1954 the French had lost control of the countryside.
4. The French were decisively defeated in 1954 when a French army under General Navarre, which had sought to lure the Vietminh into the open and destroy them, was surrounded and forced to surrender in May after a 50-day siege at **Dien Bien Phu.**

The Reasons for the French Defeat

1. Ho and the Vietminh had the support of the mass of the people.
2. The Vietminh were masters of **guerrilla warfare**.
3. From 1950 the Vietminh were supplied with weapons from communist China.
4. The **war-weary** French failed to prosecute the war effectively. Many of the French soldiers were young conscripts, so that the war became very unpopular at home.
5. The French were experiencing problems in other parts of the world by hanging on to their colonial empire.
6. The attempt to lure the Vietminh into a battle in the open at Dien Bien Phu was a grave error of judgement.

The Significance of the Indo-China War

1. This war was a war of national liberation. Throughout much of South-East Asia the colonial powers were leaving. In the case of French Indo-China and Malaya, they chose to stay. In both places this was resisted.
2. It was seen by the Americans as a proxy war* in the Cold War, Ho Chi Minh acting as proxy for the Kremlin, and the French acting as proxies* for the Americans.

The Truce

1. A peace conference was arranged at Geneva in 1954 under the joint chairmanship of the USSR and UK in consultation with France, the USA, China and the states of Indo-China.
2. By the terms of the Geneva Agreement of 1954:
    (a) Laos and Cambodia were to be independent.
    (b) Vietnam were **temporarily divided** into two states at the 17th parallel. Ho Chi Minh's Government was recognised in the north, while an American puppet regime under Ngo Dinh Diem was set up in the south.
    (c) In 1956 elections were to be held throughout Vietnam, after which it was to be united.
3. The French left the country. They had more pressing problems to deal with in Algeria.

Ngo Dinh Diem

The Vietnam War

"In an incredible perversion of justice, former soldiers who sprayed festeringly poisonous chemicals on Vietnam, and now find today that they themselves have been damaged by them, appeal to the people for sympathy and charity. The effects of the defoliant "Agent Orange" are discussed at length, but not one single newspaper article or hearing that we are aware of has even mentioned the effects of the people who still live in those regions of Vietnam. It's as outlandish as if Nazis who gassed Jews were now to come forward and whine that the poisons they utilized had finally made them sick. The staggering monstrousness goes unlaughed at and even unnoticed, as in a Kafka novel." (Fred Woodworth)

"The draft is white people sending black people to fight yellow people to protect the country they stole from red people." (Gerome Gragni and James Rado)

"Contrary to what virtually everyone -- left or right -- says, the United States achieved its major objectives in Indochina. Vietnam was demolished. There's no danger that successful development there will provide a model for other nations in the region." (Noam Chomsky)

The Outbreak of the Vietnam War

1. In 1955 Diem refused to make preparations for the promised elections. The US supported him, since they expected that Ho would win any genuine elections overwhelmingly.
2. The Diem government became very unpopular because:
   (a) A Catholic, he discriminated against Buddhists, who made up 75% of the population.
   (b) He blocked demands for land reform, as was being carried out in the north under Ho.
   (c) His regime was notoriously corrupt, and ruled the country as a family property.
   (d) He was seen as an American puppet.
   (e) Diem accused his opponents of being communists, and imposed a police state.
3. In 1960 various groups, including communists and former Vietminh, formed the **National Liberation Front (NLF),** known by the Americans as the Vietcong, to demand a democratic coalition government which would negotiate a peaceful union of the two parts of the country. When this was refused, a guerrilla war began in the south, waged by the Vietcong, who attacked government buildings. Buddhist monks burned themselves alive in protest at Diem's regime.
4. Traditionally, the South supplied the north with food. Diem refused to do this.

5. US President Kennedy sent 16,000 advisers to assist Diem, together with military equipment.
6. As in Korea, the Americans tried to involve their allies. Only Australia, New Zealand, Thailand and the Philippines ever sent any troops.
7. Local peasants were moved *en masse* into so-called "fortified villages" where they could be controlled by the ARVN. These were, in effect, concentration camps.
8. The Vietcong singled out government officials for attack.
9. The Vietcong were supplied by North Vietnam, since it was clear that the only way that the promised elections could be held was by overthrowing Diem and expelling the Americans.

The Causes of the Vietnam War

1. The Vietnamese wished for their independence, and under a popular leader, they were prepared to fight for it.
2. In order to retain US influence in the region, Eisenhower had used the Truce to set up a client state in the South, in violation of the terms of the Geneva Agreement.
3. The puppet government of this client state tried to suppress the independence movement and failed, leading to civil war.
4. Kennedy, in order to retain US influence in the region, sent US troops to prop up the regime in the South.
5. His pretext was the **Domino Theory** of the previous administration. If South Vietnam were allowed to become a Communist state, then one by one, all the other states of the region would follow suit. This suggested a singular lack of faith in the inherent attractiveness of the "capitalist, democratic Western way of life" championed by the USA.
6. It has been claimed that the since US had lost the Asia specialists of the State Department, who had been hounded out of office as "communists" by Senator Joseph McCarthy, they did not know who the Vietcong were. But there is no reason to suppose that if they had known, they would have behaved any differently. The issue was not whether the Vietcong were communists or not, but US control over the region.

The Course of the Vietnam War

Under US President Kennedy

1. "Fortified villges" were set up to control the population.
2. The CIA spread rumours that the communists were torturing Catholics in the North, in order to get them to flee to the South to buttress Diem.
3. "Communist villages" were bombed by US pilots using Vietnamese aeroplanes.
4. US forces began using:
    (a) napalm, burning Vietnamese peasants alive;
    (b) "free-fire zones", where they could kill anyone at will;
    (c) defoliants, to destroy the natural environment.
5. Thousands fled from the South to the North. Diem ordered them to return to fight the NLF.
6. Diem began to lose effectiveness:
    (a) His support was reduced to his dependants and Roman Catholics.
    (b) He became resentful that American aid had turned into American control.
7. During 1963 demonstrations against the Diem regime led to a declaration of **martial law**.* Many Buddhist monks burned themselves alive as a protest. US special forces raided Buddhist monasteries in reprisal.
8. On 1st November 1963, Diem was overthrown by the army, and murdered. Afterwards, the south

was ruled by a succession of generals, of which Nguyen Van Thieu survived longest (1967-75).

9. Increasing numbers of US forces were sent in.

10. The legend, based upon a popular film, that Kennedy had decided to withdraw from Vietnam just before his assassination, is inherently unlikely:

    (a) There is no evidence for it;

    (b) It was Kennedy who had taken the USA into the war in the first place.

Under President Johnson

1. US President Johnson chose to decide that the Vietcong were really northerners who had infiltrated the South, and used this as a reason to bomb North Vietnam, hoping that this would lead Ho to call off the campaign.

2. The pretext was a supposed attack upon a US destroyer in the Gulf of Tonkin off North Vietnam by North Vietnamese patrol boats in international waters. The US Congress almost unanimously endorsed the **Gulf of Tonkin Resolution**, authorising the president to take "all necessary measures to repel attacks . . . and prevent further aggression." This resolution in effect gave the president the authority for full-scale US intervention in the Vietnam War. Johnson ordered US planes to bomb North Vietnam.

    A State Department official, Daniel Ellesberg subsequently leaked to the press the *Pentagon Papers,* which revealed that:

    (a) The resolution had been prepared a month before the incidents reported.

    (b) The US destroyers had been in North Vietnamese waters, trying to land marines of the South Vietnamese Army on the shore to engage in acts of sabotage.

3. After 1965, US involvement in the war escalated rapidly in response both to the growing strength of the Vietcong (who had 35,000 troops in South Vietnam by 1964) and to the inability of the ARVN to suppress the Vietcong on its own.

4. On the night of Feb. 7, 1965, the Vietcong attacked a US base at Pleiku. In retaliation, Johnson ordered a reprisal bombing of North Vietnam. When, three days later, the Vietcong raided another US military base at Qui Nhon, Johnson ordered more bombing of Hanoi and NLF-controlled areas in the South.

5. Small contingents of the North Vietnamese army began fighting with the Vietcong in South Vietnam, which they reached via the Ho Chi Minh Trail west of the Cambodian border.

6. NLF forces gained control of more and more areas of the countryside, and a communist victory seemed imminent. President Johnson sent more troops. By the end of 1965, 180,000 Americans were in South Vietnam under the command of General William C. Westmoreland.

7. The US troops depended heavily on bombing, superior fire power, and helicopters for rapid deployment in rural areas. The Vietcong, by contrast, fought a guerrilla war.

8. The US concentrated on killing Vietnamese, and every Vietnamese killed was counted as Vietcong. Many were murdered and raped by US soldiers who wore necklaces of ears as trophies. Only one incident was punished, selected as a propaganda example to prove that the US punished its soldiers who committed war crimes, the massacre of over a hundred women and children at **My Lai** in 1967. Yet even here, only one soldier was found guilty of any crime: Lieutenant William Calley. He was sentenced to life imprisonment. In fact, he served less than four years, and that under "house arrest."

9. Both sides tortured prisoners and the Geneva Conventions were ignored.

10. US troop strength in South Vietnam rose to 389,000 men in 1967, but, despite their vastly superior resources, sophisticated weapons and equipment, the Americans could not defeat the insurgents. Instead, more North Vietnamese troops arrived to bolster the NLF in the South.

11. A presidential election, in which all candidates who favoured negotiating with the NLF were banned, was held in South Vietnam in September, and General Nguyen Van Thieu became president.

12. At the beginning of 1968 the Vietcong lured US forces into the countryside by an attack on a US base at Khesan. Then on Jan. 30th they launched a massive surprise offensive during the Tet (lunar new year) Vietnamese festival, attacking 36 cities and towns. The **Tet Offensive** was especially fierce in Saigon, where the NLF attacked the presidential palace, airport, radio station and US embassy, and in the city of Hué, which the NLF held for several weeks, executing a thousand citizens. This campaign convinced many Americans that the insurgency in South Vietnam could not be crushed, and that the war would continue for many years.

13. In the USA, sentiment against the war mounted from 1967.

(a) This was in part due to some war reporting which was not entirely the usual propaganda. In particular two images on the television screen moved the public:

(i) A kneeling Vietnamese being summarily shot in the head by a policeman;

(ii) A girl running down the street with her clothes and skin being burned off her by napalm.

(b) Much of the opposition was due to the introduction of a selective draft. Some Americans left the country to avoid the draft.

There were:

(a) peace marches;

(b) acts of civil disobedience.

Growing numbers of Americans began to question:

(i) if the US could win the war;

(ii) whether the war was morally justifiable.

14. General Westmoreland requested more troops in order to widen the war after the Tet Offensive, but Americans wished for "de-escalation" of the conflict. On March 31, 1968, President Johnson announced in a television address that:

(a) bombing north of the 20th parallel would be stopped;

(b) he would not seek re-election to the presidency in the autumn.

Under President Nixon

1. Hanoi responded to the decreased bombing by de-escalating its insurgency. The USA and North Vietnam agreed to peace talks in Paris. In October Johnson ordered a total halt to bombing.

2. In September 1969, Ho Chi-min died.

3. In March 1970 Prince Sihanouk of Cambodia was deposed by his prime minister, General Lol Nol. The new government asked for US arms, but the US and ARVN invaded. This extension of the war was stopped when the US Congress cut off the funds to wage it.

4. In June 1970, US President Richard M. Nixon announced the withdrawal of 25,000 US troops from South Vietnam.

5. The USA began a program of **Vietnamization*** of the war, whereby the South Vietnamese would gradually assume all responsibilities for their own defence, while being supplied with US arms, equipment and economic aid. US commanders were instructed to keep US casualties to "an absolute minimum." This was known as the **Guam Doctrine**.

6. In Paris the peace talks dragged on, but the South agreed to negotiate directly with the NLF and the North Vietnamese.

7. The war expanded during spring 1970:

(a) US and ARVN troops invaded border areas of Cambodia, allegedly to destroy North Vietnamese bases.

(b) US planes bombed northern Laos, where North Vietnamese forces were fighting with the pro-Communist Pathet Lao (Lao Country) against the US-supported Vientiane government. The Ho Chi Minh Trail was the constant target of B-52 bombers. The expansion of the war into Cambodia sparked a new wave of demonstrations and protests in the United States.

8. By late 1970, the number of US military personnel in South Vietnam had been reduced to 335,000. The gradual withdrawal of US troops from Vietnam proceeded as announced, but the peace talks remained deadlocked.

9. In 1971, the US and ARVN invaded Laos, but faced North Vietnamese forces which defeated them.

10. By the end of 1971 the South Vietnamese had accepted responsibility for all fighting on the ground, although they still depended on US air support. The number of US military personnel in South Vietnam had dropped to about 160,000.

11. In March 1972 the North Vietnamese invaded the DMZ and captured Quang Tri province. President Nixon ordered:
   (a) the mining of Haiphong and other North Vietnamese ports;
   (b) carried out an intense bombing of the North.

12. Peace talks resumed in July, but the talks broke down in mid-December with each side accusing the other of bad faith. Hanoi and other North Vietnamese cities were subjected to eleven days of intensive US bombing.

13. By the end of 1972 the western half of South Vietnam was in the hands of the Vietcong.

14. Talks started again in Paris and resulted on Jan. 27, 1973, in an agreement between the South Vietnamese communist forces which Nixon called "Peace with honour."
   (a) A cease-fire would go into effect the next morning throughout North and South Vietnam.
   (b) All US forces would be withdrawn and all bases dismantled.
   (c) All prisoners of war would be released.
   (d) An international force would keep the peace.
   (e) The South Vietnamese would have the right to determine their own future.
   (f) North Vietnamese troops could remain in the South but would not be reinforced.
   (g) The 17th parallel would remain the dividing line until the country could be reunited by "peaceful means."

15. Angered by:
   (a) President Johnson's lies about the staged Gulf of Tonkin incident;
   (b) President Nixon's secret invasion of Cambodia;
   the US Congress passed the **War Powers Act** which banned any further US military activity sanctioned by the President alone in Indochina.

Under President Ford

1. By the end of 1973 there were few US military personnel left in South Vietnam, but the fighting continued, and North and South Vietnam each denounced the other of violations of the truce.

2. During 1974 a series of offensives took place as each side sought to seize land from the other.

3. The North Vietnamese prepared for a major offensive to be launched in either 1975 or 1976.

4. The capture of Phuoc Binh in December 1974 by the North Vietnamese convinced the North Vietnamese that an invasion of the South feasible.
   In early March, North Vietnamese forces began a large-scale offensive in the central highlands. When President Thieu ordered a withdrawal of all ARVN forces from the central highlands and from the two northern provinces, there was a panic. The South Vietnamese army began to melt away. By early April the ARVN had abandoned the northern half of their country to the North

Vietnamese. Remaining Americans left in a panic evacuation by helicopter from the Embassy.

5. On April 21st, President Thieu resigned and fled to Taiwan.
6. On April 30th the South Vietnamese government officially surrendered unconditionally, and North Vietnamese tanks occupied Saigon.
7. A military government was installed, and on July 2, 1976, the country was united as the Socialist Republic of Vietnam, with its capital in Hanoi. Saigon was renamed Ho Chi Minh City.
8. The collaborators with the US either fled as "boat people" or were interned in prison camps.

Reasons for US Failure

1. The Vietcong and NLF had overwhelming support among the people.
2. The Vietcong were experienced in guerrilla warfare,
3. The Vietcong were fighting on their own territory.
4. The Vietcong received some help from North Vietnam, the USSR and China, although this was in no way decisive.
5. The Vietcong were dedicated fighters for their country and its independence.
6. In Ho Chi Minh, the Vietcong had a trusted leader.
7. Ho Chi Minh had good generals: Vo Nguyen Giap and Hoang Van Thai.
8. The North Vietnamese dispersed their factories, hospitals and population to avoid US bombing campaigns.
9. US atrocities alienated most of the Vietnamese.
10. The ARVN* was thoroughly corrupt and demoralized, and suffered from increasingly frequent desertions.

The Consequences of the War

1. The effects of the long conflict were harsh for all involved.

(a) Casualty figures for the Vietnamese are uncertain, estimates range from 185,000 to 225,000 killed and 500,000 to 570,000 wounded. The North Vietnamese and Vietcong suffered about 900,000 troops killed and 2 million wounded. In addition, more than 1,000,000 North and South Vietnamese civilians were killed during the war.

More than 47,000 Americans were killed in action, nearly 11,000 died of other causes, more than 303,000 were wounded in the war.

(b) More bombs had been dropped on Vietnam than during the whole of the Second World War. Many cities and towns were heavily damaged.

(c) For a decade the USA dropped tens of thousands of tons of defoliants, such as agent orange, over three million acres of South Vietnam, Laos and Cambodia to kill vegetation used as a cover by the enemy and to destroy their crops. This included dioxin, one of the most toxic substances known. It produces metabolic disorders, immunological abnormalities, reproductive abnormalities, neuro-psychiatric disorders and death. About two million people were affected by these poisons in Vietnam, which have produced birth defects in 500,000 children. Deformed births in the area continue until today.

(d) By the war's end much of the population of South Vietnam had become refugees seeking an escape from the fighting.

(e) Agriculture, business, and industry had been disrupted, and Vietnam's economic resources partly destroyed.

(f) In the USA Johnson's economic program for a "Great Society" had been halted by the economic and military demands of the war. The cost of the war has been estimated to have totalled about $200 billion.

(g) With the Communist victory in South Vietnam and in neighbouring Cambodia and Laos, Vietnam emerged as an important Southeast Asian power.

2. Neighbouring Laos and Cambodia were destabilized. The Communist Khmer Rouge, under Pol Pot, instituted a reign of terror. Town dwellers were forced into the countryside in order to build a new society. All educated people, were massacred or died in death marches. Perhaps one fifth of the Cambodian nation perished. Laos fell to the Communists after the fall of Saigon.

3. In the end, the area fell under Soviet influence.

4. The War made East-West relations much more difficult.

5. It made the USA unpopular among Third World states and before world public opinion.

6. It introduced profound divisions into US society.
   (a) The draft was unfairly applied. It could be avoided by staying at college indefinitely (Bill Clinton) or by joining the State Militias, performing only nominal duties (George W. Bush).
   (b) A disproportionate number of casualties were black Americans, revealing discrimination within the armed forces. ie. Black Americans were more likely than the average to be sent abroad, to Vietnam, and in Vietnam into the jungle. This provoked calls for minority civil rights.

7. The demoralized US army was infected with a narcotics problem. US soldiers returned from Vietnam and imported a drug culture into the USA.

8. US prestige around the world suffered a great blow.

9. The immense amount of money and resources lavished on the war reduced the resources available for Johnson's "Great Society Programme," designed to improve education health and social services in the inner cities. Thus the war had the effect of preserving social and economic inequalities within the USA.

10. The conduct of US policy created a "credibility gap" between US governments and the rest of the world.

11. The conduct of US policy created a "credibility gap" between US governments and the American people. Presidents became very unpopular. Congress legislated to limit the power of the US president to wage war unaccountably. This scepticism about the motives and abilities of US leadership was to be reinforced by the Watergate Affair.

12. Thousands of "boat people," usually people who had collaborated with the French and then the Americans, fled in small boats to escape reprisals.

13. The Japanese economy boomed as it was used as a base for industrial production for the war.

14. The vindictiveness of US policy ensured that Vietnam would continue to suffer the effects of economic warfare. The USA imposed a trade embargo on Vietnam from 1975 to 1995, and pressured other countries to do the same.

The Significance of the War

1. The Vietnam War was:
   (a) a civil war, fought between:
       (i) the ARVN and the Vietcong;
       (ii) later the Vietcong were aided by the North Vietnamese; but if the country was a unity by the terms of the Geneva Agreement (1954) this was still a civil war.
   (b) It was interpreted by the USA as part of the Cold War in the usual self-serving way, as part of the struggle between international communism on the one side, and "freedom and democracy," i.e. US dominated capitalism, on the other.
   (c) It was really a national liberation struggle against foreign colonial oppression. In the eyes of the Vietnamese, the Americans had simply replaced the French as would-be imperial masters, and the ARVN were collaborators, willing or not.

2. It was an example of **asymmetrical warfare*** in which one side has overwhelming resources, and the other has few, but wins nevertheless.
3. US misinterpretation of the liberation movement as part of a worldwide Communist conspiracy of is an example of a government and people believing their own propaganda. Fear of Communism and the collective paranoia generated by the media, and employed by governments for their own ends, distorted US perceptions of reality at the highest levels.
4. The war showed the readiness of the US to use chemical warfare to destroy the environment in conflict against small nations to extend or maintain their dominance across the world.
5. The destabilization of the entire region of Indo-China, with terrible consequences for the people, demonstrated a fundamental lack of responsibility in the conduct of US foreign policy.
5. The war showed that it was possible for a small country to resist superpower domination, although at terrible cost.
7. The war showed the isolation of the USA. Despite considerable pressure, no European allies sent troops to Vietnam.
8. The war revealed the imbalance which has grown up between the power of the "imperial presidency" and the legislature in the USA, with presidents waging war by stealth, and lying to justify wars.
9. Even though news coverage was heavily (self) censored so as to avoid undue distress to US administrations or citizens, the Vietnam War was the first televised war. Much of the opposition to the war within the USA was due to the fact that for the first time civilians in the aggressor country could see something of what their soldiers were doing in their name. This led to a reappraisal of war coverage, and to the measures since taken by governments and military to exercise control over the media coverage during subsequent wars.

Glossary

ARVN: the South Vietnamese Army

asymmetrical warfare: warfare between very unequally balanced forces of different levels of military sophistication, in which the more sophisticated usually call the less sophisticated "terrorists" and use this as a pretext themselves to evade the rules of war.

client state: a state which, while being officially independent, is in fact under the control of a hegemonic power

guerilla warfare: warfare fought in small groups using hit-and-run tactics

martial law: the normal human rights protections of the civilian population are removed, giving the military the power to execute summary justice.

National Liberation Front (NLF) or Vietcong: a Vietnamese movement formed to demand independence, led by Ho Chi-minh

NLF: the National Liberation Front or Vietcong

proxies: those fighting on behalf of others

proxy war: a war fought on behalf of other powers

Vietcong: the military wing of the National Liberation Front (NLF)

Vietminh: the League for the Independence of Vietnam

Vietnamization: Nixon's policy of handing over the war to the ARVN, as a cover for US withdrawal

Willy Brandt

11. DÉTENTE (1963-79)

"In the nuclear area, there is no rational alternative to accords of mutual restraint between the United States and the Soviet Union, two nations which have the power to destroy mankind." (US President Ford)

By "**détente**" is meant a long-term state of relaxation of east-west tensions, as opposed to a short "thaw." Détente may be said to have begun shortly after the resolution of the Cuban Missile Crisis at the end of 1962, and finally ended with the Soviet invasion of Afghanistan at the end of 1979.

The Causes of Détente

Causes Relating to Both Superpowers

1. The Cuban Missile Crisis had revealed the dangers of confrontation and brinkmanship.* The continued arms race and nuclear stand-off posed a permanent threat to the planet.
2. The super-powers were alarmed at the possibility of the proliferation of nuclear weapons. This possibility was increased by:
   (a) the number of fast-breeder reactors in nuclear power stations producing small amounts of plutonium as a by-product of the process of producing nuclear energy;
   (b) new methods of enriching uranium to weapons' grade standard.
3. The superpowers were alarmed at the development of weapons technology:
   (a) The development of multiple independent re-entry vehicles (MIRVs), which allowed separately targeted warheads to be carried on a single missile;
   (b) The development of anti-ballistic missile systems (ABMs) to counter a first-strike threatened to destroy the stability of deterrence.
The increasing complexity of weapons systems led to the possibility that the development of new weapons or delivery systems could allow one side to jump far ahead of the other, when it would be tempted to launch a pre-emptive first strike.
4. The "Allies" of both superpowers began to show a new independence in themselves improving relations with "the other side," e.g. France and Rumania, and especially West German *Ostpolitik*.

Causes Relating to the USA Alone

1. A series of revelations about the working of the US brought about a widespread loss of faith in the USA in the justice of US institutions and policies:

    (a) The horrors of the Vietnam War,

    (b) Involvement in the coup in Chile and support of the Allende dictatorship,

    (c) The Watergate Affair, when President Nixon was directly implicated in the burglary of the Democratic Party election HQ

    (d) The **Church Committee** examined CIA activities across the Third World, revealing:

        (i) attempts to assassinate foreign leaders;

        (ii) involvement on coups d'etat;

        (iii) ties to the Mafia;

        (iv) improper storage of dangerous materials.

    (e) The **Rockefeller Committee** investigated the FBI and found that the Agency:

        (i) carried out illegal surveillance on political groups and civil rights leaders;

        (ii) carried out illegal acts to discredit anti-war and civil rights groups;

        (iii) carried out experiments with behaviour-changing drugs on unsuspecting suspects.

As a result, the Congress passed measures to limit the power of the president and oversee the intelligence services. e.g.

        (i) The War Powers Act (1973) gave Congress the power to review and cancel executive orders to send troops overseas;

        (ii) In 1975 the CIA was required to inform a Congressional Committee of its secret operations;

        (iii) The Freedom of Information Act was strengthened;

        (iv) In 1976 President Gerald Ford banned peacetime assassinations of foreign leaders;

        (v) The attorney-general banned secret operation within the USA;

        (vi) Limits were placed on aid to regimes such as those of Turkey, South Korea, Indonesia Uruguay and Chile;

        (vii) Various covert activities, e.g. in Angola, were reined in.

2. The Sino-Soviet split reduced pressure on the USA.

3. By expanding economic and cultural ties, the US hoped to open up Soviet society to Western (i.e. US) propaganda and influence.

Causes Relating to the USSR Alone

1. Détente had been the strategy of the USSR ever since the death of Stalin. It had been referred to as "peaceful coexistence."

2. Dominant people in the party (e.g. Kosygin) wished to reduce spending on defence to bring the standard of living of Soviet citizens to Western levels.

3. There was a perceived need to repair the image of the Soviet Union because of the suppression of the Prague Spring.

4. The Soviet government did not wish to be isolated by the Sino-Soviet split and improving US/Chinese relations

5. The failure of Soviet agriculture made the USSR dependent upon grain imports from the US and Canada.

6. Parity* in the arms race and the improvement of the Soviet economy required access to new western technology, particularly in computers.

7. Brezhnev came to like his image as a man of peace, and came to believe in what had initially been merely a matter of tactics.
8. The leadership of the USSR was disabled. Under Brezhnev and Chernenko it became a gerontocracy,* That generation of leaders wished to end their lives in office peacefully. The younger Yuri Andropov governed from a hospital bed for much of his period in office.
9. The Soviet economic system, the command economy, was showing signs of decay, which suggested that a cautious policy was advisable.

Ostpolitik

An important factor in bringing about détente was the *Ostpolitik* of West German Foreign Minister Willy Brandt.

1. The official West German attitude towards eastern Europe was expressed in the **Hallstein Doctrine** propounded by Konrad Adenauer in 1955: The Federal Republic of Germany (FDR) would have no diplomatic relations with any state which recognised the German Democratic Republic (DDR).
2. For this reason the FDR broke off diplomatic relations with Yugoslavia (1957) and Cuba (1963).
3. In December 1966 a coalition was formed of the SPD, the CDU and the Christian Social Union. The SPD leader, Willy Brandt, became Foreign Minister.
4. He outlined his proposals for a reduction in east-west tension (***Ostpolitik***) at a NATO foreign ministers' meeting:
    (a) An improvement in east-west relations, beginning with Poland and Czechoslovakia;
    (b) This to be part of a wider European détente;
    (c) Support for moves to reduce arms levels and to control the spread of nuclear weapons (i.e. no West German nuclear bomb to be developed).
5. On 3rd. Jan. 1967 Diplomatic relations were established between the FDR and Rumania. This showed that the Hallstein Doctrine was no longer operational.
6. April 1967 The **Karoly Vary (Czechoslovakia) Conference** of Warsaw Pact communist parties discussed "problems of European security". It was agreed that:
    (a) No state would establish diplomatic relations with the FDR without getting agreement from the DDR;
    (b) A European security conference should be called.
7. Feeling threatened, the DDR signed treaties of "mutual assistance and friendship" with Poland and Czechoslovakia.
8. Jan. 1968 The FDR re-established diplomatic relations with Yugoslavia.
9. The FDR opened a trade mission in Czechoslovakia.
10. Progress was halted, but only temporarily, by the Soviet invasion of Czechoslovakia.
11. In September 1968 the FDR lifted the ban on the communist party imposed since 1955.
12. The DDR allowed more citizens to visit the FDR (one and a half million senior citizens).
13. In October 1968 the SPD and FPD (liberal) coalition formed a government in the FDR with Willy Brandt as Chancellor.
14. In November 1969 the FDR signed the nuclear Non-proliferation Treaty.
15. In December 1969, a Warsaw Pact meeting was held in Warsaw to work out a common response to *Ostpolitik*. Ulbricht demanded that the FDR recognise the DDR. Brandt spoke of "Two states within one nation."
16. In January 1970 the East Germans introduced random road blocks on access routes to West Berlin.

17. In March 1970 the Prime Minister of the DDR, Willi Stoph, met Brandt in Erfurt.
18. In August 1970, the USSR and DDR signed a "non-aggression treaty" in Moscow, setting the seal of soviet approval on Ostpolitik.
19. In December 1970, Brandt visited Warsaw and:
    (a) Signed a non-aggression treaty with Poland;
    (b) Recognised the Oder-Neisse line as the boundary of Germany with Poland;
    (c) Knelt before the memorial erected to Hitler's victims in the old ghetto quarter of Warsaw. This was a recognition of German war guilt.
    This diminished Poland's need for dependence on the USSR for its defence.
20. Only the DDR dragged its feet. May 1971 Walter Ulbricht was replaced as First Secretary by Erich Honecker.
21. On 19th September 1971, a four-power agreement on Berlin was reached, by which:
    (a) The joint responsibilities of Great Britain, the USA, France and the USSR as occupying powers were recognised as unchanged.
    (b) Links between the FDR and West Berlin were to remain.
    (c) West Berliners were to have easier access to East Berlin and the DDR.
22. In December 1972, the DDR had to sign the "Basic Treaty" with the FDR by which they would:
    (a) cultivate good neighbourly relations;
    (b) enjoy increased personal and cultural contacts;
    (c) respect each others' frontiers and alliances;
    (d) exchange permanent diplomatic missions; (but not embassies, so the exchange fell short of recognition).
    The United States, Britain, and France seconded Brandt's efforts by concluding a new Four Power accord with the USSR on Berlin in September 1971. The Soviets made what they considered a major concession by agreeing to retain their responsibility under the Potsdam Accords for access to West Berlin and achieved in return Western recognition of the status quo in eastern Europe and access to West German technology and credits.

Reasons for *Ostpolitik*

1. East-west tensions were dangerous to the FDR. If the cold war turned into fighting in Europe, it would probably begin in Germany.
2. This was particularly true with the adoption by NATO of a "flexible response strategy" and the development of tactical "battlefield" nuclear weapons* after 1967. The obvious place in which they would first be used was Germany, where NATO and the Warsaw Pact confronted each other directly.
3. With the development of détente, it was thought desirable for the FDR to establish good relations with eastern bloc countries in order not to be outflanked by the USA or France.
4. It would perhaps lead to increased trade.

East-West Relations during Détente

1. Following the Cuban Missile Crisis, in 1963 a "hot line' telephone link was established between Washington and Moscow in order to allow the leaders to contact each other directly during future crises.
2. In 1963 the **Nuclear Test Ban Treaty** was concluded, banning all nuclear tests except underground tests (because it was impossible to verify them).

3. The USA began to export wheat to the USSR.
4. The Soviet invasion of Czechoslovakia in 1968 hardly caused *détente* to pause.
5. In 1973 the Conference on Security and Cooperation in Europe (CSCE) began talks to increase mutual security in the continent. The final accord was signed in 1975 at Helsinki. It:
    (a) recognised the legitimacy of the postwar borders of Europe
    (b) called for closer cultural and technological cooperation
    (c) called upon signatory states to protect human rights.
The USA used the last point to criticise the Soviet Union's human rights record in Eastern Europe (while conveniently ignoring its own in Central and South America and elsewhere).
6. 1969 Strategic Arms Limitation talks (SALT) began. This led to several agreements in 1972:
    (a) Banning nuclear weapons on the ocean floor;
    (b) Updating the "hot line" to take account of new developments in satellite communications;
    (c) Limiting each side to two ABM systems of limited size and effectiveness;
    (d) Freezing the development of new systems of offensive weapons until 1977.
7. SALT II talks led first to agreement in 1974 to:
    (a) a ban on all underground tests above 150 kilotons (which could be independently verified);
    (b) a new SALT Treaty should extend until 1985.
8. The treaty was signed in 1979:
    (a) Limiting delivery systems on each side to 2,400, declining to 2,250 in 1985;
    (b) Missiles over a certain size were banned;
    (c) Limits were set on the number of warheads per missile;
    (d) Very modest restrictions were placed upon the development of new delivery systems;
    (e) The parties agreed to notify each other of tests and stocks.
    It was never ratified by the US Congress.
9. NATO and the Warsaw Pact held talks on mutual and balanced force reductions (MBFR) from 1969. Little was achieved until 1979 when Brezhnev unilaterally announced the withdrawal of 1,000 tanks and 20,000 men from East Germany.
10. Many agreements between the USA and USSR were signed, dealing with space research, trade and environmental pollution:
    (a) The Outer Space Treaty (1967) banned the placing of nuclear weapons in orbit around the earth or in outer space.
    (b) The Nuclear Nonproliferation Treaty (1968) whose signatories agreed not to exchange nuclear knowledge or hardware. China, France and Israel did not sign it.
    (c) The Seabed Pact (1971) banned placing nuclear weapons on the sea bed outside a country's twelve-mile limit of territorial waters.
    (d) The Biological Warfare Treaty (1972) banned the development, production and stockpiling of biological toxins and weapons.
11. Yet by 1971 the US had developed the doctrine of **strategic sufficiency**, by which the USA would seek to possess:
    (a) a wide range of weapons to enable a flexible response to all "threats"
    (b) a capacity to retaliate against the USSR even after an all-out surprise attack with nuclear weapons.
    In pursuit of this aim, the USA began developing new weapons and delivery systems.
12. In 1972 and 1974 Nixon visited Moscow, and 1973 Brezhnev visited Washington.
13. During 1973 the US began to withdraw significantly from Vietnam.

14. In July 1975 The Helsinki Agreement involved:
    (a) The acceptance by the USA, Canada, and almost all European states of all post-war frontiers; (thus tacitly recognising the permanent division of Germany).
    (b) The communist countries agreed to extend human rights to their peoples, e.g. the right to leave the country, to freedom of speech.
15. The Eastern European satellites were allowed to develop their economies with more freedom.

Nuclear Détente

1. The Cuban Missile Crisis led to a new awareness of the dangers of the nuclear arms race, and to serious attempts to "manage it" so as to make it less perilous.
    (a) In 1963 a crisis "hot line" was set up between the White House and the Kremlin. This was a direct link between the leaders so that rapid communication could be achieved in the event of a nuclear accident and was also set up to help prevent an accidental nuclear war. Generally thought to have been a telephone, it was actually a teleprinter.
    (b) By 1963 nearly 500 nuclear weapons had been tested in the atmosphere as well as others in the oceans. In that year the first major attempt at limiting the testing of nuclear weapons came into the existence with the Nuclear Test Ban Treaty, banning all but underground testing. It was signed by the USSR, USA and Britain.
    (c) In 1967 the US and USSR jointly presented the **Nuclear Non-Proliferation Treaty** to try to limit the **proliferation** of nuclear weapons. This treaty was signed in 1968 by the five nuclear nations, as well as by 59 non-nuclear states. It placed severe limitations on the transfer, by states with nuclear weapons, to other states of the knowledge or materials required to manufacture, test or deploy nuclear weapons.
    Some nations with the capability to develop a nuclear weapons program, and who wished to do so, refused to sign, e.g. Israel, Argentina, Brazil, India and Pakistan. The treaty went into effect in 1970.
    (d) The Outer Space Treaty (1967) banned military installations in outer space and on orbiting satellites..
    (e) The Seabed Arms Control Treaty (1971) banned nuclear weapons from being placed on the seabed outside the twelve-mile limit of any nation.
    (f) In 1972 the **Anti-Ballistic Missile Treaty** (ABMs) allowed each side two sites for the deployment of ABMs:
        (i) one to protect the capital city;
        (ii) one to shield a single complex of ICBM silos.
    ABMs were not to be transferred to another country.
    (g) The Strategic Arms Limitation Talks (SALT 1) of 1972 obliged the superpowers for five years to:
        (i) reach parity in land and sea launchers
        (ii) allow site verification by satellite photographs.
2. However, the arms race continued apace. The Cuban Missile Crisis had made the Soviet leadership determined never again to be humiliated by being exposed in a position of military inferiority. Thus Khrushchev and his successors thus began the largest peacetime **arms race** in history.
3. The Soviets developed **Multiple Independently Targettable Re-entry Vehicles (MIRVs)**. A single rocket would carry many warheads, which would split off from the "parent" rocket to reach their own targets.

4. The USA developed radar-evading Cruise missiles.
5. The primary focus of the arms race was to develop an effective first strike capability, the ability to effectively disable the enemy's weapons, making retaliation impossible. Once each side had reached an effective first strike capability, the need arose to develop a second strike force, which would let the nation surprised by a nuclear attack retaliate with a full nuclear blow.

   Once each side had an effective second strike force, there would be stability, as each side would realize the pointlessness of nuclear weapons, since even with their first strike, they would still be vulnerable to the other's second strike force. This concept became known as **mutually assured destruction (MAD).**

   The number of nuclear weapons held by the two superpowers increased dramatically because of this need for a first strike and second strike force. At one point they had enough to destroy all life on earth more than 1,500 times.
6. SALT II talks led first to agreement in 1974 to a ban on all underground tests above 150 kilotons (which could be verified). The treaty was signed in 1979:
   (a) Limiting delivery systems on each side to 2,400, declining to 2,250 in 1985;
   (b) Missiles over a certain size were banned;
   (c) Limits were set on the number of warheads per missile;
   (d) Very modest restrictions were placed upon the development of new delivery systems;
   (e) The parties agreed to notify each other of tests and stocks.
   It was never ratified by the US Congress.

The Significance of Détente

1. It could be argued that détente had been the policy of the USSR ever since the death of Stalin in 1953, under the title of "peaceful coexistence," but it had never been reciprocated by the USA.
2. Both sides meant different things by détente:
   (a) For the USA it was a way to
      (i) contain Soviet power and Communism in a less confrontational manner, e.g. by using trade to restrain it from promoting and supporting revolutionary movements in the Third World
      (ii) liberalize the USSR
      (iii) undermine Soviet control over its satellites
   (b) For the USSR it was a safe way to wait for the inevitable economic and social crisis in the West which would bring about the Revolution.
   (c) For both it was a way to make the nuclear world safe for a non-military ideological struggle.
3. Détente was presented to the US public as a less confrontational method of containing Communism and Soviet power. It was claimed that there would be a system of rewards and punishments (carrots and sticks) by which Washington would change the policies and behaviour of the Soviet Government. The United States would link positive inducements, such as the transfer of technology and grain sales, to some expected response from the Soviet Union, such as their restraint in promoting revolutionary movements. This extremely (but typically) patronizing policy was called "**linkage**".*

Glossary

ABMs: antiballistic missiles

CSCE: Conference on Security and Cooperation in Europe

détente: a long-term reduction in hostile relations

DDR: German Democratic Republic (East Germany)

Dergue: the Ethiopian military junta

ghetto: an area of a city set aside for the Jews

FDR: Federal Republic of Germany (West Germany)

gerontocracy: rule by old men

hot line: a direct communications link between the White House and the Kremlin, for use during emergencies

INF: Intermediate Nuclear Force Reduction talks

linkage: the US policy of linking positive inducements, such as the transfer of technology or grain sales, to some desired response from the Soviet Union, such as their restraint in supporting Third World revolutionary movements.

MBFR: mutual and balanced force reductions

MIRVs: multiple independent re-entry vehicles

NATO: North Atlantic Treaty Organisation

neutron bomb: a "small" nuclear bomb which had enhanced radiation to kill people without harming property.

Nuclear Use Theorists (NUTs): a school of US strategists who thought that a nuclear war could be winnable

Ostpolitik: West German policy of reduction of tension with its eastern neighbours

rapprochement: a reconciliation between nation

SDI: Strategic Defence Initiative, or "star wars"

START: Strategic Arms Limitation Talks

tactical nuclear weapons: short range nuclear missiles

Third World: that part of the world which was neither part of the West nor of the Soviet bloc

Bibliography

Griffith, William E., *The Ostpolitik of the Federal Republic of Germany* MIT Press (Cambridge Mass.,1978)

George Papadopoulos

12. The Junta of the Greek Colonels

"We are the government, you are nothing. The government isn't alone. Behind the government are the Americans." (Inspector Basil Lambrou, Head of the Athens secret police)

Background

1. In 1964 a new king, Constantine II, and a new prime minister with a majority in Parliament, George Papandreu, seemed to indicate a period of stability ahead:

    (a) The government increased expenditure on education and social services.

    (b) Releases of Communists from prison camps suggested the beginning of the end of the bitterness of the Civil War.

2. However, the government faced problems:

    (a) the unwillingness of the EEC to absorb Greece's agricultural surplus;

    (b) inadequate military aid from NATO;

    (c) communal violence in Cyprus;

    (d) the constant threat from Turkey:

    > (i) of an invasion of Cyprus;

    > (ii) pressure on the Greeks of Constantinople to force them to leave;

    > (iii) threats towards the ecumenical patriarchate.*

    (e) The King considered that as Commander-in-Chief he had sole right to run the armed forces.

3. Papandreu, afraid of right-wing army conspiracies from officers' groups such as IDEA sought to replace higher officers appointed by the previous government.

4. Rumours of a left-wing conspiracy in the army, **Aspida** (Shield), were connected to Andreas Papandreu, the prime minister's son.

5. In May 1965 Papandreu dismissed his Minister of Defence and decided to do the job himself. The king refused to appoint him. Papandreu offered his resignation, and the king accepted it.

6. Several attempts were made to form a government which could command a majority in the

*Vouli,** before Stephanos Stephanopoulos formed a government in September. This managed to hold on until April 1966, when a caretaker government took over with a mandate to hold elections in May 1967. During this period

   (a) the alleged murderers of Grigorios Lambrakis, a left wing politician, were tried.

   (b) Officers involved in the Aspida conspiracy were also put on trial. No connection with Andreas Papandreu was established, and he could not be tried as he enjoyed parliamentary immunity. This would lapse if the government fell, so his father tried to persuade the leader of the opposition, Panagiotis Kanellopoulos, to agree to extend his immunity until after the elections. He refused and the caretaker government resigned.

7. The king then asked Kanellopoulos to form a government. Knowing that he would not have a majority in the *Vouli*, he asked for a dissolution and new elections before facing the *Vouli*, and the king granted his request.

8. George Spandidakis and other generals had been plotting a coup with the king's approval, using a NATO-approved plan to seize power, but they vacillated.*

The Colonels' Coup

1. The elections never took place, because in the early hours of the morning of 21st April 1967, a group of middle-ranking army officers led by Colonel George Papadopoulos, Colonel Nicholas Makarezos and Brigadier Stylianos Pattakos, seized control of the state.

2. George Papadopoulos a former member of the Security Battalions, belonged to the Central Intelligence Service (KYP) founded by, and working with, the CIA. All were members of right-wing societies IDEA and the Union of Young Greek Officers (EENA). They had decided to pre-empt their superiors with their own coup.

3. During the night many prominent people were arrested.

4. The pretext was that the king had requested the army to intervene to "protect" the state from imminent danger of a Communist coup. The newspapers of that day appeared with identical headlines, leading articles and commentaries supplied by the military Press Service.

5. The King was initially alarmed. The US Defence attaché called on him and was told: "Incredibly stupid ultra-right wing bastards, having gained control of tanks, have brought disaster to Greece." Later, as his own arrest appeared increasingly unlikely, the king calmed down. The US embassy assured the State Department that the coup leaders "declare themselves one thousand per cent pro-American."

Reasons for the Coup

1. C. M. Woodhouse, probably representing the "official" British point of view, claimed that the coup was due to the "irascible character and impetuosity of George Papandreu, exacerbated by the wrong judgments of the King."

2. It has also been attributed to the generally inept management of the Greek political class.

3. Strains set up by the Civil War contributed to the unwillingness of all sides to abide by constitutional practices.

4. The issue about US involvement in the coup is not *whether* the US Government was involved, but *how deeply* and *how intimately* they were involved. Although the CIA probably did not actually organize and direct the overthrow of democracy:

   (a) The plotters used American weapons;

   (b) and a plan devised under the umbrella of NATO to ensure US control of Greece;

   (c) The coup leader had been in receipt of CIA pay since 1952, and was chief liaison officer between the Greek KYP and the CIA.

(d) There is evidence that the CIA knew of the plot a month beforehand.

(e) The CIA was in close contact with the colonels. Greece's most decorated soldier, General George Koumanakos, had been approached as early as 1965 by a senior official of the US embassy and asked why he was not "coming in with us."

It seems that the CIA wished to pre-empt a royalist coup by people under British influence with their own coup organized by people on their own payroll.

5. Although the initial justification for the coup was that it was "to ward off the imminent danger of a Communist seizure of power," later, seeking legitimacy, the junta tried to present revolutionary credentials, referring to "the Glorious Revolution." It was suggested that the army acted on the mandate of the people, and were preparing a new, "healthy" democracy in the future.

6. It soon became evident from their actions that the real purpose of the Junta was the systematic subordination of Greece to US interests.

The Government of the "Colonels"

1. Initially, the Colonels found few respectable politicians prepared to collaborate with them, but they did find a compliant king to swear their government into office.

2. Over the next few days, the regime tightened its grip on the country:

    (a) Some 6,000 people were arrested as "Communists" and interned without trial in prisons and concentration camps on islands.

    (b) A powerful secret police (ESA) under military control spied on citizens.

    (c) Many were imprisoned. Torture became commonplace. Prisoners were beaten, hung suspended from their wrists. There was jumping on the stomach, pulling out finger nails, use of electric shock. In addition there was psychological torture. Prisoners were threatened with being maimed, raped and killed, and there were mock executions.

    (d) Many more people simply lost their jobs, or had their pensions revoked.

    (e) The press was censored, many books, songs and public meetings of over five persons were banned.

3. This provoked a mild show of disapproval by foreign governments:

    (a) The US Government, anxious to distance itself in public from the junta, suspended some arms sales for a while, and asked for vague reassurances that democracy would at some point be re-established; then recognized the regime, and fully resumed arms sales. The US vice-president visited Greece to express his solidarity with the regime.

    (b) Only the Scandinavian, Dutch and Yugoslav governments resolutely refused to countenance the overthrow of democracy in its original home.

    (c) The European Investment Bank withheld a promised loan.

    (d) In December 1969 Greece left the Council of Europe to avoid expulsion.

4. The self-proclaimed purposes of the Junta were:

    (a) to purge Greece of Communism;

    (b) to replace the effete democracy which had been unable to secure union with Cyprus;

    (c) to defend Hellenism.

5. Under the slogan "Greece of the Christian Greeks", the Junta claimed to represent nationalism and Orthodoxy. The socially conservative Colonels regarded them selves as the guardians of the traditional values of Greek Christianity. They condemned long hair and short skirts, cutting the hair of male tourists whose locks were deemed long enough to offend Christian sensibility. Historian C. M. Woodhouse records that "It was almost impossible to name any Greek of international reputation ... who did not regard them with contempt."

6. The Junta quickly consolidated its hold on power:

(a) The Church was purged, Thirty-three bishops were replaced, and later another twelve;

(b) Civil servants were forced to sign loyalty declarations;

(c) many army officers were forced to resign;

(d) nearly one third of the university teaching staff were forced to resign;

(e) In 1969, twenty-one senior judges and prosecutors were dismissed.

(f) Prominent citizens were placed on trial, e.g. former prime minister George Papandreu, composer Mikis Thodorakis, and newspaper editor Eleni Vlachou.

7. By December 1967, even the king was finding it difficult to work with the junta, and planned a counter-coup, which failed miserably. The king then fled into exile. A regent* was appointed, and Papadopoulos became prime minister.

8. In an attempt to gain popular approval, the Junta adopted some populist measures:

(a) the cancellation of farmers' debts to the Agricultural Bank;

(b) the provision of housing loans for workers;

(c) the provision of free textbooks and loans for university students.

9. In reality it favoured big business with:

(a) huge tax breaks for large foreign companies;

(b) the suppression of trades unions and strikes;

(c) corruption;

so that the gap between rich and poor grew.

10. In 1968 a new constitution was approved, but never fully put into effect.

11. Despite the police surveillance, opposition to the Junta within Greece began to grow:

(a) On 1st November 1968 the funeral of George Papandreu was the signal for a massive demonstration of public opposition to the dictatorship.

(b) The Communists were fractured into many rival groups by internal splits.

(c) A young officer unsuccessfully tried to assassinate Papadopoulos.

(d) On the centre left the Panhellenic Liberation Movement (PAK) of Andreas Papandreu led opposition.

12. Feeling confident, in 1969 the Junta suspended press censorship and restored some freedoms, but martial law remained in force.

13. In 1971 Papadopoulos reshuffled his government, removing or demoting many who had helped him to power.

14. During 1972, after the Regent had criticised him, Papadopoulos took the post himself, and an attempt was made to develop a personality cult:

(a) his portrait adorned public buildings;

(b) his symbol, the phoenix, replaced the king's head on coins.

15. In 1972 the US Sixth Fleet was granted home port facilities in Greece, possibly fulfilling the real purpose of the coup.

16. During the early years the economy benefited from measures taken before the Junta came into power, but by 1973 problems were beginning to surface. The dictators engaged in public works projects, borrowed heavily to pay for them, kept wages down by repression, and so brought about inflation at 30% *per annum*.

The Fall of the Junta

1. The US wanted President-Archbishop Makarios out of Cyprus, since his government was pursuing a course of non-alignment, even occasionally voting on issues in the UN with the Soviet Union. Such independence earned him the title "Castro of the Mediterranean" in Washington.

2. The junta withdrew the Greek soldiers from Cyprus which guaranteed the security of the majority Greek community there, leaving the island open to invasion from Turkey.
3. On March 8th 1970, the Junta tried to assassinate Archbishop Makarios but failed. They then began to infiltrate Cypriot society in preparation for a coup.
4. When the Junta cancelled the routine deferments of eighty-eight students, and forcibly conscripted them into the army, students and staff held a sit-in at the Athens Law School. After two days, police suppressed the sit-in, chasing and beating students in nearby streets.
5. In May 1973 units of the Greek Navy mutinied and a destroyer was taken to Italy. Many naval officers were arrested.
6. Convinced that the king was behind the mutiny, Papadopoulos abolished the monarchy, made himself president, and confirmed the process with a rigged plebiscite.
7. In November 1973, students began a "sit-in" in the Athens Polytechnic, and transmitted radio broadcasts calling upon the people to rise up against the tyranny. On the night of 16-17th November army tanks bulldozed the locked gates, and armed police swarmed into the grounds. At least twenty students were killed.
8. Senior officers decided that Papadopoulos was incompetent. The blame for the Polytechnic massacre was laid on him, and he was replaced by Brigadier Ioannides, head of the military security police. Described by C. M. Woodhouse as "a man who would be perfectly at home in the Gestapo," he arrested Papadopoulos and installed a puppet of his own in his place. Under his leadership, repression increased in efficiency and ruthlessness.
9. Ioannidis decided to launch a coup on Cyprus in which Archbishop Makarios would be replaced by journalist Nikos Sampson, who would proclaim union with Greece. The US knew about the plan, but Henry Kissinger wanted nothing done to prevent it, as it would provide a pretext for a desired Turkish invasion. Makarios escaped death, but the Turks used the pretext to invade the island anyway, and carved out twenty-five per cent for the small Turkish population.
10. This spelled the end for the Junta. When the government ordered mobilization, the result was a shambles. It was clear that the Junta could not even organise their own forces efficiently.
11. Three days after the Turkish invasion of Cyprus, Ioannides allowed himself to be sidelined as senior officers of all three branches of the armed forces invited Constantine Karamanlis to return to restore the rule of law and democracy.
12. The new government:
    (a) restored the pre-Junta constitution, with a president replacing the king;
    (b) suspended martial law;
    (c) released all political prisoners;
    (d) legalized the Communist Party.
13. Although the UK, Turkey and Greece had agreed to guarantee the independence of Cyprus, the Turks seized the opportunity to launch a second attack on Cyprus and seized 40% of the island. In protest, Karamanlis withdrew Greek forces from NATO command.

Assessment

1. This was the first time that a state in Europe had fallen to a military dictatorship since the Second World War.
2. The "Colonels" were:
    (a) provincial people, puritanical and self-righteous social conservatives, who had risen through the ranks of the army;
    (b) C. M. Woodhouse pointed out: "... they had almost no experience as fighting soldiers. Most of the generals whom they displaced had fought with distinction: in Albania, in the

Greek Army of the Middle East, in the civil war, against the communists in Korea. The ex-colonels had a different sort of career: one in the military police, another in the security battalions (which the Germans formed to resist the resistance), and so on. To most of my Greek friends it is discreditable that not one of them took any part in the resistance during the German occupation (when they were all in their twenties): to the ex-colonels themselves it is a matter of congratulation."

(c) They were a group of right-wing Nazi collaborators originally enrolled by the British to ensure their control of post-war Greece, who later transferred their allegiance to the Americans.

3. The Colonels' pathological anti-Communism, and their brutally repressive conduct towards their political opponents, shows that this was a postscript to the Civil War.
4. The Junta never established a base of popular support, and could command little talent since few would work for them.
5. The experience of the rule of the Junta brought left and right together in a new appreciation of democracy, and highlighted the worse features of the post civil war system:
   (a) police files and supervision;
   (b) arbitrary arrest and imprisonment of political opponents;
   (c) the use of torture.
6. Among the lasting effects of this episode was a deep, widespread scepticism in Greece about US claims to moral leadership. The police, as agents of the junta, were also discredited. This led to a strengthening of traditional Greek dislike for the authorities and lack of respect for the law.

Glossary

Aspida: a left-wing conspiratorial group of army officers

CIA: Central Intelligence Agency - US espionage agency

ecumenical patriarchate: the headquarters of the Christian Orthodox Churches

EEC: European Economic Community (the Common Market)

EENA: Union of Young Greek Officers - a right-wing conspiratorial group of army officers

IDEA: a right-wing conspiratorial group of army officers

KYP: The Greek Central Intelligence Service - Greek espionage agency

martial law: military rule

regent: the representative of an absent king

vacillated: could not make up their minds when or how to act

Bibliography

Anonymous, *Inside the Colonels' Greece,* Tr. Richard Clogg, Chatto & Windus (London, 1972)

Clogg, R., & Yannopoulos, G., *Greece Under Military Rule*, Secker & Warburg (London, 1972)

Gallant, Thomas W., *Modern Greece*, Arnold (London, 2001)

Murtagh, Peter, *The Rape of Greece*, Simon & Schuster, (London, 1994)

Woodhouse, C. M., *The Rise and Fall of the Greek Colonels*, Granada (London, 1985)

Alexander Dubček

13. Eastern Europe (1979-85)

"One may hope that the next Dubček will appear in the nerve centre of the system: Moscow." (François Fejtö)

Czechoslovakia

Background

1. Czechoslovakia was:
   - (a) the most Western oriented and industrially advanced of the Soviet satellites;
   - (b) the one initially with the largest Communist Party;
   - (c) the last of the countries occupied by the Red Army to be incorporated into the Soviet system.
2. After the Yugoslav crisis there was a purge of nationalist-leaning leaders and Communists, with executions of some of the leaders.
3. Under Antonin Novotný, Czechoslovakia seemed the most docile of the Soviet satellites.
4. During the mid-1960s discontent began to develop, with:
   - (a) An industrial country, its progress was hampered by:
     - (i) inability to trade with the West, e.g. importing its iron-ore from Sweden;
     - (ii) by overcentralized control.
   - (b) Economic growth was poor, and the standard of living had fallen
   - (c) Restrictions on personal liberty.
   - (d) Slovaks were discontented with their position in the country, particularly under Novotný, a Czech who despised Slovaks.
5. This led to:
   - (a) meetings of intellectuals;
   - (b) student demonstrations over living conditions in Prague in November 1967, which were brutally suppressed by the police.
6. In January 1968, Novotný was voted out of office. Alexander Dubček became first secretary, General Jan Svoboda president, and Černík as prime minister.

The Prague Spring

1. Immediately upon his appointment, Dubček visited Moscow and assured the Soviet leadership of his loyalty.
2. The new triumvirate* sought to liberalise society, to develop "socialism with a human face."
3. Censorship was relaxed. This provoked a lively public debate.
4. At the beginning of April reformers produced an Action Programme:
   (a) This attacked:
       (i) The suppression of liberty under Novotný;
       (ii) Central management of the economy;
       (iii) The party monopoly of power.
   (b) It promised:
       (i) the rehabilitation of the victims of the 1949 purges;
       (ii) changes in the status of Slovakia;
       (iii) the democratization of the Communist party;
       (iv) the revival of the Czech Parliament;
       (v) freedom for political parties within the Communist-controlled National Front;
       (vi) the right to travel abroad;
       (vii) freedom of speech;
       (viii) a free press;
       (ix) the curbing of the secret police;
       (x) judicial reforms.
5. The Soviet and other Warsaw Pact leaderships became alarmed at these developments because they raised issues of personal and national freedom which might destabilise other satellites.
6. Popular pressure induced the bringing forward to early September of the Party Congress.
7. In early May the Czech leadership went to Moscow to reassure the Soviet leadership that they did not intend to leave Comecon* or the Warsaw Pact.*
8. A series of warnings were issued by the Kremlin:
   (a) Kosygin and later Marshall Grechko and General Epishev, head of military intelligence, visited Prague.
   (b) In June, Warsaw Pact forces held military manoeuvres in Czechoslovakia, and delayed leaving.
   (c) Warsaw pact leaders met in Warsaw, the Czechs not being invited, and issued a warning to the Czechs that they were letting power slip away from the Communist Party.
   (d) On 29th July a four day Russo-Czech meeting was held at the border.
   (e) Several days later there was another meeting at Bratislava.
9. The Czech leaders repeatedly assured the Soviets of their loyalty to the Warsaw Pact, but refused to backtrack on reforms.
10. In August, Tito of Yugoslavia and the independent-minded Ceausescu of Rumania visited Prague to rapturous receptions.
11. On 10th August the new statutes of the Czech Communist Party were published. They were to be submitted to the Party Congress in September. They ended democratic centralism* and granted rights to other parties.

The Invasion of Czechoslovakia

1. On 20th August, Soviet troops invaded, accompanied by troops from all the other Warsaw Pact countries except Rumania. There was no resistance, but a massive passive public hostility.

2. The Soviets intended to pre-empt the approval of the reforms at the September Party Congress
3. The Czech leadership was seized and taken to Moscow. The Soviets may have expected the Czech Central Committee to:
    (a) replace them with more compliant leaders
    (b) issue an invitation, retrospectively to justify the invasion
    This did not happen, and the triumvirate was reinstated. However, they had agreed to:
    (a) accept Soviet troops indefinitely on Czech soil
    (b) the restoration of censorship
    (c) the end of the rehabilitation
    (d) the watering down of economic reforms.
4. The invasion was justified by the **Brezhnev Doctrine**: that the USSR would intervene in any Communist state where the supremacy of the Party was threatened. This was a Soviet counterpart to the Truman Doctrine.
5. The invasion was condemned by China, Rumania, Yugoslavia and Albania, as well as the West.
6. The USSR vetoed a censure motion in the UN.

The Aftermath

1. Dubček was replaced by Gustav Husák.
2. The reforms were slowly reversed.
3. A new federal constitution was adopted to resolve Czech-Slovak differences.
4. In March 1969 the victory of the Czech ice-hockey team over their Soviet rivals led to an anti-Soviet demonstration.
5. Dubček was successively demoted, expelled from the Party, and employed as a forestry worker.
6. It brought the process of destalinization in Eastern Europe to an end.
7. Surprisingly, it did not affect the progress of détente.

Significance

1. It demonstrated the fragility of the Soviet system. All change was a threat.
2. It showed that the way forward was likely to come from within the Communist Party.

Poland

Background

1. During the period of détente the Polish government had embarked upon a wide-ranging development plan financed by western European credits.
2. Economic performance was not as expected, and the country's foreign debt mounted to $28,000,000,000.
3. The government imposed a series of price rises on staple goods.
4. In 1979, the Polish pope, John Paul II, visited Poland, giving a boost to nationalist forces.
5. By 1979–80 a popular protest movement had grown up around the unofficial Solidarity trade union in the Lenin shipyard at Gdansk (formerly Danzig) under its leader, an electrician, Lech Walesa. Strikes took place there and elsewhere across the country.
6. The government was forced to compromise with the strikers:
    (a) Edward Giereck resigned, as did other officials responsible for the near bankruptcy of the state.
    (b) Solidarity was officially recognised as a trades union.

7. In September, the USSR held large scale military manoeuvres on the Soviet-Polish border.
8. NATO countries warned against a Soviet military intervention, holding in reserve the threat of declaring Warsaw in default on its debts.
9. General Wojciech Jaruzelski replaced Stanislaw Kania, and prepared to deal more firmly with Solidarity.
10. By this time the union had thirteen million members, compared with three million in the Polish Communist Party. The Polish intelligentsia had allied themselves with it, and the powerful Roman Catholic Church supported it. In December 1981, Solidarity demanded:
    (a) the right to foreign travel
    (b) free elections
    (c) a referendum to demonstrate the size of its following
    (d) a share for Solidarity in the running of the economy.

Martial Law

1. In December 1981, General Wojciech Jaruzelski declared martial law. This avoided the necessity for a Soviet invasion. He:
    (a) imposed military rule
    (b) suppressed Solidarity
    (c) arrested many of its leading members
2. The United States responded by:
    (a) suspended Poland's most-favoured-nation trade status
    (b) blocked further loans from the International Monetary Fund.
    (c) Reagan also tried to impose an international embargo on high-technology exports to the USSR, but this angered the Western Europeans.
3. Martial law was lifted in July 1983.
4. With a ban on strikes, the economic situation improved significantly.
5. The Roman Catholic Church remained a centre of opposition to the government and Party.
6. In April 1986, there was a terrible accident at the Chernobyl nuclear power station in Ukraine. People in Western Europe were afraid to buy Polish food in case it had been contaminated.
7. Yet in the same year, Poland became a member of:
    (a) the International Monetary Fund
    (b) the World Bank
8. The new five-year plan in 1986 provided for:
    (a) a plan to rapidly develop precision and electronic engineering
    (b) new incentive schemes for industrial workers
    (c) encouragement for free enterprise in agriculture.
9. Jaruzelski held a referendum in 1987 to confirm the popularity of his policies, but 56% voted against them.

Glossary

Comecon: The Soviet-dominated common market

democratic centralism: the absolute party discipline demanded by Lenin

détente: a permanent relaxation of tension between the superpowers

triumvirate: a three-man group leadership

Augusto Pinochet

14. Chile

"Not a nut or bolt shall reach Chile under Allende. Once Allende comes to power we shall do all within our power to condemn Chile and all Chileans to utmost deprivation and poverty." (Edward M. Korry, US Ambassador to Chile)
"I don't see why we need to stand by and watch a country go communist due to the irresponsibility of its own people." (Henry Kissinger)

Background

1. Chile was one of the most developed and urbanised nations of the continent.
2. In the countryside landless peasants worked the estates of large landowners.
3. Industrialisation created a large industrial working class.
4. Until the 1920s the chief export was nitrates, and after the 1920s copper. The economy was dependent upon the world price of these products.
5. The copper mines were owned by US companies, which exported the profits to the USA and did not invest them in Chile.
6. The industrialists and landowners formed a wealthy oligarchy which conspired with the US companies to suppress trades unions and depress the living standards of the mass of the people.
7. Nevertheless, Chile had functioning parliamentary institutions.
8. As the elections of 1964 approached, public discontent with the *status quo* made it seem likely that a Socialist-Communist alliance under the Marxist Salvator Allende would gain power. To prevent this the parties of the right decided to compromise with the more moderate reformist Christian Democrats led by Eduardo Frei Montalva. CIA money was channelled into the election contest to support Frei, and won the election.

The Reforms of Eduardo Frei

1. The programme put forward by Frei and the Christian Democrats was called "Revolution in Liberty." It promised reforms with the aim of improving the conditions of the lower classes.
2. Frei instituted a program of "Chileanization" of the copper industry. 51% of the shares of the US copper companies were purchased.

3. US aid was poured into the country to assist Frei's reforms.
4. With this wealth the government set about improving the economy:
    (a) New industries, paper and petrochemicals, were developed.
    (b) The Andean Pact created a common market with Colombia, Bolivia, Ecuador and Peru.
    (c) Banking Reforms were effected.
    (d) A graduated income tax, where the wealthier pay proportionally more of their incomes in tax than the poor, was introduced.
    (e) The housing of the poor was improved.
    (f) Standards of literacy were raised following educational reforms.
    (g) In 1967, with the support of the Socialist and Communist parties, an agrarian reform law was approved. The government would:
        (i) limit the amount of land that could be held by one person;
        (ii) expropriate uncultivated land;
        (iii) set up peasant cooperatives on these lands.
        (iv) teach the peasants better farming methods.
    The agrarian reforms, however, proceeded slowly because of the need to:
        (i) provide better housing;
        (ii) provide better agricultural equipment;
        (iii) set up irrigation systems.
    But by 1970 about 5,000,000 acres had been expropriated.
5. With new elections approaching, the government had lost some of its support.
    (a) They had alienated the middle class by trying to obtain the support of the peasants and the urban unemployed.
    (b) A drop in world copper prices led to inflation, which led to strikes and repression.
6. The reforms encouraged poorer people to take an active role in political life. This encouraged the radicalization, not only of the Communist and Socialist parties, but also of some of the Radicals and Christian Democrats. In 1969 the left-wing parties formed the Popular Unity (Unidad Popular) coalition, under Salvador Allende.
7. The US tried to prevent Allende's election as they did not want Marxism to spread in the American continent, where it would:
    (a) threaten US financial interests,
    (b) end Cuba's isolation.
8. The CIA planned a coup d'état to prevent Allende becoming president. When the commander-in-chief of the army, General René Schneider, would not agree to an illegal coup, three attempts were made to abduct him. On the third attempt, he was murdered. This annoyed the army, which refused to cooperate, and another commander-in-chief who would respect the constitution was appointed.
9. Allende was elected president in 1970.

The Presidency of Salvator Allende

1. Allende began to put into effect the Popular Unity program:
    (a) He nationalised, without compensation, the US owned copper and nitrate companies, some heavy industries and the larger banks.
    (b) He expanded the programme of agrarian reform, using the same expert who had managed Frei's reforms. The intention was to divide up all holdings of more than eighty irrigated hectares.

(c) He sought to provide employment, either in the new nationalised enterprises or on public works projects.

(d) He reformed the health care system.

(e) He continuing his predecessor's reforms of the educational system,

(f) He instituted a scheme for providing free milk for all children as a dietary supplement. He had said at an international conference: "[Chile has] 600,000 children who, for want of proteins in their first eight months of life, will never attain their full mental vigour."

This was called "The Chilean Way to Socialism."

2. The economic situation was not favourable. A fall in world copper prices led to inflation. The price fell from $66 per ton in 1970 to only $48-9 in 1971. For a while Allende managed to improve the workers' situation by wage rises and price controls.

3. Between 1970 and 1972, however, support for Popular Unity among the middle class declined because of economic difficulties resulting from the nationalization programme.

4. Difficulties in maintaining production levels were caused by

(a) boycotts, mainly by US capital,

(b) the reduction of agricultural production due to agrarian reform.

5. Inflation and stagnation of production led to a union of:

(a) the oligarchy of industrialists and landowners,

(b) the right-wing National Party,

(c) the centre Christian Democrats,

(d) the Roman Catholic Church (which was displeased with the direction of the educational reforms,

(e) the armed forces,

(f) the US companies which had owned the copper mines.

6. Late in 1971, Fidel Castro toured Chile. His visit was used to panic some of the middle class.

7. In October 1972 a wave of politically motivated strikes by the middle classes began, e.g.

(a) owners of trucks

(b) small businessmen,

(c) professional unions

(d) student groups.

8. Despite the economic difficulties, the Popular Unity coalition increased its vote in parliamentary elections in 1973. However, the Christian Democrats joined the right-wing National Party in the Confederación Democrática (CODE) to block further reforms.

9. On June 29, 1973, a tank regiment under Colonel Roberto Souper surrounded the presidential palace (la Moneda) in a failed coup attempt.

10. A strike at the end of July was joined by some copper miners. Terrorist incidents began.

11. On August 9, General Prats was made Minister of Defence, but he was forced to resign this and his position as Commander-in-Chief of the Army; and was replaced by General Augusto Pinochet Ugarte, a graduate of the military academy in Santiago (1936), a career military officer.

12. The government was afraid to call upon the national police, fearing their lack of loyalty. In August 1973, the Supreme Court complained about the government's inability to enforce the law.

13. On August 22 the Chamber of Deputies accused Allende's government of unconstitutional acts and called on the military ministers to assure the constitutional order.

14. In early September 1973, Allende floated the idea of resolving the crisis with a plebiscite.

The Coup d'état

1. On Sept. 11, 1973, the armed forces staged a **coup d'état**.
2. The rebels bombed the Presidential Palace.
3. During the coup, Allende was killed. His doctor said that he committed suicide with a machine gun(!) and his death was officially described as suicide. Witnesses testified that he was murdered by Pinochet's soldiers while defending the palace.
4. A junta composed of three generals and an admiral, with General Augusto Pinochet Ugarte as president, was installed. Besides Pinochet from the army were Gustavo Leigh Guzmán of the Air Force, José Toribio Merino Castro of the Navy, and César Mendoza Durán of the Gendarmerie. The Coup leaders named Pinochet head of the victorious junta's governing council. The headship was to be rotated among all members.
5. At the outset the junta received the support of
      (a) the oligarchy,
      (b) a sizable part of the middle-class,
      (c) the right-wing movements,
      (d) many Christian Democrats.
6. In June 1974 Pinochet assumed sole power as president, relegating the rest of the junta to an advisory role. This was a coup within a coup.
7. Soon it became evident that the military had their own agenda, the repression of all left-wing and centre political forces.
      (a) On September 13, the junta dissolved the Congress and set aside the constitution, declaring a "state of siege."
      (b) On the same day, the National Stadium was temporarily converted into an immense prison. Approximately 130,000 individuals were arrested over a three-year period, with the number of "disappeared" reaching into the thousands within the first few months. Some 5,000 were murdered. Many were tortured. Most had been supporters of Allende.
      (c) The Communists, Socialists, and Radicals were banned, while the Christian Democratic, National, and Radical Democracy parties were declared to be in "indefinite recess."
8. In his memoirs, Pinochet claims that he was the originator of the coup and used his position to coordinate the plan with the other branches of the military. High ranking military officials have said that Pinochet only reluctantly got involved in the coup a few days before it was due to occur.

US Involvement

1. The CIA provided funding and propaganda support to Chilean opponents of Allende in the 1964 and 1970 elections, and during the Allende administration.
2. Documents declassified in 2000 show that the CIA had supported an attempt to kidnap Chile's army chief of staff, in the hope of preventing the congressional confirmation of Allende as president.
3. US President Richard Nixon expressed his determination to "do everything we can to bring Allende down." Documents released during the Clinton administration show that the US government and the CIA sought the overthrow of Allende from 1970, immediately after he took office. Many potentially relevant documents still remain classified.
4. Nixon ordered the CIA to "make the economy [of Chile] scream." Immediately after the

Allende government won office the US began high-level planning to ensure the reforms would not succeed. This would be achieved by sabotage of the Chilean economy.

5. US planning of a coup in Chile is evident in a secret cable from Thomas Karamessines, the CIA Deputy Director of Plans, to the Santiago CIA station, (October 16, 1970), after the election but before Allende's inauguration. "It is firm and continuing policy that Allende be overthrown by a coup ... it is imperative that these actions be implemented clandestinely and securely so that the USG [Unites States Government] and American hand be well hidden."

6. The CIA was notified by contacts of the impending coup in advance, but claims that it "played no direct role in" the coup. After Pinochet assumed power, US Secretary of State Henry Kissinger told US President Richard Nixon that the US "didn't do it" but had "created the conditions as great [sic] as possible."

7. The document *CIA Activities in Chile* revealed that the CIA actively supported the military junta after the overthrow of Allende and that it paid many of Pinochet's officers as contacts of the CIA or US military. In a 2003 interview, US Secretary of State Colin Powell conceded the US role in the coup.

8. The US government consistently supported Pinochet's government after he came to power.

The Pinochet Regime

The Police State

1. Pinochet was determined to:
   (a) extirpate leftism;
   (b) reassert free-market policies in the country's economy.
2. A repressive police state was imposed on the country.
   (a) People were arrested on the street and simply "disappeared."
   (b) Torture was routine.
3. His government was widely condemned for its harsh suppression of dissent, but he was protected by the USA. Large amounts of aid flowed to Chile, including for the purchase of weapons.
4. A modest political liberalization began in 1978 after a "managed" plebiscite had resulted in a 75% vote of support for Pinochet's rule.
5. The policies of the military government, encouraged the development of free enterprise and a new entrepreneurial class, This caused:
   (a) mass unemployment,
   (b) a decline of real wages,
   (c) a worsening of the standard of living of the lower and middle classes.
6. In 1980 a new constitution, as well as an eight-year extension of Pinochet's presidential term, was "approved" by another plebiscite. This promised a transitional to civilian constitutional government over the eight-year period. In 1989 he would be submitted to a national referendum for either approval or rejection by a majority of the voters.

The Economic Experiment

1. The economist Milton Friedman visited Chile and persuaded the junta to adopt the free market economics of the Chicago School. The government:
   (a) cut public spending by 27%;
   (b) deregulated finance;
   (c) removed restrictions on foreign investment; Multinational companies were given the right to take out of the country 100% of their profits.

(d) removed price controls;

(e) drastically lowered import tariffs;

(f) swept away progressive legislation designed to protect the interests of workers;

(g) privatised many government run activities, including 400 state industries, mostly sold at prices below their value to cronies of the junta, and even health care and public pensions;

(h) fixed the escudo to the US dollar.

2. As a result:

(a) There was mass unemployment;

(b) GNP* fell 13%, and industrial production by 28%;

(c) Purchasing power fell by 40%. The number of poor rose from one million to seven;

(d) The public wealth had been looted by private interests, many of them foreign;

(e) Many businesses were bankrupted;

(f) The health and well-being of the general population suffered;

(g) Industrial unrest was brutally suppressed;

(h) Massive environmental degradation, including desertification took place.

3. Between 1978 and 1981 the economy expanded by 32%.

This was due to:

(a) Massive US aid;

(b) The liberalization of credit to consumers.

4. In 1982 the economy collapsed.

(a) The price of copper fell;

(b) GDP* fell by 15%;

(c) The escudo was devalued;

(d) The private banking system collapsed.

5. Pinochet's government was forced to:

(a) Reimpose controls over finance, banking, industry, prices and wages.

(b) Ask the IMF to rescue the country;

(c) Promise to repay debtors

The End of the Dictatorship

1. Pinochet continued to repress political opposition. After a failed assassination attempt in 1986 he had political leaders arrested.

2. In 1988, wishing to improve his image, he finally lifted the "state of siege" and invited exiles to return.

3. He held the plebiscite scheduled for 1989 in October 1988, saying that if he won he would stay until 1997. 55% voted "no" to a "yes" vote of 43%.

4. Though rejected by the electorate, Pinochet remained in office until after free elections installed a new president, the Christian Democrat Patricio Aylwin, on March 11, 1990. He remained the commander of the armed forces until 1998.

5. Later that year, while visiting London, he was detained after Spain requested his extradition in connection with the torture of Spanish citizens in Chile. The case caused the USA and other governments to release classified documents relating to the "disappeared." In January 2000 Pinochet was released by UK Home Secretary Jack Straw on "medical grounds."

Assessment

1. The history of Chile during this period demonstrates the vulnerability of all developing states

whose economies largely depend upon the export of a single resource, crop or product.

2. The provision, cutting off, and subsequent provision, of aid by the USA illustrates the way in which the US controls its client states,* and ensures governments acceptable to itself.

3. CIA participation in successive elections and in the coup shows how covert US actions determine the rise or fall of governments in Latin America, even when these appear to result from the democratic process.

4. US support for the Pinochet regime, despite its unconstitutional seizure of power and its appalling human rights record demonstrates that it is not democracy which the USA supports and tyranny and terrorism which it opposes. It is forms of economic organisation which protect privilege and foreign exploitation which it supports, and forms of economic organisation which redistribute wealth to the general population and resist foreign exploitation which it opposes.

5. Allende demonstrated that Communists could come to power by the normal democratic processes, but that if they did, the USA would undermine them and not allow them to govern.

6. There would be no fair test of the rival economic systems under democratic conditions, the USA would not allow it. However, the fortunes of the Chilean economy under Pinochet demonstrates the failure of the free market economics of the Chicago School.

7. It is noteworthy that it is normal to blame conditions in Eastern Europe upon the failure of the Communist system, but not to blame conditions in central America upon the capitalist system.

Glossary

agrarian: to do with farming or the land

Chicago School: the proponents of economic doctrine that the free market should be allowed to operate without any support or restrictions imposed by governments, so-called because they were centred upon the (US Government-supported) Department of Economics of the University of Chicago

CIA: US Central Intelligence Agency - US espionage agency

client states: states which are supposed to be independent, but which have to have a government and policies acceptable to a more powerful state, otherwise it will intervene to change them by force directly or indirectly.

CODE: Confederación Democrática

GDP: Gross Domestic Product - The total market value of all goods and services produced within a state during one year, the government's measure of how much an economy produces.

GNP: Gross National Product - the total market value of all goods and services produced by the citizens of an economy during one year, now known as GDP.

IMF: International Monetary Fund - a body established by the United Nations in 1945 to monitor and stabilize foreign exchange markets.

Bibliography

Debray R. *Chilean Revolution: Conversations With Allende.* Pantheon (New York, 1972)

Grandin, Greg, *Empire's Workshop*, Henry Holt & Co (New York, 2006)

Lavretski J. S*alvador Allende.* Editorial Progreso (Moscow, 1978)

Medhurst, K. ed., *Allende's Chile* Hart-Davis, MacGibbon, (London, 1972)

Henry Kissinger

15. China and the Cold War

"[Major General Patrick J. Hurley] ... was appointed American ambassador to Chungking... Hurley, [who had been born in Choctaw Indian country] liked to demonstrate a blood-curdling Comanche yell. He chose to loose this salutation to the Chinese Communists at Yenan - Mao Tse-tung, Chu Teh, Chou En-lai, and others - when he first met them on an official ambassadorial visit at the airport of their city. He admittedly did not like the Communist leaders. He referred to them as Mouse Dung and Joe N. Lie.")" (Robert H. Ferrell)

Background

1. China had long been seen in the USA as a soft area for exploitation. American missionaries were sent out during the late nineteenth and early twentieth centuries. This had led to rivalry with Japan, which had similar hopes for expansion in that region.
2. A civil war broke out in the 1930s between the Nationalists, under Jiang Kaishek (Chang Kaishek) and the Communists, under Mao Zedong. This was brought to a pause by the Sino-Japanese War of 1937.
3. During the war, the USA and USSR both recognised Jiang as head of the legitimate Chinese government.
4. When the Second World War was coming to an end, US generals were sent to China to establish a presence. Their main aim was to:
    (a) secure an end to the civil war;
    (b) create a strong central government;
    (c) ensure that it would be firmly under US influence.
5. The US hoped:
    (a) to reform the GMD under its supervision. General Wedemeyer recommended this in July 1947. The China Aid Act and the Sino-American agreement of 1948, by which the GMD would put its house in order, were passed as a consequence.
    (b) to bring the GMD and the CCP together under the moderates of the Democratic League. These attempts failed as both sides were too suspicious of each other. The talks broke down

over the failure to merge the two armies.

6. The GMD received US aid, and was assisted by US forces in taking over all those areas occupied by the Japanese.

7. After the war Stalin's policy was to:

    (a) Prevent the rise of a strong central government;

    (b) To nibble away at China's borderlands.

    Since Stalin thought that Mao would make a stronger ruler of China than Jiang, his policy was also supportive of the Nationalists and hostile to the Communists.

    (a) An anti-Chinese revolt was engineered in Xinjiang (Sinkiang) in 1944, and a secessionist republic was set up.

    (b) By declaring war on Japan in the last days of the war the Red Army was able to occupy Manchuria.

        (i) Japanese industrial plant was removed to the USSR;

        (ii) The area was returned to the GMD.

    (c) Outer Mongolia, nominally under Chinese sovereignty but really controlled by the USSR, was abandoned by the Chinese at the Russo-Chinese Treaty of August 1945.

8. Following the Japanese surrender there was a race by GMD and CCP forces to occupy the lands vacated by the Japanese, including valuable arms and military supplies. In this race the Communists were better placed to liberate most occupied areas.

9. The USA and the USSR handed over areas they took over to the GMD, yet the GMD government collapsed during 1949, and the Communists came to power.

[For a fuller treatment of the Chinese Civil War, see the companion volume "Wars and Warfare"]

Initial Alignment

1. When the Communists came to power there was a division among the leadership about which way to lean in the Cold War:

    (a) Lio Shaoqi favoured the USSR and the Eastern bloc;

    (b) Zhou En-lai favoured the USA and the West.

    Mao Zedong decided to lean towards the USSR:

        (i) as a fraternal socialist country;

        (ii) because the USSR had aided Sun Yatsen and the Chinese Communist Party (CCP) in the past;

        (iii) because Mao insisted that foreign powers respect Chinese sovereignty, while the US government demanded the same special privileges for its diplomats and citizens resident in China that the colonial powers had demanded before the revolution.

2. In July 1949 the Truman administration issued the *China White Paper* condemning China's "subservience to a foreign power" (i.e. the USSR).

3. Mao visited Moscow and in February 1950 signed the **Treaty of Friendship, Alliance and Mutual Assistance.**

    (a) China received $300 million for 5 years at 1% interest;

    (b) loan of Soviet technicians;

    (c) training of Chinese students in the USSR;

    (d) The USSR received joint stock companies in Xinjiang and Manchuria.

4. The USA:

    (a) imposed trade restrictions on China;

    (b) vetoed attempts to replace Jiang and the Nationalists with Mao and the People's Republic for China's seat at the UN.

The Korean War

1. During the Korean War, when UN (largely US) forces approached the 38th parallel, Zhou warned that US control of North Korea would not be acceptable to China, and that if they crossed the 38th parallel, China would intervene.
2. US forces crossed the 38th parallel, in an attempt to take the whole of Korea, and approached the Yalu River, the Chinese border.
3. The Chinese were concerned:
    (a) They feared a US-backed attempt by Chinese Nationalists to attack China.
    (b) General MacArthur had expressed his desire to invade China.
    (c) The Chinese wished to keep North Korea as a buffer between themselves and US forces. Over 300,000 Chinese "volunteers" from the Peoples' Liberation Army (PLA), renamed the Chinese Volunteer Force, crossed the border and drove the US army back beyond the 38th parallel. Pyongyang and then Seoul was captured by the Chinese.
4. The US forces were soon driven south, and then a stalemate was reached at the 38th parallel.

Consequences

1. Chinese casualties were over 300,000.
2. The USA persuaded the UN to declare China an aggressor in Korea and to deny it the seat belonging to China on the Security Council still held by the government of Jiang Kaishek on Taiwan (Formosa).
3. The USA imposed a total trade embargo on China.
4. Chinese plans for invading Taiwan (Formosa) were set back. The US moved the seventh Fleet into the Taiwan Straits to prevent any action by the Chinese against Taiwan. Mao regarded this as interference in the internal affairs of China.
5. China gained in prestige as it had forced the superpower to a stalemate. The USA had learned to treat China with circumspection.
6. The niggardliness of the Soviets when asked for support was not forgotten.

The High Cold War

1. China gave support and aid to Ho Chi Minh and the Viet Minh in the Indo-China War, and assisted in reaching the Geneva Armistice of 1954. They felt betrayed when the USA did not keep to the agreement but set up a South Vietnamese administration and failed to hold promised elections, leading to the Vietnam War.
2. In September 1954, the USA created the **South-East Asia Organisation (SEATO)** to encircle or "contain" China. It was a failure as few South-East Asian countries joined.
3. In December 1954 the USA signed a defence treaty with Taiwan (Formosa).
4. In response to Jiang's attacks on the mainland, the Communists bombarded the nationalist-held islands of Jinmen (Quemoy) and Mazu (Matsu) just off the mainland. In response:
    (a) Jiang's air force bombed the mainland.
    (b) Eisenhower threatened the Chinese with nuclear weapons.
5. In May 1957, the USA supplied the Nationalists on Taiwan with missiles capable of reaching the mainland and capable of carrying nuclear warheads.
6. In 1958, Mao again bombarded the island of Jinmen (Quemoy) and Mazu (Matsu), and China was again threatened with nuclear weapons.
7. The USA continued to fortify Taiwan as a military base, and used it to conduct illegal flights over Chinese territory by U-2 spy planes.

The Sino-Soviet Split

1. When, in 1956, Khrushchev denounced Stalin, Mao was annoyed at not having been warned in advance.
2. When in 1958 Mao bombarded the island of Jinmen (Quemoy) and Mazu (Matsu), Khrushchev was annoyed at not being informed in advance.
3. In September 1959, Mao and Khrushchev met in Beijing and Khrushchev asked for wireless stations on Chinese soil. Mao refused. The two men quarrelled.
4. In April 1960, China attacked the Soviet doctrine of peaceful co-existence with the West as undermining the world revolution.
5. In August 1960 all Soviet experts in China were withdrawn.
6. In 1961 the USSR did not help in the famine which followed the failure of the Great Leap Forward. Instead, Canada and Australia supplied China with grain.
7. In 1962 there was a border conflict between China and India in the Himalayas provoked by India. In his comments, Khrushchev supported the Indian side.
8. In 1962 Mao criticized Khrushchev for giving way to Kennedy over the Cuban Missile Crisis.
9. During 1963 the quarrel was conducted in the press in both countries. Ideological differences were accentuated. Splits began to occur in Communist Parties throughout the world, between pro-Soviet and pro-Maoist factions.
10. In July China attacked the Nuclear Test Ban Treaty as an attempt by the superpowers to consolidate their joint nuclear monopoly.
11. With the change of leadership in the USSR in 1963, there was a lull in the controversy.
12. During the Vietnam War, each side accused the other of failing to support the National Liberation Front (NLF)
13. Nearly 40 Soviet divisions were moved from Eastern Europe to the Sino-Soviet border. In 1959 there was a confrontation over a disputed island in the Usuri River.
14. Moscow began to pursue a policy of containment of China, improving relations with Pakistan, Afghanistsan, India, Burma, Laos, Cambodia, Japan and Mongolia, and suggesting an Asian security pact.
15. In 1966 the Great Proletarian Cultural revolution began. Mao claimed that part of the purpose of the movement was to eradicate Soviet-style Communism in China.
16. In 1968 Mao condemned the Soviet invasion of Czechoslovakia. The Brezhnev Doctrine was described as "out and out gangster logic put out by the new Tsars to justify their aggression."
17. In 1969 cashes broke out at disputed points of the border. There was a major build-up of forces on each side of the border.
18. The Indo-Pakistani War of 1974 was a tense period in Sino-Soviet relations.

The Causes of the Sino-Soviet Split

1. The roots of Sino-Soviet hostility go back a long way. China and Russia were rivals in the nineteenth century, when the expanding Russian empire took territory from a weak China. These territorial disputes were to surface again in the Sino-Soviet dispute.
2. Stalin had:
   (a) insisted upon giving the wrong advice to the Chinese Communist fighters in the civil war
   (b) collaborated with the Guomindang (GMD) during the Sino-Japanese War
   (c) handed over Manchuria to Jiang Kaishek
   (d) suspected Mao of being another "Tito" (the independent-minded Communist leader of Yugoslavia).

3. A rivalry developed between Khrushchev and Mao, based upon mutual resentments.
4. Ideological differences grew up, particularly relating to the Soviet belief in peaceful coexistence. The Chinese accused the Soviets of being revisionists,* of altering the ideological inheritance of Marxism-Leninism.

The Significance of the Sino-Soviet Split

1. It is sometimes said that the Sino-Soviet split shattered the unity of the Communist bloc; however, there never had been any real unity between the USSR and China.
2. During the 1970s, the USSR became obsessed with the prospect of a hostile China.
3. It showed the *realpolitik* which lay behind the rhetoric of Chinese and Soviet foreign policy. It was determined not by idealistic or ideological considerations, but by the needs of power politics.

The Sino-American *Rapprochement*

1. Nixon's plan for a settlement in Vietnam involved détente with both Moscow and Peking. President Nixon sent "low level signals" to the Chinese that he was interested in improved relations as soon as he came to power. These were either ignored or were not recognised.
2. In March 1969 the US lifted restrictions on its citizens to visit China.
3. In April the US trade embargo against China was eased.
4. In the same year Nixon put out peace feelers to Beijing through General de Gaulle of France and Yahya Khan of Pakistan.
5. Army commander Lin Biao opposed improving relations with the United States but died when his plane crashed under mysterious circumstances.
6. Zhou Enlai sought:
    (a) an American counterweight to Soviet hostility;
    (b) concessions on the status of Taiwan;
    (c) the transfer of Western technology to China.
    The Nixon Doctrine also promised to remove the obnoxious US military presence in Asia
7. In April 1970 some Japanese companies accepted Chinese terms for trade:
    (a) No trade or investment with Taiwan or South Korea;
    (b) No export of weapons for US use in Indochina;
    (c) No affiliation with US companies.
8. In April 1971 a US table tennis team was invited to play in China.
9. The US ended its veto on the entry of Communist China into the United Nations Organisation. The People's Republic of China was formally admitted in October 1971.
10. This was followed by a secret visit to China by Henry Kissinger, when he secured an invitation for Nixon to visit China. The visit took place in February 1972.
11. A **Sino-Japanese rapprochement** followed. The Chinese insisted upon:
    (a) Recognition of the People's republic of China as the sole legitimate government of China;
    (b) Recognition that Taiwan was Chinese territory;
    (c) The abrogation* of the treaty between Japan and Taiwan.
    The Japanese agreed. Prime Minister Tanaka then visited China.
12. Many nations subsequently established diplomatic relations* with China.
13. Jiang Kaishek died in 1975, but the status of Taiwan remained a contentious issue.
14. In December 1978, President Carter withdrew US recognition of Nationalist China, and in January 1979 entered into full diplomatic relations with the People's Republic of China.

The Reasons for the Sino-American *Rapprochement**

1. The US:
   (a) Sought help in getting out of Vietnam; the Chinese might be willing to offer this;
   (b) Perhaps realised that their policy of containment of China had failed;
   (c) Wished to end the dangerous isolation of a nuclear China;
   (d) Wished to cause anxiety to the Soviets;
   (e) Saw some popularity at home, and an honourable place in the history books, by ending the long and dangerous hostility between the USA and China.
2. The Chinese wanted:
   (a) An American counterweight to Soviet hostility. The threat of a hostile nuclear-armed Soviet Union and a hostile nuclear-armed USA and the prospects of US-Soviet collusion*, faced China with unacceptable isolation.
   (b) Concessions on the status of Taiwan;
   (c) Trade with the USA and its Allies;
   (d) The transfer of modern technology.

The Results of the Sino-American *Rapprochement*

1. The Chinese achieved:
   (a) Security from the danger of a US-Soviet or Soviet attack;
   (b) Acceptance of a **One China*** policy by the USA, and withdrawal of US military installations from Taiwan;
   (c) Some trade;
   (d) The end of China's diplomatic isolation from much of the Western world.
   However:
   It undermined China's standing in the Communist world.
2. The USA achieved the weakening of the Soviet position in the world.

The Significance of the Sino-American *Rapprochement*

It showed the *realpolitik** which lay behind the rhetoric of US policy and Chinese policy, which was determined not by idealistic or ideological considerations, but by the needs of power politics.

Glossary

CCP: Chinese Communist Party

collusion: a deliberately deceptive secret understanding between conspirators

GMD: Guomindang or Kuomintang (KMT) - party founded by Sun Yat-sen

KMT: Kuomintang or Guomindang (GMD) - party founded by Sun Yat-sen

One China policy: recognising only the government of the Peoples' Republic of China, and not that of the Chinese Nationalists on Taiwan

rapprochement: the re-establishment of cordial relations between two parties

Sinification: developing in a Chinese way

Sino-: Chinese

xenophobia: fear and hatred of foreigners

Ronald Reagan

16. The Cold War 1979-85

"The crusade against the 'Evil Empire' to which - at least in public - President Reagan's government devoted its energies, was ... designed as therapy for the USA rather than as a practical attempt to re-establish the world power balance." (Eric Hobsbawm)

"It really got to them. They didn't know what it all meant. A squadron would fly straight at Soviet airspace, and other radars would light up and units would go on alert. Then at the last minute the squadron would peel off and return home." (Dr. William Schneider, US undersecretary of state for military assistance and technology,)

"Whoever does not understand that when it comes to nuclear weapons the whole concept of relative advantage is illusory—whoever does not understand that when you are talking about preposterous quantities of overkill the relative sizes of arsenals have no serious meaning—whoever does not understand that the danger lies not in the possibility that someone else might have more missiles and warheads than you do, but in the very existence of these unconscionable quantities of highly poisonous explosives, and their existence, above all, in hands as weak and shaky and undependable as those of ourselves or our adversaries or any other mere human beings; whoever does not understand these things is never going to guide us out of this increasingly dark and menacing forest of bewilderments into which we have all wandered." (George Kennan)

The Causes of the New Cold War

1. During the last years of détente, the Soviet Union made many advances, while the USA faced significant setbacks.

   (a) In the Vietnam War the USA suffered an ignominious defeat. *[See Chapter 10, "The Vietnam War"]*

   (b) Cambodia and Laos fell to revolutionary insurrections.

   (c) The bloody overthrow of Allende in Chile and the installing of Pinochet alienated world opinion from the USA. *[For a full treatment see Chapter 14, "Chile"]*

   (d) Communists performed well in Europe:

       (i) The fall of fascist, or quasi-fascist regimes in Spain and Portugal allowed the local Communist Parties to function legally once more.

     (ii) In Italy the Communists were about to be included in government in 1978, and this was only prevented by the murder of prime minister Aldo Moro.

     (iii) Communists played key roles in the governments of President Mitterand in France.

.   (e) Soviet policy met with success in Africa:

     (i) Soviet aid and advisors were accepted in Somalia;

     (ii) The USSR supported Haile Mengistu and the Dergue in Ethiopia, which sought to introduce a Marxist-socialist society. A Soviet airlift of supplies saved Mengistu in the war against Somalia.

     (iii) The former Portuguese colonies of Angola and Mozambique fell to pro-Soviet regimes. A Cuban, Soviet-financed expedition was sent to Angola to support Aghostino Neto and the MPLA, against rival Angolan groups supported by the USA and South Africa. The new regimes sheltered members of the South African National Congress Party, which opposed the white apartheid regime in South Africa.

     (iv) Southern Rhodesia fell to an insurrection.

  (f) The Soviet navy acquired bases in the Indian Ocean.

  (g) In the Middle East the US became unpopular as the chief supporter of Israel.

  (h) In 1979, the Shah of Iran, a US puppet, was overthrown by a Muslim fundamentalist-led revolt. The staff of the US embassy in Teheran was held hostage. A US attempt to rescue them failed.

  (i) The West was disappointed at the failure of the USSR to liberalise its society in accordance with the Helsinki agreement. Neither free speech nor free travel was allowed, and dissidents continued to suffer harassment.

  (j) Increased Soviet oil and gas exports enabled the USSR to purchase foreign technology.

It was argued in the USA that détente (i.e. peaceful coexistence) favoured the Soviets, allowing them to win trade and espionage advantages without their conceding anything in return.

2. In fact:

  (a) Many of these developments were not so much due to Soviet actions as to:

     (i) the reaction of world opinion against the USA;

     (ii) the US refused to enter into constructive relationships with new states on the basis of respect for their independence and their neutrality in the Cold War.

  (b) The new allies of the Soviets were more of a burden than a gain in global power.

  (c) The leadership of the USSR was becoming a gerontocracy* and unable to take advantage of the situation.

  (d) The Soviet system was already sclerotic an unable to take advantage, e.g. of new computer technology it was able to acquire indirectly from the West.

  (e) Political successes hid economic weakness.

3. The Soviet invasion of Afghanistan 25th December 1979 was chosen as the pretext for cooling relations. This was disingenuous. Afghanistan had been under Soviet influence for many years, but it was packaged as a threatening Soviet advance..

President Carter:

  (a) imposed a grain embargo on the USSR;

  (b) broke off the SALT talks.

  (c) called for a boycott of the Moscow Olympic Games of Summer 1980.

4. Then new Western leaders, Margaret Thatcher (1979) and Ronald Reagan (1980) determined to act in a confrontational manner towards the USSR.

US **neoconservatives*** rebelled against détente.

5. A small but influential group of thinkers known as **Neo-Conservatives** gained influence in Washington. They believed that:

  (a) Liberal US society was doomed because individual freedom eroded the basis of society.

(b) In order to bind society together and provide stability myths were needed in which the mass of people could believe. These myths did not have to be true to be useful.

(c) The myths which American people could be unified around were:

    (i) religion, particularly fundamentalist Christianity;

    (ii) extreme nationalism - the belief that the USA was a unique nation, alone standing for goodness in a world full of dark and evil forces, of which the chief was Communism.

They argued for:

(a) the right of the USA to use its military power to exercise an imperial dominance over the entire planet;

(b) The strengthening of the US executive at the expense of thew individual freedom of US citizens;

(c) The reduction of government controls over the ability of big business to make profits;

(d) Reductions in social spending.

They included names which became well known under the administration of George W. Bush: Paul Wolfowitz, Robert Kagan, Elliott Abrams, Dick Cheyney and Donld Rumsfeld.

Many were led by Senator Henry Jackson, a Democrat, and pressured President Carter into taking a more aggressive stance towards the USSR. Later they aligned themselves with Ronald Reagan and the conservative wing of the Republican Party, who promised to "win the Cold War", and with socially conservative Christian fundamentalists.

The New Freeze

1. As in the early days of the Cold War, Communism was built up in the public mind as an ever-present threat to the American way of life. In particular:

    (a) All manifestations of opposition to US policy anywhere in the world, and particularly terrorism, were portrayed as part of a single diabolical master plan to take over the world.

    (b) The military power of the USSR, rapidly decaying, was portrayed as threatening by the simple process of taking the *absence* of evidence of new weapons systems as itself evidence of the possession by the Soviets of terrifyingly sophisticated *hidden* systems..

2. Through figures such as Dick Cheyney and Donald Rumsfeld, the neo-conservatives came to dominate US foreign policy. They determined to go on the attack against Communism to win the Cold War in order to unite the American people and make them more easily governable.

3. Despite his anti-Communism, Reagan ended Carter's ban on US grain exports to the USSR, since it hurt the profits of US farmers. However, he unsuccessfully tried to stop the construction of a natural gas pipeline supplying the European Union from Siberia.

4. Reagan decided to foster and support irregular forces to overthrow pro-Soviet governments in the Third World, e.g. in Angola, and Nicaragua. This was called the **Reagan Doctrine**.

5. When Israel invaded the **Lebanon** in 1982, Reagan sent in US marines. After over two hundred were killed in a truck suicide bomb attack in 1983, they were soon withdrawn.

6. From 1981 the Reagan administration funded terrorists to try to destabilize the government of the **Sandinistas** in **Nicaragua**. The CIA mined the harbours of Nicaragua. A secret deal had been done selling arms to the Iranians in return for releasing US hostages they had taken, and in order to bypass Congress, this money was illegally used to fund the Contras. When this **Irangate** scandal was uncovered, the president claimed he could not recall authorising it. No move was made to impeach him.

7. When a left-wing government took over in tiny **Grenada** in the Caribbean, in October 1983 a US invasion of the country was staged.

8. In October 1983 a South Korean (KAL) commercial passenger airliner was shot down when it strayed over the sensitive Kamchatka Peninsula in Siberia, the USA made as much capital out of it as they could. (This contrasts with the later downplaying of the US shooting down of an unarmed Iranian civil airliner over the international waters of the Persian Gulf five years later.)
9. Communist China became offended by Reagan's degree of support for the Nationalist Government on Taiwan, so that there was a cooling in Sino-American relations. Brezhnev and then Andropov took this opportunity to improve Sino-Soviet relations.
10. Under Reagan the USA waged economic warfare on the USSR, intentionally using suprior US resources to outspend the Soviet Union in order to strain their economy, hoping to create an internal revolution which would destroy the Soviet Union.

The Nuclear Arms Race

1. The most serious consequence of the collapse of détente was an acceleration of the arms race.
2. In the mid 1970's, a Comprehensive Nuclear Test Ban Treaty, was proposed, in an attempt to stop all testing of nuclear weapons. It was rejected by US president Ronald Reagan.
3. The neo-conservatives claimed in December 1976, that the Soviets were achieving military superiority and were preparing to fight a nuclear war. When CIA professionals found that the Soviets aimed only at parity, CIA head George H. W. Bush, appointed a group of hardliners who came up with another sufficiently frightening report which became official doctrine.
4. In 1977 the USSR deployed 150 SS20 missiles and 50 Backfire bombers in Europe.
5. Doubts were arising in the USA about the effectiveness of Mutually Assured Destruction (MAD) as an effective deterrent. Improved targeting enabled strategists to consider targeting a single site, and receiving a proportionate response, and so waging **limited nuclear war**. This might have tempted one side to a first strike.
6. The US Senate refused to ratify the SALT II Treaty limiting numbers of missiles on both sides.
7. Predictions made by many scientists based upon computer models revealed that a nuclear war would result in a universal "**nuclear winter**," from which no one would survive. In a full scale nuclear war, a vast cloud of dirt, smoke, and radiation would cover the earth, blocking out the sun. This would last for over four months. Anyone surviving the war and the radiation for this long would face starvation, as almost all plant life on earth would die. The temperature of the earth's surface would drop drastically, as the temperature inland could reach -30 degrees Celsius. This projected drop in temperature led to the term, nuclear winter. There would also be a 70% destruction of the ozone layer, so that solar radiation would flood into the atmosphere.
8. Despite this, Reagan was surrounded by people who believed that the USA could fight and survive a nuclear conflict. These **Nuclear Use Theorists (NUTs)** discussed:
    (a) the possibility of a nuclear war confined to Europe;
    (b) launching "decapitating strikes" at Soviet command and control centres.
    (c) the deployment of the neutron bomb in Germany.
9. In December 1979 NATO announced it would deploy 500 Pershing and Cruise missiles in Europe. In 1983 they were deployed in Western Europe. The Soviets broke off the INF and START talks.
10. The US began psychological operations against the USSR in mid-February 1981 and continued intermittently through 1983.
    (a) US submarines demonstrated how close they could approach important Soviet military bases in the North Atlantic and Pacific Oceans and in the Black, and Baltic seas.
    (b) US bombers would fly directly towards Soviet airspace, peeling off at the last moment, sometimes several times per week.

11. Not surprisingly, in May 1981 the Soviets became so alarmed about a US first strike that at a meeting with high-ranking KGB officials, Leonid Brezhnev and KGB chairman Yuri Andropov announced that the USA was preparing a secret nuclear attack. To detect and prevent a US nuclear first strike Operation RYAN, an intelligence gathering operation was set up to monitor all those who would make the decision to launch a nuclear attack, and the technical personnel who would implement it, and the facilities from which the attack would be made.

12. In March 1983, Reagan announced the intention to develop antiballistic missile defences based in outer space. This **Strategic Defence Initiative (SDI)**, known as "Star Wars" was based upon laser and particle-beam technology to shoot down incoming long-range missiles. This:

    (a) was ridiculed by scientists as

        (i) scientifically naive

        (ii) incredibly expensive

        (iii) counterproductive, as it might invite a first strike if it ever looked like becoming possible.

    (b) It was in direct breach of the 1972 ABM Treaty which the USA had signed.

Soviet CP First Secretary Yuri Andropov accused Reagan of "inventing new plans on how to unleash a nuclear war in the best way, with the hope of winning it."

13. The Able Archer 83 exercise in November 1983 was a realistic simulation of a coordinated attack held by NATO throughout Western Europe. It involved participation by heads of state and radio silences. It led the USSR to believed a nuclear strike against them might actually be taking place, and Soviet nuclear forces were placed on the highest alert. This was the closest the world has come to nuclear destruction since the Cuban Missile Crisis. Again, this was caused by aggressive US actions and attitudes.

The Consequences of the "New" Cold War

1. The world was once more in danger of destruction by nuclear catastrophe from either misundertstanding or miscalculation.

2. Central America was devastated. *[See Chapter 18]*

3. The USA had fostered Muslim fundamentalism as a weapn to employ against the Soviets in Afghanistan. They would regret this when it subsequently turned upon them.

4. The spread of "**Reaganomics**"* the dismantling of social safety nets in favour of the unfettered operation of the market (except where powerful US interests were involved), led to increases in the gap between rich and poor, and immense social suffering. The USA was waging war on the poor.

5. It took Reaganomics 8 years to increase the US national debt from the $1 trillion, which had accumulated since Indpendence, to $3.5 trillion.

6. The orthodox view is that Reagan's policies hastened the **collapse of the Soviet Union** by forcing the USSR to compete in a new arms race. However, Georgi Arbatov, head of the Moscow-based Institute for the Study of the USA and Canada, testified his memoirs in 1992 that in fact the extreme aggressiveness of US policy strengthened hard-liners in the Soviet Union. Similrly, George Kennan said that it *delayed* rather than hastened the changes that overtook the Soviet Union. Reagan was in office for over four years before Gorbachev came to power, but during that period no significant Soviet reforms took place. It was only when Gorbachev came to power that the changes occurred.

Glossary

ABMs: anti-ballistic missile systems

apartheid: the racist doctrine that proposes separate (and unequal) development of the races within national borders, often by the construction of reservations or bantustans.

ICBMs: inter-continental ballistic missiles

inter-continental ballistic missiles (IBMs):

INF: Intermediate Nuclear Force

Intermediate Nuclear Force (INF):

IRBMs: intermediate range ballistic missiles

KGB: The Soviet espionage agench, the Committee for State Security

MIRVs: Multiple independent re-entry vehicles

Multiple independent re-entry vehicles (MIRVs):

Mutually Assured Destruction (MAD): each side would not attack the other because both sides had more than enough nuclear weapons to completely destroy the other side and make the entire planet uninhabitable. Therefore, for either side, launching an attack on the other side would be suicidal, so neither side would launch an attack.

neo-conservatives: a movement of influential people in the USA characterised by:

   (a) extreme US nationalism;

   (b) militarism: desire to use US military power in an expansionist foreign policy;

   (c) support for a strong executive and shrinking of human rights and freedoms;

   (d) support for big business;

   (e) social conservatism;

   (f) opposition to social spending.

neutron bomb: a "small" nuclear bomb which had enhanced radiation to kill people without harming property.

NUTs: Nuclear Use Theorists, who believed it would be possible for the US to fight and win a nuclear war.

proliferation: spreading

Reaganomics: (a) tax cuts would increase Federal revenues enough to pay both for the cut itself and for increased defense spending to force the USSR into a new arms race;

   (b) the market should operate with a minimum state interference, and state enterprise rolled back by privatization

SDI: Strategic Defence Initiative - "Star wars", a**Strategic Arms Reduction Talks (START)**: talks on the mutual reduction of strategic weapons

Strategic Defence Initiative (SDI): "Star wars" - projected anti-missile defence system

tactical nuclear weapons: "small" short-range nuclear weapons designed for use on the battlefield.

Babrak Karmal

17. The Afghan War

"We can do a lot of damage to the Soviet Union." (William Casey)

Background

1. Afghanistan was traditionally a buffer zone, a disputed area between the British and Russian empires. Rival attempts to gain influence over the country were known as the "Great Game."
2. It is an area of mixed ethnicities:
    (a) The Pathans, living in the south east and straddling the border with Pakistan
    (b) The Tadjiks in the north, straddling the border with the Russian Empire/USSR.
    Modern Afghanistan has been mostly governed by the Pathans, a fact resented by the Tadjiks.
3. There was little of the infrastructure of a modern state, and a medieval fiscal system.*
4. Since 1945, Afghanistan was ruled by the Emir Mohammoud Zahir Shah.
5. In 1953 Mohammoud Daoud, cousin of emir Zahir, became Prime Minister.
6. Daoud wanted to modernize the army. He first approached the USA to purchase military equipment. When the US rejected his request, Daoud turned to the USSR. This led, over a period of time, to Afghanistan becoming a client state of the USSR.
7. King Zahir instituted a constitution in 1964, permitting multi-party elections.
8. A group of intellectuals established the **People's Democratic Party of Afghanistan (PDPA)** in 1965.
9. The PDPA soon split into two competing factions:
    (a) the **Khalq**, led by Nur Mohammad Taraki and Hafizullah Amin. This party was largely made up of Pathans, and was stronger in the south-east and in rural areas.
    (b) **Parcham**, led by Babrak Karmal. It was largely Tadjik, and was stronger in the north and in urban areas.
    This division was to lead to a protracted power struggle between the two factions.

The Causes of the War

1. Mohammoud Daoud seized power in a military coup on July 17, 1973. He abolished the monarchy and established a Republic, with himself as President and Prime Minister.
2. His non-Marxist but pro-Soviet government employed 3,500 Soviet advisers, who were attached to the Afghan army.
3. Daoud's rule soon gave rise to discontent:
     (a) He failed to carry out much-needed economic and social reforms.
     (b) He repressed his political opponents.
4. In Spring 1978, he tried to eliminate the PDPA by arresting its leaders
5. This provoked a coup by army leaders in the PDPA, during which Daoud was killed. PDPA leader Nur Mohammad Taraki became president of the "Democratic Republic of Afghanistan." Babrak Karmal was deputy Prime Minister and Hafizullah Amin a member of the government.
6. Very quickly the Khalq leaders found ways to remove Karmal and other leaders, by appointing them as ambassadors.
7. Soon after seizing power, Taraki tried to introduce Marxism. He promoted the establishment of
     (a) women's rights and
     (b) land reform.
8. These threatened
     (a) Afghan cultural traditions,
     (b) the wealth of the landowners
9. This led to widespread resistance in the summer of 1978. In incidents during riots:
     (a) the US ambassador was shot
     (b) 50 Soviet advisers were murdered in Herat.
10. On 28th March 1979, Hafizullah Amin became Prime Minister with Taraki, while demoted, retaining some of his party posts.
11. Amin began punitive razzias,* traditional massacres, throughout the countryside.
12. Into this volatile situation , US President Carter began to arm Muslim fundamentalist groups of religious militants hostile to Moscow, known as *mujahiddin**, in an attempt to destabilize the region at the expense of the Soviets. This included not only Afghanistan, but also Soviet Central Asia, with its large Muslim population.

The Soviet Invasion

1. Anarchy spread through the country. Alarmed at disorder, the USSR decided:
     (a) to get rid of Amin
     (b) to take control of the country
2. Taraki was encouraged by the Soviets to remove Amin, but his potential victim acted first. On September 14th, Taraki was killed in a confrontation with Amin's supporters.
3. Amin was tricked into inviting Soviet aid. Instead of aid, on Christmas Day 1979, Soviet forces invaded, executing Amin.
4. Babrak Karmal was brought back from the Soviet Union and became the new Prime Minister, President of the Revolutionary Council and Secretary General of a Parcham government.
5. Widespread resistance against Babrak's regime and his Soviet backers led to the Afghan war.

Reasons for the Soviet Invasion

1. The USSR was intervening in a the affairs of a chaotic client state on its borders, in order to restore order.
2. The Soviet leadership was afraid that the Muslim militancy in Iran might spread into a disorderly Afghanistan, and from there into the central Asian Republics of the USSR, where there was a large Muslim population. This was particularly likely as:
   (a) The Pathans of Afghanistan were one people with the Pathans of Pakistan
   (b) the Tadjiks of Afghanistan were one people with the Tadjiks of the USSR
   The borders were porous. Tribesmen would pass from one side to the other, e.g. to attend the marriages of distant relatives.

The US Reaction

1. The Soviet invasion of Afghanistan was conducted within the Soviet sphere of influence and for an obvious reason, but the US chose to make political capital out of it because:
   (a) By this time, the USA wished to end detente, and was seeking a pretext.
   (b) The invasion would be unpopular with the Muslim world. The US saw an opportunity to side with the Arabs, normally hostile to the USA for its support of Israel, against the USSR.
2. Thus they chose see the Soviet invasion as:
   (a) part of the onward march of Communism
   (b) the extension of Soviet Power into the oil-rich Middle East, in an area where they themselves had recently lost control of Iran with the overthrow of the Shah.
3. It was a distraction from the humiliation of the USA in the region, as the personnel of their Iranian embassy had been taken hostage during the Iranian Revolution and the US had thus far been unable to do anything at all about it.
4. Thus the USA:
   (a) tried to sabotage the summer 1980 Moscow Olympic Games by leading a boycott
   (b) banned grain sales to the USSR, which led the Soviets to purchase grain from elsewhere
   (c) broke off the Strategic Arms Limitations Talks (SALT).

The Course of the War

1. The relatively high-technology Soviet troops fought a war of attrition against a low-technology, ill-disciplined, but highly motivated guerrilla force.
2. Considerable Soviet forces (up to 100,000) were tied up for an extensive period of time. Soviet troops controlled the cities and major strongholds, had air superiority. But in the countryside they had always to be prepared for an ambush. Soviet vehicles moved in large, protected convoys. Within Afghanistan there were remote regions the Soviets never got under control.
3. From the first, the United States, through the CIA, provided funds, weapons and general support for the *mujahiddin,* but day-to-day operations and direct contact were usually left to the Pakistani Inter-Services Intelligence agency. CIA officers helped the Pakistanis to set up training camps for the *mujahiddin,* giving instruction in guerrilla warfare, urban sabotage and the use of heavy weapons.
4. From 1985, the CIA supplied the *mujahiddin* with:
   (a) satellite reconnaissance data of Soviet targets;
   (b) plans for Soviet military operations inferred from satellite intelligence;
   (c) intercepts of Soviet communications;

(d) secret communications networks;

(e) delayed timing devices for plastic explosives for urban sabotage and guerrilla attacks;

(f) long-range sniper rifles;

(g) a targeting device for mortars that was linked to a US Navy satellite;

(h) wire-guided anti-tank missiles;

(i) stinger ground-to-air missiles, so that they were able to shoot down Soviet Helicopters. As a result, the USSR lost air superiority.

This was the largest US "aid" program since World War II.

5. By 1987 specialist US teams were accompanying the *mujahiddin* across the border to supervise attacks, especially of airports, railroads, fuel depots, electricity pylons, bridges and roads.

6. With no serious progress being made, no end of the fight in sight, and body bags coming in, Soviet morale dropped.

7. In 1988, Gorbachev announced a policy of gradual withdrawal from Afghanistan. This was completed in 1989.

8. After the Soviet withdrawal, the war continued inside Afghanistan between the forces of Mohammad Najibullah and the Mujahiddin, until the former was defeated in 1992.

The Effects of the War

1. Soviet losses amounted to 15,000 dead and 37,000 wounded; an estimated 1 million Afghanis died during the war.

2. The Afghan *Mujahiddin* consisted of several different groups, with no unified organization. When the Soviets withdrew, the Afghan factions fought each other for power, beginning a long civil war. This led to the rise of the Taliban, a movement fostered by the Pakistanis under US supervision. The Taliban were to establish a Muslim fundamentalist regime.

3. Afghanistan was an opium growing country, and Soviet forces picked up a narcotics problem, which they took back with them to the USSR.

4. The Soviet Union was regarded as aggressor by Third World* states, and particularly by Muslim states.

5. The Soviet invasion assisted the belligerent Western leaders Reagan and Thatcher in manufacturing anti-Soviet propaganda to justify a return to the Cold War and to increase defence spending.

6. The *Mujahiddin* subsequently sold the US Stinger missiles on the international arms market. In order to try to prevent them falling into the hands of terrorists, the US offered to buy them back at $100,000 each, but the offer was not taken up.

7. The *Mujahiddin*, trained and equipped by the CIA, later turned their attention elsewhere:

(a) to destabilise Algeria;

(b) Among the many foreigners drawn to Afghanistan to fight with the *Mujahiddin* was a young, wealthy Saudi, Osama Bin Laden. Osama bin Laden and Al Quaida would later turn their attention to the role of the USA in the:

(i) exploitation of the oil wealth of the Middle East;

(ii) support of corrupt authoritarian regimes which collaborated in this;

(iii) support for Israel in its continued oppression of the disinherited Palestinians.

Thus the seeds of the terrorism of 9/11 were sown by the US Government and the CIA during the Afghan War. The forces they created and fostered at that time as a weapon to destabilise the region to obstruct the USSR would later turn upon themselves.

The Significance of the Afghan War

1. Although the Soviet invasion of Afghanistan was greeted in the West with shock and horror, this was a deliberate choice, not a genuine reaction. Afghanistan had been part of the Soviet sphere of influence for decades before.
2. The US support for the Mujahiddin was a deliberate attempt to mire the USSR in its own unpopular and costly "Vietnam War". This was largely successful, except that the USSR was committed less to the war than the USA had been, and withdrew more speedily.
3. The Afghan War was another example of **asymmetrical warfare**.*
4. Together with the Vietnam War, this war demonstrates, under certain circumstances, the ability of a Third World people to resist a superpower.
5. The USA played a major role in boosting and arming the rise of Islamic fundamentalism for use as a Cold War weapon against the Soviets, giving rise to the Taliban, and Osama bin Laden and Al Quaida

Comparison of the Vietnam and Afghan Wars

1. Causes (Global)
   - (a) The Vietnam War was fought for the containment of Communism.
     The Afghan War was fought to fend off Islamic fundamentalism.
   - (b) The Vietnam War was fought for the preservation of US control over South Vietnam.
     The Afghan War was fought for the preservation of Soviet control over Afghanistan.
2. Causes (Local)
   Both were fought in support of an unpopular and threatened client regime.
3. Nature
   - (a) Both pitted the invaders' high technology against third world guerrillas (asymmetrical warfare).
   - (b) In both cases the fighters had conflicting ideologies (ideological warfare).
   - (c) the guerrillas were supplied from outside, giving the war a Cold War dimension (proxy warfare).
   - (d) The War was unpopular with the soldiers from the super-power, whose morale dropped quickly.
   However:
   - (e) the Vietcong were a single united force; while the Mujahiddin were divided.
   - (f) American strength in Vietnam rose to over 500,000 troops, who were employed in sizable operations; the Soviet force varied from 90,000 to 120,000. Up to 20% of its strength went to man over 860 picket posts throughout the country, and much combat strength was drained by convoy duties.
   - (g) The Vietcong had tree cover; the Mujahiddin did not.
4. Result: In both cases the invasion failed to achieve its ends. Technology was no match for:
   - (a) highly-motivated guerrillas;
   - (b) fighting on their own territory;
   - (c) with the support of most of the local population;
   - (d) against unpopular puppet regime and their unpopular outside backers.
5. Outcome: In each case the superpower concerned:
   - (a) alienated the non-aligned;
   - (b) incurred the hostility from the other super-power;

(c) paid a prohibitive material and propaganda cost;

(d) suffered casualties resented at home.

(e) Returning soldiers imported narcotics problems.

However:

In the USA after some years the effects were more public; in the USSR they were less vocal because of overt censorship.

6. Withdrawal

The US departure was undignified: panic evacuation by helicopter from the roof of the US embassy in Saigon; the Soviet departure was reasonably dignified: marching out with bands playing, the officers at the rear.

Glossary

asymmetrical warfare: warfare between very unequally balanced forces of different levels of military sophistication, in which the more sophisticated usually call the less sophisticated "terrorists" and use this as a pretext themselves to evade the rules of war.

fundamentalism: a literal appreciation of religious beliefs. Christian fundamentalists tend to believe in the literal truth of the Bible.

Khalq: Pathan branch of the People's Democratic Party of Afghanistan (PDPA)

Mujahiddin: disparate groups of fighters united against the Soviet Union in Afghanistan

Parcham: Tadjik branch of the People's Democratic Party of Afghanistan (PDPA)

Pathans: People living in south-east Afghanistan and north-west Pakistan

PDPA: People's Democratic Party of Afghanistan

Shah: emperor of Persia (Iran)

Tadjiks: People living in northern Afghanistan

Taliban: Afghan Muslim fundamentalist movement founded by the Pakistani Army

Third world: that part of the world not part of the developed West or the Soviet bloc

Bibliography

Arnold, Anthony, *Afghanistan, the Soviet Invasion in Perspective*, Hoover Institution (Stanford, CA, 1985)

Bonosky, Phillip, *Washington's Secret War against Afghanistan*, International (New York, 1985)

Cooley, John, *Unholy Wars: Afghanistan, America and International Terrorism*, Pluto (New York, 2001)

Corkery, Michael, *End Game: The Road to the Soviet Intervention in Afghanistan (1976-1979)* Wayland Press (Providence, RI., 1997)

Galeotti, Mark, *Afghanistan, the Soviet Union's Last War*, Frank Cass (London, 1994)

Giradet, Edward, *Afghanistan: The Soviet War*, St. Martin's (New York, 1985)

Urban, Mark, *War in Afghanistan,* St. Martin's, (New York, 1990)

Colonel Oliver North

18. Central America

"The High ... Parties declare inadmissible the intervention of any one of them, directly or indirectly, and for whatever reason, in the internal or external affairs of any of the Parties." (Declaration of the Buenos Aires Conference (1936) signed by US President Roosevelt)

General Background

1. Throughout the twentieth century the states of Central America were client states of the USA. Most people were landless peasants, while a very rich minority collaborated with US companies, especially the United Fruit Company, which owned much of the land.
2. At the beginning of the century US President Theodore Roosevelt had added a rider to the Monroe Doctrine, to the effect that the US had the right to intervene anywhere in the continent if they were dissatisfied with the performance of the government. US forces invaded the countries of Latin American to preserve or remove governments repeatedly during the century.
3. The power of the US-trained military became dominant throughout Latin America. High-ranking officers removed governments at will, and set themselves up as dictators. Only in Costa Rica was there a liberal democratic tradition.
4. This made the US almost universally loathed by the people throughout the continent. On a tour of Latin America in 1985, Vice-President Nixon was greeted with insults and violence. In attempts to create a more acceptable impression:
  (a) President Eisenhower instituted the:
   (i) Inter-American Bank;
   (ii) Inter-American Fund for Social Development.
  (b) President Kennedy set up the Alliance for Progress.
5. Little was actually achieved.
  (a) Latin American governments were trapped by huge interest payments on loans.
  (b) Loans were provided on condition they were spent with US companies, which prevented local industries from developing.
  (c) US aid was blatantly employed to exert political control.
  (d) Much of the aid disappeared into the hands of the military and the wealthy oligarchies.*

6. The 1979 oil-price increase, together with a fall in world coffee and cotton prices led to a **slump** throughout Central America, with:

    (a) negative growth;

    (b) high inflation;

    (c) high unemployment;

    (d) increased foreign borrowing, although debtor nations could not even pay the interest on previous loans;

    (e) the constant drain of capital to the USA;

    (f) the imposition of austerity programmes.

7. This led to discontent, the growth of the political left and insurrection,* in many countries. This was often supported by priests influenced by **liberation theology.***

8. In turn this provoked right-wing repression with the aid of the military and the USA. Attempts at reform were systematically sabotaged by a coalition of:

    (a) the local wealthy oligarchies;

    (b) the local army command;

    (c) US agencies, such as the CIA.

    One country would be used by the USA as a staging post for the suppression of reform in another, e.g. Guatemala for the launching of the bay of Pigs invasion of Cuba, Honduras as a base for attacks upon the Sandinistas of Nicaragua.

9. Repression was given free rein and made more efficient when Ronald Reagan came to power and the neo-Conservatives were allowed a free hand in Central America.

10. At the same time, pressure was exerted by the USA to move to unrestricted capitalism:

    (a) to cut taxes;

    (b) lower wages;

    (c) exempt foreign (i.e. US) companies from labour and environmental laws and allow them to repatriate all their profits;

    (d) cut social spending, e.g. on health care and education;

    (e) sell off state industries and utilities (mostly to US interests or tiny wealthy oligarchies).

Glossary

liberation theology: a movement within the Roman Catholic Church, particularly among the Jesuits, which argued that a minimal social justice for the poor was demanded by their religion. It was suppressed by Pope John Paul II.

neo-conservatives: a movement of influential people in the USA characterised by:

    (a) extreme US nationalism;

    (b) militarism: the desire to use US military power as an instrument of an expansionist foreign policy;

    (c) support for a strong executive and shrinking of human rights and freedoms;

    (d) support for big business;

    (e) social conservatism;

    (f) opposition to social spending.

oligarchies: small but wealthy and powerful minorities who see themselves as an elite

Jacobo Arbenz Gúzman

Guatemala

"Sabotage, like all things in life, is good or bad depending on whether its object is good or bad." (CIA guide inciting Guatemalans to acts of sabotage against their own government).

Background
1. One of the poorest states of Latin America, the economy of Guatemala is largely dependant upon the export of coffee and bananas. Most of the people are landless peasants. The land was owned by US companies, particularly the United Fruit Company.
2. For most of the time between 1838 and 1950, Guatemala was ruled by military dictators.

The CIA Overthrows Democracy
1. In 1950 Jacobo Arbenz Gúzman won an election.
2. Gúzman was regarded by Washington as:
    (a) "too left wing";
    (b) an enemy of foreign capitalist exploitation of Guatemala, especially of the powerful United Fruit Company.
3. In office, President Gúzman:
    (a) confiscated uncultivated land belonging to the United Fruit Company, paid the company compensation, and distributed it to the peasants;
    (b) supported strikers against foreign companies;
    (c) legalised the Communist Party;
    (d) introduced a basic minimum wage;
    (e) required the US companies which owned the estates to provide adequate housing for their workers;
    (f) built new schools and hospitals.
4. At the 10th inter-American Conference, held in Caracas in 1954, US Secretary of State John Foster Dulles tried to persuade the other states to condemn Gúzman's government. When they refused, he stormed out of the conference.

5. Then the USA put pressure on Guatemala:
    (a) All US aid was stopped.
    (b) Gúzman was accused of being a Communist.
    (c) The neighbouring states of Honduras and Nicaragua were pressured to complain of guerilla* incursions from Guatemala;
    (d) Isolated the country diplomatically through the OAS.
    (e) The USA pressured other states not to sell arms to Guatemala;
    (f) CIA Operation PBSUCCESS:
        (i) spread rumours that the government was going to confiscate bank accounts, seize private property, force children into re-education centres, persecute the Catholic Church, etc.;
        (ii) conducted a terrorist bombing campaign, bombing roads, bridges, military installations and the property of supporters of the government;
        (iii) dropped leaflets inciting local people to commit acts of sabotage;
        (iv) put out propaganda radio programmes about non-existent resistance movements within Guatemala with staged on-air "battles";
6. Finally, the CIA armed mercenaries and arranged an invasion from the neighbouring states.
7. Guatemala appealed to the UN Security Council. The US tried to secure the referral of the matter to the US controlled Organisation of American States (OAS), but this was vetoed by the USSR.
8. The invasion was successful because the Guatemalan armed forces failed to defend the government, fearing the retribution of the USA if they did so.
9. Colonel Carlos Catillo Armas took over the country.
10. There followed a period of "suppressed civil war" (Peter Calvocoressi), assassinations and coups, under a succession of dictators, who fought each other for a share of US "aid":
    (a) 120,000 were killed in fighting;
    (b) 40,000 political opponents, union leaders, student leaders, teachers, human rights advocates, etc. just "disappeared" as right wing "death squads" terrorized the towns.

Reform and Reaction

1. In 1978, the liberal General Garcia became president.
2. He promised to redistribute uncultivated land to the peasants. When the wealthy protested, this land was awarded to them.
3. Virtual civil war followed, with thousands of political murders.
4. In 1982, when it was announced that General Guevara, a nominee of Garcia, had won, a right-wing group of army officers declared the result a fraud and installed General Efraín Ríos Montt.
5. Montt, a "born-again" Christian Protestant ordered the massacre of the entire population of selected Indian villages thought to be supporting guerillas. Within six months he had killed nearly one hundred thousand Mayans, and created a quarter of a million refugees. Children had been systematically beaten on rocks and thrown into rivers in front of their parents, and their parents then subjected to mass rapes, amputations and burning alive.
6. In 1983 he was replaced by General Oscar Meija. Meija, who complained that the US was pressuring him either to denounce the Sandinistas in neighbouring Nicaragua, or be himself deposed. He did denounce them. However, he also introduced elections for civilian democracy.
7. In November 1985 elections returned a Christian Democrat majority. Vinicio Cerez Arévajo became prime minister.

Napoleon Duarte

El Salvador

"[The country must be] destroyed totally, the economy must be wrecked, unemployment must be massive ... a cleansing ... of some 3 or 4 or 500,000 people [must be carried out.] (Robert White, US Ambassador to El Salvador)

Background

1. Like other countries in the region El Salvador was firmly in the hands of US companies and a tiny local oligarchy .
2. In 1932, Augustín Farabundo Martí, a founder of the Central American socialist party, led a popular revolt. The Salvadorian army responded by killing Indians. 30,000 people died during *la Matanza*, (the Massacre).
3. By the 1970s, most Salvadorians were suffering from poverty, unemployment and lack of land.
4. In 1979, a junta of military officers and civilians overthrew the president. They pledged to implement reforms but reneged on their promises.

On March 24, 1980, the popular Archbishop Oscar Romero, was assassinated while celebrating mass in San Salvador.

The Civil War

1. The Farabundo Martí National Liberation Front, FMLN, launched its armed struggle against government forces on January 10, 1981.
2. They quickly conquered territory in eastern and northern El Salvador. The guerrillas then tried to bring the economy to a standstill by destroying bridges and coffee plantations, cutting down power lines, and killing livestock.
3. The military responded by attacking villages and murdering the inhabitants. The most notorious of these was in El Mozote in Morazán district, where 900 people, including children, were massacred.
4. In 1982, the leader of the extreme right ARENA party, Major Roberto d'Aubuisson, set up death squads to eliminate suspected leftists and trade union members. They murdered thousands of

people.

5. The United States spent 6 billion dollars to bolster the government. They provided:
   (a) special training for army officers at Fort Benning, Georgia;
   (b) equipment and weapons;
   (c) an intelligence and reconnaissance system.

6. In 1984 the US took the remnants of the Christian Democrat Party, a reformist party under Jose Napoleon Duarte, which had not joined the civil war, and set it up as a "democratic" front. Elections were held, which Duarte "won."

7. Whenever Duarte tried to:
   (a) introduce reforms;
   (b) institute criminal actions against members of the military for crimes committed against non-combatants;
   the army threatened to overthrow him.

8. He also had to follow Reagan's line on economic liberalization and cutting back on social spending.

9. Duarte came to rely upon force to impose his will on the disaffected population.

10. Sensing his increasing unpopularity, Washington decided to support ARENA instead, and secured their "election in 1989.

11. In 1989, the FMLN launched a major offensive on the capital, San Salvador, but it failed.

12. This prompted both the government and the rebels to begin peace negotiations, under United Nations mediation.

13. An agreement was reached on January 16, 1992 which provided for military and political reforms.

14. The 12-year civil war claimed the lives of 75,000 people. Over 300,000 people fled the country.

Glossary

Farabundo Martí National Liberation Front: the Salvadorean national liberation movement

FMLN: Farabundo Martí National Liberation Front

Daniel Ortega

Nicaragua

"Daniel Ortega is an enemy of everything the United States represents. Further, he is a friend of our enemies. Ortega has a relationship of more than thirty years with states and individuals who shelter and condone international terrorism." (Jeb Bush, governor of Florida and brother of president George W. Bush, in a full-page advertisement in *La Prensa*, Nicaragua's major newspaper, during the Nicaraguan election campaign, 2001)

Background

1. In 1911 US troops intervened to prop up a favoured president and suppress the opposition. They stayed on.
2. In 1933 US troops suppressed a rising by Colonel Augusto Cesar Sandino. In the same year Anastasio Somoza became dictator, assassinating Colonel Sandino, and the US forces left.
3. The Somoza family ruled over Nicaragua as hereditary military dictators for almost fifty years:
    (i) Anastasio 1933-56;
    (ii) Luis 1956-63;
    (iii) Anastasio II 1963-79.
4. As time went on, the rule of the Somozas became increasingly repressive and corrupt.
5. During this period, the US employed Nicaraguan troops:
    (a) against Guatemala in 1954;
    (b) against Cuba in 1961;
    (c) against the Dominican Republic in 1965.

The Revolution

1. During the 1960s the **Sandinista Liberation Front** was formed, and began insurgency. The SLF was composed of nationalists, socialists (including Marxists), liberals, Catholics and progressive

capitalists. They were helped by Costa Rica.

2. In 1972, Mangua, the capital, was razed to the ground by a severe earthquake. Aid sent by Nixon was mostly stolen by the Somozas and others, while the wealthy profited from the rebuilding.

3. When guerilla war flared up, the repression was so harsh that the Catholic Church protested.

The Government of the Sandinistas

1. In 1979, Antonio Somoza was finally driven out, and the country was governed by a collective leadership, dominated by the Marxists. They:
    (a) nationalised foreign owned enterprises
    (b) redistributed land to the poor
    (c) conducted a literacy campaign
    (d) conducted a public health campaign, eliminating polio.

2. The USA decided to get rid of the Sandinistas:
    (a) They instituted a trade and credit blockade, and pressured their allies to follow.
    (b) They financed and trained the **Nicaraguan Defence Force (NGF), the contras**.

3. Using neighbouring Honduras as a base, the CIA, Argentine officers and the Honduran army launched the **contras** on raids into Nicaragua. They:
    (a) destroyed the cotton and coffee crops.
    (b) demolished roads, bridges, schools and hospitals.
    (c) committed atrocities, including maiming children, cutting off arms, gouging out eyes, bayoneting pregnant women in the stomach, and amputating genitals.

4. During the early 1980's, the US trained Nicaraguan Contras to use of high speed boats for attacks against Sandinista shipping, and mined the ships in Managua harbour.

5. As expected, this forced the postponement of elections and the mobilisation of the people (CF Castro's Cuba), enabling the Americans to denounce the Sandinistas as undemocratic.

6. The contras were not very successful:
    (a) Their destruction of the crops and infrastructure, and atrocities, were unpopular.
    (b) Much of the money received from the USA was diverted to the contras' personal use.

7. A controversy developed in the USA, and Congress voted that aid to the contras be stopped.

8. In 1985 Daniel Ortega was elected president of Nicaragua.

9. At the Latin American Parliament, 16 out of 18 countries condemned the USA for its persecution of Nicaragua.

10. Late in 1986 the **Irangate*** affair broke out. The profits had been used, illegally, to finance the contras.

11. The Nicaraguan economy was devastated by:
    (a) The US-led trade and credit embargo;
    (b) The cost of the war against the contras.

12. In 1986 the World Court:
    (a) condemned the USA for "unlawful use of force" against Nicaragua;
    (b) demanded that it stop;
    (c) demanded that it pay extensive reparations of $17 billion dollars in damages for mining the harbour in Managua;
    (d) declared all US aid to the contras, whatever its character, to be "military aid," not "humanitarian aid."

13. The Court was either denounced in the USA or ignored. The United States never recognized that debt.

14. The Democrat-controlled Congress immediately authorized new funds to step up the unlawful

use of force.

15. The USA vetoed a Security Council resolution calling on all states to respect international law. Although the resolution did not specify any state by name, it was clear that the USA was intended.

16. When the General Assembly passed a similar resolution, the US voted against it, joined by Israel and El Salvador. In another vote during the next year, only the Israelis supported them.

17. In 1987, President Arias of Costa Rica persuaded the Latin American presidents to support a peace plan for the region. This was an attempt to solve the region's problems without American interference. He received the Nobel Prize, but the plan was difficult to implement because:

(a) The US was still trying to destabilize Nicaragua.

(b) Under US pressure, Honduras and El Salvador were forced to refuse to cooperate.

18. In April 1990 free elections were held. The US government:

(a) through its "National Endowment for Democracy," poured millions of dollars into the coffers of the UNO Party;

(b) President Bush let it be known that the Contras would resume their attacks if he UNO Party did not win;

thereby ensuring the defeat of the Sandinista government. Violeta Chazamorro claimed to follow a policy of national reconciliation.

Glossary

Contras: right-wing mercenary guerilla fighters who committed atrocities against the Nicaraguan people when they sought to topple the Sandinista regime using illegal funds supplied by the US Government

Irangate: US President Reagan, boasted that he would never bargain with terrorists, but secretly sold US missiles to the Iranians in order to secure the release of the hostages in the US embassy in Teheran. The secret funds obtained in this way were used to finance the Contras, enabling the government to hide US support of them from the Congress. The funds were transmitted using the services of cocaine and marijuana dealers, such as General Manuel Noriega of Panama. This deal was organised by CIA chief William Casey and Colonel Oliver North and Most of those responsible, including President Reagan, who said that he did not remember authorising the deal, escaped punishment.

Sandinista Liberation Front (Sandinistas): a national liberation movement formed during the 1960s to overthrow the dictatorship of Anastasio Somoza. It was named after a national hero, Colonel Augusto Cesar Sandino, who had successfully resisted US domination of his country during the 1930s.

The Significance of US Policy in Central America

1. The states of Central America fell firmly within the US sphere of influence throughout the twentieth century. Their condition, therefore, illustrates what US hegemony produces in the countries most firmly under its control:
    (a) endemic poverty;
        (i) The Pan-American Health Organisation estimated that of 850,000 children born in Central America each year, 100,000 will die before the age of five years, and two-thirds of those who survive will suffer from malnutrition.
        (ii) According to the World Health Organisation, 60% of the population of Central America lives in poverty; nearly ten million in extreme poverty.
        (iii) The US imposes severe restrictions on trade to prevent Central American goods being sold at lower prices than US goods.
    (b) social underdevelopment;
    (c) rampant government corruption;
    (d) severe environmental degradation: deforestation, pesticide poisoning, soil erosion, etc.
    (e) military rule, coups, assassinations, death squads, government terrorism, etc.
    The history and the state of Central America should be compared with that of Eastern Europe, the corresponding region most firmly under Soviet control.
2. It is clear that in its treatment of Central America, the Cold War had little to with US policy. When President George H. W. Bush ordered the invasion of Panama, the Cold War was already over. There was no danger at all that Panama would become a Soviet satellite. The aim of US policy was clearly the uninterrupted maintenance of US domination and exploitation.
3. Central America was where three streams of thought in modern US politics came together:
    (a) the USA is somehow special, God's new chosen people, who are always, by definition, on the side of goodness;
    (b) the absolute value of unrestricted market capitalism;
    (c) Christian **fundamentalism.**
    and where these were used as a tool by the neo-conservatives.
4. The treatment of Central America from the 1980s marks a step in the development of open US illegality and militarism, that was to lead to US governments:
    (a) ignoring or bypassing congress and "reinterpreting" US law to their own advantage;
    (b) repudiating international law and norms of civilised behaviour, e.g. in the setting up of a gulag of prison camps, in seeking to justify the practice of torture, etc.
    (c) seeking to impose its will by relying upon US military might;
    as these subsequently became evident to the world community during the administration of George W. Bush.
5. It was a triumph of Wetern (US) propaganda that virtually no one compared the suffering of the Soviet satellites of Eastern Europe with that of the US satellites of Central Ameica, which would have shown Soviet hegemony to have been very mild, and in some ways beneficial, compared with that of the USA.

Bibliography

Grandin, Greg, Empire's Workshop, Henry Holt & Co (New York, 2006)

Mikhail Gorbachev

19. The End of the Cold War

"And now what shall become of us without any barbarians?
Those people were some kind of solution." (Constantine P. Cavafy)

"We should shed a tear in recognition of the millions of our best and our brightest who -- through the 1920's and '30's in the Soviet Union when it was still possible to believe in a brave new world, through the Spanish Civil War, through the resistance to Hitler -- sacrificed their lives for an idea. For behind the original communist idea was a vision of the human race that was essentially optimistic and idealistic: the notion that men and women could function by giving to society the best of their abilities, and in return receive from that society what they needed to live decently.
"So, we should shed a tear, it seems to me, for ourselves; for burying this notion; for coming to the conclusion that the human race does not have this potential; for deciding that a society functions more efficiently when it appeals to the profit motive, to greed, to the instinct that transforms ordinary people into consumers and then pushes them to accumulate for the sake of accumulation." (Robert Littell)

"In 1990, a year of the greatest upheaval and revolutionary change since World War II, a look at President Bush's proposed $15 billion foreign aid package would indicate that the five most deserving countries in the world for the United States are Israel, Egypt, the Philippines, Turkey and Pakistan." (John M. Goshko, *Washington Post*)

"For a part of this past century, there were some constraints on our capacity for arbitrary military action — what you might call the inhibitions of the Cold War — but with the collapse of the Soviet Union, we've acquired a headier sense of what we can get away with." (Former US Attorney General Ramsay Clark)

"Prospects are pretty dim for Eastern Europe. The West has a plan for it -- they want to turn large parts of it into a new, easily exploitable part of the Third Word." (Noam Chomsky)

The Years of Stagnation

1. During the Brezhnev years belief in Marxist-Leninist ideology largely died out. The population had become cynical and apathetic, while the ageing leadership served out their time in comfort.
2. Increasingly, signs of the failure of the sclerotic command economy began to multiply.
3. The leadership reluctantly realised this and sought to provide for the reform of the system under the next leader.
4. Andropov sought to "tighten" up the system, to make it more efficient, but his campaign against corruption threatened the gerontocracy. When he died, he was replaced by Chernenko precisely to give a breathing space for the gerontocracy to die in office.

Gorbachev's Reforms

1. When Gorbachev became First Secretary, with the intention of reforming the system, his power was limited within the collective leadership. Reform would have the wide support of two groups with quite opposite aims:
   (a) Neo-Stalinists: who wished to bring Stalin's system back to its full vigour;
   (b) Pro-western liberal democrats, who wished to replace the existing system with something else.
   Of the two, the neo-Stalinists were the more powerful group. Gorbachev later said to economist Abel Abanbeygan: "They had me surrounded."
   Any reform at all would be likely to be resisted by the cadres, who benefited from special privileges.
2. During 1985 and 1986 Gorbachev set about building his power base.
   (a) Influential Brezhnevites were retired
   (b) New figures from the provinces were introduced into the leadership: e.g. Ligachev, Ryzhkov and Yeltsin.
3. Initially, Gorbachev followed the example set by Yuri Andropov in stressing discipline: instituting a crackdown on the inordinate vodka consumption, slackness and absenteeism thought to be responsible for "stagnation".
4. Late in 1986, Gorbachev moved more openly towards reform. Key concepts were:
   (a) *glasnost* (openness)
   (b) *perestroika* (restructuring)
5. *Glasnost* led to a breakdown of the closed society. In 1988, censorship was abolished.
   (a) Books by previously banned writers began to appear, e.g. by Trotsky, Solzhenitsyn and Pasternak. Independent newspapers appeared.
   (b) A debate was opened about Soviet history in books, press and television. By 1989 the work of Lenin himself was being questioned.
   (c) Political organizations reflecting many different points of view were set up. The Democratic Union organized mass street demonstrations.
   (d) Persecution of the Orthodox Church ended, and state and church became partners in restoring historic church buildings. Religious texts and artifacts became freely available.
6. *Perestroika:* New legislation freed the economy from rigid state control:
   (a) The **Law on Enterprises** gave enterprises the rights to:
      (i) seek their own resources
      (ii) dispose of their output

(iii) pay their workers differentially.

(b) Workers were allowed to leave collective farms.

(c) Private cooperative enterprises were allowed by mid-1988. The first examples were retail kiosks and small restaurants.

7. By 1988 the new spirit was evident everywhere:

(a) new goods were appearing on the streets created by private enterprise

(b) there was a new preparedness to discuss and question.

Some considered these things hopeful, and others that the reforms were getting out of control.

8. The Congress of Peoples Deputies, elected by indirect elections in March 1989, met in May, and began to criticize all aspects of Soviet life.

The End of East-West Confrontation

1. When Mikhail Gorbachev became First Secretary, he immediately announced:

(a) a 6-month freeze on the deployment of missiles in Europe; (If the US responded with a similar freeze of Cruise and Pershing missiles, the freeze could be renewed.)

(b) his wish to meet US President Reagan;

(c) a unilateral moratorium* on all nuclear tests.

2. In France he proposed:

(a) a 50% reduction in strategic nuclear weapons;

(b) direct talks with France and the UK over their nuclear weapons;

(c) a continuing freeze of deployment of INF in Europe.

3. At a summit in Geneva, the discussions were cordial. Gorbachev proposed:

(a) a call for the abolition of all nuclear weapons;

(b) a call for the abolition of all bases on foreign soil.

4. In October 1986 at a summit at Reykjavik, in Iceland, US President Reagan proposed the elimination of all INF and strategic missiles, the "**zero option**". Gorbachev insisted that SDI be included and Reagan refused. Under pressure from "hawks" such as Margaret Thatcher, Reagan then backtracked on his original offer.

5. However, in December 1987 the USA and USSR agreed to the INF Treaty which involved:

(a) the dismantling of all medium-range missiles;

(b) onsite verification.

6. In December 1988 at the United Nations, Gorbachev announced:

(a) a unilateral reduction in Soviet army forces of half a million men;

(b) the withdrawal from eastern Europe of 10,000 tanks;

(c) the USSR would henceforward adopt a "defensive posture";

(d) invited the NATO countries to do the same.

The Collapse of Soviet Eastern Europe

1. In December 1988 Gorbachev announced at the UN that every nation had the right to choose its own government, and that there were no exceptions to this. He repeated assurances given to leaders of Eastern bloc countries as far back as 1985, that the USSR would no longer interfere in the internal affairs of any other state. The Brezhnev Doctrine was dead.

2. This placed the Eastern bloc leaders in a dilemma, since their own power ultimately depended upon the threat of Soviet force.

Hungary

1. In May 1989 in Hungary, a group of reformers within the higher reaches of the Party forced János Kadar to resign, replacing him with Karoly Grosz, and then with a "Gang of Four".
2. During Summer 1989, this government:
   (a) opened its borders with Austria;
   (b) announced that the uprising of 1956 had not been a counter-revolution, and rehabilitated its leaders. The body of Imre Nagy was publicly reburied.
   (c) announced free parliamentary elections for the following year.
3. Gorbachev took no action against them.
4. On October 18th, the Hungarian National Assembly:
   (a) abolished the leading role of the Communist Party in society;
   (b) legalized non-Communist political parties;
   (c) dropped the term "People's Republic" from the name of the country.

Poland

1. In Poland, the Solidarity union demanded democratic reforms.
2. In 1988, the government of General Jaruzelski approved partially free elections to be held on June 4th, 1989. In those elections:
   (a) Solidarity won 160 of the 161 seats up for election, and then won the remaining seat in a runoff. Poland had chosen a non-Communist government.
   (b) The new prime minister, Tadeusz Mazowiecki, who was the choice of Lech Walesa, was immediately invited to Moscow and treated in a friendly and supportive manner.
3. Power had already begun to pass to Solidarity. The new government immediately began the change-over to a capitalist economy.

East Germany

1. Under Erich Honecker, East Germany had one of the most hard-line governments of the Eastern bloc. Honecker had even censored the news of Gorbachev's reforms.
2. In October Gorbachev attended the fortieth anniversary celebrations of the German Democratic Republic (GDR). Gorbachev was fêted by the crowds.
3. During August and September, many thousands of East Germans, under pretext of vacationing in Hungary, took the opportunity to flee to the West via that country.
4. By October huge crowds were gathering in Leipzig and Dresden to demand the end of Communist control. Honecker decided to order the soldiers to fire on the demonstrators. Egon Krenz suppressed this order, and a week later forced Honecker into retirement.
5. Krenz then promised reform. On November 1 the border with Czechoslovakia was opened to allow emigration to the West. People began to stream across the border.
6. On November 3 the ministers in charge of security and the police resigned. The next day perhaps a million demonstrators demanded democracy, prompting the resignations of the rest of the cabinet.
7. When new arrangements for travel to the West were announced on the evening of the 9th, reporters asked the government spokesman when the checkpoints would be opening. He said: "Right away." Almost immediately, thousands of East Berliners began gathering at the checkpoints, to the surprise of the border guards, who had received no orders. The crowds told the guards that they had heard on the television that the Wall was to be immediately thrown open. Shortly before 11 p.m., the commander of one of the check points decided to let the crowd through, and raised the barrier. The border guards on the other side soon gave up trying to stem

the tide of people which flooded into West Berlin. Soon crowds were clambering all over the wall, and many began to break it up with hammers.

8. A week later the *Stasi* (state security police) were disbanded. Then the *Volkskammer* (the East German Parliament) renounced the Socialist Unity Party's "leading role" in society. A new coalition government took control and planned free national elections for May 1990.

9. On December 3rd, Krenz' government collapsed. Since there had been little organised opposition, there was no alternative government ready to take over. After some confusion, Hans Modrow became caretaker chancellor, and the elections were moved up to March.

10. Honecker and the *Stasi* leaders were arrested. The offices of the *Stasi* and Communist Party were sacked by mobs.

Czechoslovakia

1. In 1988 in Czechoslovakia, Gustav Husák and Miloš Jakeš had long ago purged all independent voices in government.

2. However, large crowds had demonstrated against their Communist regime on the anniversary of the 1968 Soviet invasion.

3. On November 17th 1989 the authorities allowed a demonstration commemorating the 50th anniversary of the suppression of a student demonstration in German-occupied Prague. The police brutality which took place at the commemoration set off a protest movement throughout the towns of the country. Demonstrations and strikes were organised by **Civic Forum**, led by Václav Havel.

4. The cabinet resigned, and the Communist Central Committee promised a special congress to discuss the party's future. Václav Havel denounced this as a trick. Crowds demanded genuine multi-party elections, and Czechoslovak workers declared a two-hour general strike as proof of their solidarity.

5. The government abandoned the Communist party's "leading role" on November 29, opening the border with Austria on the 30th, and announcing a new coalition cabinet on December 8. President Gustav Husák resigned on the December 10th, and free elections were scheduled for the 28th.

6. By the end of the year, Václav Havel had been elected president by the communist members of parliament. Former party leader Alexander Dubček had become the new speaker of the parliament.

7. This non-violent revolution was known as the **velvet revolution**.

Bulgaria

1. In 1984 in Bulgaria, Communist party secretary and president, Todor Zhivkov, decided to "Bulgarise" the Turks who lived inside the country. They were:
   (a) forced to adopt Bulgarian names
   (b) forbidden to practice Islam.

2. When the resisted, they were expelled from the country.

3. Petar Mladenov forced Zhivkov to resign on November 10th, 1989.

4. Within a month crowds in Sofia called for democratization.

5. The Central Committee:
   (a) voluntarily surrendered the party's "leading role" in society;
   (b) announced multi-party elections for the next year;
   (c) ended the persecution of the Turks;
   (d) arrested Todor Zhivkov.

Rumania

1. Ceausescu's Rumania was a Stalinist state, in the grip of the Securitate (Rumanian secret police).
2. Demonstrations in the Transylvanian city of Timisoara, when the government tried to evict a Protestant pastor, spread to other cities. People formed a human chain around the church. Army officers who refused to shoot the demonstrators were themselves shot by the Securitate, who attacked the crowd.
3. Riots spread across the country.
4. When Ceausescu addressed a crowd in Bucharest, he was shouted down and forced to flee, ordering the Securitate to attack the crowd. In the fighting, the Army supported the people.
5. Ceausescu was arrested, tried, and executed on December 25th. The Securitate continued fighting for some days, before they were wiped out or surrendered.
6. A conspiracy of reform communists and disaffected elements in the army formed the National Salvation Front (NSF) to lead the country to elections for May 1990.

The Collapse of the Soviet Union

The Crisis of Perestroika

1. During the mid-1980s there was a fall in world oil prices, which deprived the USSR of hard currency revenues at a critical time.
2. In April 1986 a melt-down at a nuclear reactor at **Chernobyl**, near Kiev in the Ukraine, released toxic nuclear materials into the atmosphere. The human, environmental and financial cost of cleaning up was immense.
3. In 1988 a terrible earthquake in Armenia killed 25,000 and caused massive destruction. The poor response from the rest of the USSR showed:
   (a) The degree of apathy and cynicism, and withdrawal from common enterprise which the Soviet Union had undergone.
   (b) That the USSR had already ceased to function as a unity.
4. The reforms of *perestroika* began to fail because of the inability of the central command system to absorb private enterprise and local control without large-scale collapse.
6. In February 1990 the guaranteed leading role of the Communist Party was dropped from the constitution.
7. In the elections of March, it was stipulated that officials receive 50% of the electorate to remain in office. The majority of the time-servers were swept away. Gorbachev was indirectly elected to the new non-Party post of president by the partially re-elected Supreme Soviet.
8. The elections to the Congress of People's Deputies of the Russian Soviet Federal Socialist Republic (RSFSR) were held in March and April. There was now a position of **"dual power"** in Russia once more (as in 1917). Yeltsin had a power base from which to challenge Gorbachev.
9. For Russians a central issue at this time became one of loyalty to the USSR or to Russia. In June 1990 the Congress of People's Deputies of the (RSFSR) declared **Russia** a sovereign nation. It was asserted that the laws of Russia took precedence over those of the USSR.
10. As allies deserted him, Gorbachev was forced to rely more and more upon his opponents. In December 1990 foreign minister Shevardnadze prophesied a coup and then resigned.
11. The normal trade between the republics of the USSR began to break down.
12. In September 1989 Shevardnadze, in talks with Jim Baker, dropped Soviet demands that the SDI program be included in the START negotiations.

13. In October the European Community, West Germany, and then (at the insistence of Congress) the United States, offered emergency aid totalling $2,000,000,000 to the Polish government.
14. The chairman of the U.S. Federal Reserve Board went to Moscow to advise the Soviets on how they, too, might make the transition to a market economy.

The Resurgence of Nationalism

1. The economic breakdown and new freedom fed the spirit of nationalism in the minority regions of the USSR.
2. **Nationalism** within the USSR quickly began to revive, taking advantage of *glasnost*. Gorbachev was reluctant to allow secession from the USSR, as the neo-Stalinists would draw the line at that point. Fighting broke out in the Armenian enclave of Ngorno-Karabakh in Azerbaijan between Armenians and Azeris. Azeris massacred isolated Armenian minorities in Azerbaijan.
3. In August 1989 the USSR admitted the existence of the secret protocols in the Molotov-Ribbentrop Pact under which Stalin had annexed Latvia, Lithuania, and Estonia.
4. On the 50th anniversary of the pact, on August 23rd, perhaps a million Balts formed a human chain linking their capitals to:
   (a) denounce the annexation as illegal
   (b) demand self-determination.
5. In January 1990 Gorbachev sent troops into Baku, capital of Azerbaijan in order to stop the massacre of Armenians in that country.
6. In March, Vytautas Landsbergis became head of a popular front government of Lithuania and declared independence. That led to a trade embargo.
7. In Georgia about twenty nationalist demonstrators were shot by the police.
8. Yeltsin was elected speaker of the Russian Supreme Soviet. In June Yeltsin declared Russia a sovereign state.*
9. A breakdown in relations between the various SSRs led to a need for a new Union Treaty. Gorbachev prepared one, but was constantly blocked by SSR leaders making new demands. He had to appeal over their heads to the people in a referendum in March 1991. A 76% majority favoured a new treaty, which was to be implemented in August.
10. In January 1991 Internal Ministry soldiers effectively seized power in Lithuania and Latvia, taking control of the broadcasting stations. About twenty people were killed. Yeltsin:
    (a) went to Tallin to meet Russian troops and asked them not to fire on the Balts
    (b) recognised Baltic sovereignty on behalf of the RSFSR.
    (c) He joined the Baltic presidents in making an appeal to the UN.
11. Later that month, Soviet troops attacked the Latvian Ministry of the Interior, killing four people. The determination of the Balts to gain their independence was redoubled
12. In June, Yeltsin was elected President of Russia.
13. Meanwhile, during 1991 Gorbachev's efforts to crack down on dissident Soviet ethnic groups also failed:
    (a) hundreds of thousands of Muscovites defied the ban on public demonstrations,
    (b) six Soviet republics boycotted a referendum on Gorbachev's new union plan,
    (c) Ukrainian coal miners went on strike.

The Failed Coup

1. On the eve of the implementation of the new Union Treaty, Mikhail Gorbachev went on holiday to the Crimea.

2. In his absence, on 18th August, 1991, vice-president Yanaev, Prime Minister Pavlov, Interior Minister Pugo and KGB head Kryuchkov declared Gorbachev relieved of his post on the grounds of ill-health.
3. Gorbachev and his wife were held in isolation in their Black Sea resort.
4. The plotters believed that their coup would simply be generally accepted as a *fait accompli*.
5. Some leaders of the SSRs supported the coup, many opposed it, and more stayed on the sidelines uncommitted, waiting to see what would happen.
6. Crowds demonstrated in Moscow, surrounding the White House, the Russian parliament in Moscow.
7. Elite army units disobeyed orders.
8. Yeltsin took the initiative to act as a focus of opposition by addressing the crowds outside the White House from the top of a tank.
9. When the plotters realized that their coup had failed, they rushed off to see Gorbachev, and were arrested.

Reasons for the Failure of the Coup
1. The coup plotters were visibly inadequate. Martin McCauley calls them "astonishingly inept".
   (a) They had failed to make adequate preparations, e.g. the arrest of Yeltsin.
   (b) They lost their nerve when things did not go in the way that they expected.
2. Centrifugal forces generated by loyal nationalism ensured that the peripheral republics would not necessarily conform to the will of the centre any more, making any coup liable to fail..
3. In particular, Yeltsin's relentless promotion of "Russia" as a primary focus of loyalty over the USSR meant that many of the key personnel in the Army and KGB had divided loyalties, and were inclined to listen to Yeltsin rather than either Gorbachev or the coup plotters.
4. The response of the press at their press conference, and the crowds which gathered around the White House, showed that the automatic obedience instilled by terror during the Stalin era could no longer be counted upon. This was due to:
   (a) the passage of time since the death of Stalin
   (b) a loss of deference to the leadership due to loss of ideological commitment under Brezhnev
   (c) the freedom enjoyed under Gorbachev's *glasnost*
5. In the last resort, Russian soldiers were unwilling to shed the blood of Russian citizens.

The End of Communist Rule
1. When he returned to Moscow, Gorbachev claimed that he was still a convinced socialist.
2. He replaced the head of the KGB, as crowds destroyed the statue of Felix Dzerzhinsky, founder of the Cheka, outside the Lubianka, and KGB operatives destroyed records.
3. On 23rd August, Boris Yeltsin insisted that Gorbachev read the minutes of the plot. Then Yeltsin signed a decree suspending the activities of the CPSU in Russia:
   (a) Cadres were expelled from the Secretariat of the Central Committee and the building was sealed.
   (b) The party newspaper *Pravda* was banned.
4. Two days later Gorbachev resigned as general secretary of the party and instructed that:
   (a) Local soviets should take over all party property.
   (b) Party activity in the armed forces and KGB was to cease.

The Dissolution of the USSR

1. During late August and early September the Baltic states of Estonia and Latvia declared their independence, which was recognized immediately by Russia, and later by the USSR. Beginning with the Ukraine, the other republics, with the exception of Russia and Kazhakstan soon followed suit.
2. The Congress of People's Deputies proposed a new union of sovereign states, and acknowledged that the USSR no longer had any viability as a federation. Most USSR government departments were closed down.
3. On 6th November Yeltsin formally became Russian prime minister, and soon decreed that all Soviet government resources on Russian territory were to pass to Russian government control. Other states in the USSR did the same.
4. This left Gorbachev head of a virtually non-existent government of a non-existent union. Foreign leaders still visited Gorbachev, but it was unclear what power he still exercised.
5. After much manoeuvring, in which Gorbachev tried to get agreement for a federal union of the former states of the USSR, Yeltsin's view prevailed, and only a loose confederation, the Commonwealth of Independent States (CIS), was agreed to.
7. On 17th December the Russian Supreme Soviet displaced the Supreme Soviet of the USSR in the Kremlin, and on the next day this body acknowledged its own termination.
8. On 21st December eleven former states of the USSR joined the new **Confederation of Independent States (CIS),** with its headquarters in Minsk.
9. On 25th December 1991 Mikhail Gorbachev resigned as President of the USSR.
10. At midnight on 31st December, the USSR itself officially ceased to exist.

Reasons for the failure of the Soviet System

1. Some things had never worked well in the USSR:
    (a) agriculture
    (b) the production of consumer goods.
   The Soviet system collapsed because of internal problems. The centrally controlled command -economy was:
    (c) incapable of responsiveness to the needs of consumers;
    (d) extremely difficult to dismantle without causing a general system collapse.
   This is the opinion of Mikhael Gorbachev. Once it was subjected to reform, it did collapse.
2. The leadership and the system had been sustained by ideology. This had largely died out during the Brezhnev years, when the defence of privilege was seen to be an end in itself.
3. The USSR was a Russian land empire in disguise, and suddenly subjected, under *glasnost,* to the awakened centrifugal forces of third world nationalism.
4. The Soviet system was undermined by the need to compete with the USA in the arms race. This had been deliberately fostered by the Reagan administration with the aim of causing strain and a collapse which would destroy the Soviet system.
5. The USSR was never a superpower in the same sense that the USA was. It was threatened by the nuclear-armed USA adopting an expansionist and antagonistic posture, boxing it in with hostile alliances, and then conducting an arms race designed to destroy its fragile economy and society. This held back economic and social development in the USSR, while ceaseless propaganda from the West held up "free" capitalism as a better model.
6. Certainly the USSR competed with the USA at enormous disadvantages:
    (a) It had been created out of the most backward of the Great Powers

(b) It had suffered from the First World War, revolution, civil war, foreign intervention, and in 1941-5 the most devastating war in history; by contrast with a USA whose land was untouched by war, and whose economy had flourished during the world wars.

7. The consistently aggressive policy of the USA can be seen in that the USSR directly intervened militarily outside the area agreed to be in the Soviet sphere of influence at Moscow, Yalta and Potsdam only once, with the invasion of Afghanistan, whereas during the same period the USA intervened militarily all over the world many times.

8. At several points in the history of the Cold War, US governments claimed to be lagging behind the USSR in the arms race, as a justification for increased spending. Afterwards it was always evident that the USA had been in front all the time. Therefore for US policymakers, the nuclear arms race was considered desirable in itself.

9. When Gorbachev introduced *perestroika,* Soviet citizens envisaged a move towards a humane socialist system like that of Sweden. But Western "experts" advised drastic monetarist solutions calculated to destroy the Soviet social security system, and so bring about social breakdown and mass suffering among the population. This was probably deliberate.

10. After the collapse of the Soviet system both Reagan and Thatcher triumphantly claimed to be personally responsible.

11. Yet at the time, Western intelligence experts, including the CIA, did not foresee the collapse of the Soviet system at all.

The collapse of an empire is a very dangerous time for all concerned: the collapse of an empire armed with nuclear missiles, even more so. The world was lucky that at that time, the USSR was led by such a level-headed and humane man as Mikhail Gorbachev. A Soviet "Reagan" might have brought down a nuclear disaster on the world.

The Consequences of the Collapse of the Soviet System

1. The integrated economy of the USSR collapsed, leading to the failure of many enterprises and mass unemployment.

2. The state found it almost impossible to collect taxes.

3. Hyperinflation destroyed the modest savings of ordinary citizens.

4. The social safety net which provided housing, health care, education, pensions, etc. collapsed.

5. In consequence, the nation's health has deteriorated, so that the number of premature deaths is approaching that of Stalin's purges. (Christopher Read points out that we do not have the conventions to compare political mass murder with economic mass murder).

6. Those in the *nomenklatura* class who were ruthless and well-placed made fortunes overnight by appropriating to themselves state property, such as oil wells, factories, television stations. Thus a new oligarchy of billionaires and millionaires was created in Russia almost overnight by theft. "The collapse of the Soviet system was followed by one of the most outrageous and rapid transfers of resources from poor to rich in the history of the modern world." (Christopher Read)

7. New services sprang up to cater to this class of *nouveaux riches*:* expensive boutiques, night clubs, casinos, etc.

8. Law and order broke down as organized crime, gangsterism and corruption flourished.

9. The KGB was renamed the FSB (Federal Security Service) and worked at the behest of the newly-rich oligarchy.

10. The capitalist countries moved in to take over the former markets of the USSR.

11. The collapse of the Soviet Union presented the West with an incredible opportunity to begin the creation of a peaceful world. The West could have disbanded the North Atlantic Treaty

Organisation (NATO), as the Russians disbanded the Warsaw Pact. They could have welcomed the Russians into the West; but instead, American politicians exploited Russia's temporary weakness. They could have taken on the Russians as allies in the global struggle for preventing destruction of the environment, climate change and poverty, and in building a better world, but chose not to.

12. Instead, with the end of the overt Cold War and the disappearance of the USSR as a superpower, the USA is exercising almost untrammelled world hegemony. All restraint has been removed from US imperialism. Former US Attorney General Ramsay Clark points out, "For a part of this past century, there were some constraints on our capacity for arbitrary military action — what you might call the inhibitions of the Cold War — but with the collapse of the Soviet Union, we've acquired a headier sense of what we can get away with."

This can be seen in the US:

(a) unilateral abrogation of international treaties, such as arms control treaties, the Geneva Convention (temporarily)

(b) refusal to recognise international institutions and treaties: e.g. the Kyoto Agreement, the International War Crimes Tribunal,

(c) the invasion of countries: Panama, Afghanistan, Iraq,

(d) unilateral support of Israel against the people Israel has dispossessed.

The Revealing Aftermath of the Cold War

1. Following the deliberate ending of the "Soviet threat" by Gorbachev, and immediately after the fall of the Berlin Wall, which made this apparent to all, the government of George H. W. Bush submitted an appeal to Congress, for a huge "defence" budget. This was justified as follows:

(a) "In a new era, we foresee that our military power will remain an essential underpinning of the global balance..."

(b) "...the more likely demands for the use of our military forces ... may be in the Third World, where new capabilities and approaches may be required," as "when President Reagan directed American naval and air forces to return to [Libya] in 1986"

(c) with the goal of "contributing to an international environment of peace, freedom and progress within which our democracy - and other free nations - can flourish."

(d) The primary threat to be faced is the "growing technological sophistication" of the Third World.

(e) The USA has to strengthen "the defence industrial base", creating incentives "to invest in new facilities and equipment as well as in research and development."

(f) In particular, it would be necessary to maintain intervention forces, targeting the Middle East, where there are "threats to our interests" that may require direct military engagement.

In other words, the disappearance of the Great Enemy necessitates a new arms race against no one in particular.

2. After a hiatus, during which the US pursued "threats" much less convincing than the "Red Empire" had been, such as Manuel Noriega of Panama and Saddam Hussein of Iraq, the events of "September 11th" have allowed the US administration of George W. Bush to pursue a phantom "War against Terrorism", against no visible enemy, and therefore a "war" with no end.

3. Since the end of the Cold War there has been no slow-down in the frequency of US military interventions across the world.

4. Since the end of the Cold War, the USA has sought to undermine the idea of international law, UNO and other international bodies, unilaterally broken agreements on nuclear weapons development, and obstructed agreements designed to save the environment and to assist the poorest countries.

US Military Actions 1998-2008

1998 SUDAN Missile attack on pharmaceutical plant alleged to be terrorist nerve gas plant, in fact manufacturing milk for newborn babies.

1998 AFGHANISTAN Missile attack on former CIA training camps used by Islamic fundamentalist groups alleged to have attacked US embassies.

1998-? IRAQ Bombing, Missile attacks and intensive air strikes after weapons inspectors allege Iraqi obstructions.

1999 YUGOSLAVIA Bombing, missile attacks and air strikes after Serbia declines to withdraw troops from Kossovo, part of Serbia. US led NATO occupation of Kossovo.

2001 MACEDONIA NATO forces deployed to disarm Albanian rebels.

2001 - ? AFGHANISTAN Bombing, missile attacks and invasion to overthrow the Taliban, hunt Al Qaeda fighters, install the Karzai regime, and fight Taliban resistance.

2002 YEMEN Predator drone missile attack on Al Qaeda, including a US citizen.

2002-? PHILIPPINES Naval Training mission for Philippine military fighting Abu Sayyaf rebels evolves into US combat missions in Sulu Archipelago.

2003-? COLOMBIA US special forces sent to rebel zone to back up Colombian military.

2003-? IRAQ Bombing, missile attacks and invasion to remove Saddam Hussein's (non-existent) weapons of mass destruction. Saddam regime toppled in Baghdad. US and UK forces occupy country and battle Sunni and Shi'ite insurgencies.

2004-05 HAITI Marines land after rebels oust elected President Aristide, who was "advised" to leave by Washington.

2005-? PAKISTAN Missile attacks, CIA airstrikes on alleged Al Qaeda villages.

---

5. The USA has further displayed contempt for the rights of other countries, individuals and international law by:
   (a) **rendering*, or** illegally kidnapping "suspected national enemies on soil of other countries, smuggling them out to third countries or to detention in a secret gulag of US prison camps;
   (b) holding them indefinitely without trial;
   (c) systematically torturing them, using methods similar to those employed in Stalin's USSR, and other methods developed by CIA and military-funded research in US university departments of psychology.

6. By means of US dominated international organisations, such as the International Monetary Fund (IMF) and the World Bank, the USA sought to pressure countries to open their economies and societies to economic **globalization***, in order to secure advantages for the owners of the dominant US economy, with the result that since the end of the Cold War, the gap between rich and poor, and the wealth of the world's richest and poorest nations, has increased sharply. Among the consequences of this are increased infant mortality in many poorer countries.

Did the Cold War Really Come to an End?

1. Evidence is mounting up that the Cold War never ended, as far as the US is concerned.

2. Outwardly Washington replaced previous cold war attitudes towards the USSR with a "strategic partnership and friendship" with Russia.

3. In reality there has been:
   (a) the continuation, and expansion into the formerly communist states of Eastern Europe, of NATO, despite the unilateral dissolution of the Warsaw Pact;
   (b) a continuation of the US arms build-up. In addition, US arms exports accounted for more than half of total global arms deliveries -- $34.8 billion -- in 2004, exporting more than the next six largest exporters combined;
   (c) the military encirclement of Russia, on and near its borders, by US and NATO bases, which are established or planned in many former Soviet republics, from the Baltics to the Caucasus and Central Asia;
   (d) accompanied by: "broken promises, condescending lectures and demands for unilateral concessions."
4. US economic "advisors" recommended to Russian President Yeltsin to assist in the changeover from a command economy to capitalism pushed a radical "free market" model which caused:
   (a) the breakdown of the Soviet welfare system;
   (b) the looting of the state's resources, originally paid for by the taxpayer, to be sold off at knock-down prices to cronies of Yeltsin, criminals and Western interests.
   (c) the temporary collapse of civil society and Russian state power.
5. This has recently provoked a robust response from Russia under president Putin, which has:
   (a) reversed the policy of the looting state enterprises for private profit;
   (b) recovered some lost state resources by legal action against the overnight criminal billionaires established under Yeltsin;
   (c) followed policies which are primarily designed to serve the interest of the Russian people, as opposed to those of the US Government and Western capitalists;
   (d) restored the stability of the Russian welfare system;
   (e) reasserted Russian sovereignty and power in international affairs.

Glossary

bellicosity: the quality of being warlike

Cheka: the Soviet secret police under Lenin

cognitive dissonance: a psychological explanation of the ability of people to maintain belief in some system of thought against all the facts by increasing their emotional commitment to it

confederation: a loose association of sovereign states

federation: a loose union

FSB: Federal Security Service, the successor organisation to the KGB.

globalization: the integration of national economies into the world economic system dominated by international institutions and transnational corporations operating in accordance with the ideology of free market economics.

ideologies: usually unquestioned systems of belief about society which determine the interpretation of experience and judgements of value. They usually exist to justify the existing social and economic arrangements in society, especially the privileges of the elite.

INF: Intermediate Nuclear Forces

KGB: The Committee of State Security, the secret police of the USSR

Manichaean: dividing the world into two contrasting camps, one (one's own, of course) being good, and the other evil.

manifest destiny: the US belief in their status as a "chosen people" with a God-given destiny to take the continent of North America from the native population; later expanded to include the entire American continent (embodied in the Monroe Doctrine), then control of the Pacific during the 1930s, after the Second World War extended to hegemony over the rest of the non-communist world, and today over the borderlands of the former USSR. It derives from the American Protestants' identification of themselves with the claims of the Old Testament Israelites to be "God's chosen people" and to have divine right to take the "promised land" from its indigenous inhabitants by force.

military-industrial complex: the coalition of forces and interests which benefit financially from an arms race: This is chiefly the military, and the industrialists who manufacture arms, to whom the state transfers huge amounts of taxpayers money in a form of regressive taxation, transferring wealth from the general taxpayer to the wealthy. Also benefiting to a much lesser extent are their workers, and the journalists and politicians who make capital out of raising the international temperature

Monroe Doctrine: a claim to exclusive US hegemony over the Western hemisphere, originally issued in 1823

moratorium: a pause

nomenklatura: the lists of names by which the Communist party controlled appointments to politically sensitive posts in Communist countries

nouveaux riches: those with recently acquired wealth

raison d'être: the real reason why something exists, or is the case

rendering: the practice of US governments of kidnapping suspects outside the USA, and smuggling them out of the country, either to be held without trial and tortured by US authorities, or to be handed over to third countries which will torture them for the USA, in violation of international law.

RSFSR: Russian Soviet Federal Socialist Republic

SDI: Strategic Defence Initiative, or "star wars".

sovereign state: a state subject to no higher authority outside its borders

START: Strategic Arms Limitation Talks

totalitarian: a regime which seeks to control all aspects of the lives of the citizens

verification: checking

welfare system: the system of social security - state provided pensions, health care, etc.

21. The Interpretation of the Cold War

"The poor people are the ones they [the Soviets] appeal to, and they have always wanted to plunder the rich." (US Secretary of State John Foster Dulles)

"We will mold our strength and become first again. Not first if. Not first but. But first period. I want the world to wonder not what Mr Khrushchev is doing. I want them to wonder what the United States is doing." (US President John F. Kennedy)

"... [A]s the rhetoric of J. F. Kennedy's electioneering demonstrates with the clarity of good oratory, the issue was not the academic threat of communist world domination, but the maintenance of a real US supremacy." (Eric Hobsbawm)

"For the United States, the Cold War has been a history of worldwide subversion, aggression and state terrorism, with examples too numerous to mention. The domestic counterpart has been the entrenchment of Eisenhower's 'military-industrial complex' - in essence, a welfare state for the rich with a national security ideology for population control... The major institutional mechanism is a system of state-corporate industrial management to sustain high-technology industry, relying on the taxpayer to fund research and development and provide a guaranteed market for waste production, with the private sector taking over when there are profits to be made. This crucial gift to the corporate manager has been the domestic function of the Pentagon system (including NASA and the Department of Energy, which controls nuclear weapons production); benefits extend to the computer industry, electronics generally, and other sectors of the advanced industrial economy. In such ways, the Cold War has provided a large part of the underpinnings for the system of public subsidy, private profit, that is proudly called Free Enterprise.:" (Noam Chomsky)

"Ours is a world of extremes. The poorest 40 per cent of the world population – the 2.5 billion people who live on less than $2 a day – account for five per cent of global income, while the richest 10 per cent account for 54 per cent. Never before has the goal of abolishing poverty been within our reach: there are no longer any insurmountable technical, resource or logistical obstacles to achieving it. Yet more than 800 million people suffer from hunger and malnutrition, 1.1 billion people do not have access to clean drinking water and, every hour, 1,200 children die from preventable diseases. Despite a growing world economy and significant advances in medicine and technology, many people in developing countries are not reaping the potential benefits of globalization." (United Nations Development Programme, Report 2006)

The Effects of the Cold War on World History

The Cold War has distorted the other historical trends given impetus by the world wars:

1. Independence movements were forced to declare themselves for one side or the other in the Cold War, and face the consequences of the enmity of the side they did not favour. On achieving independence, third world states were similarly forced to declare choose their camp, and face the consequences of their choice.

2. The evolution of independent Communist parties was undermined, for some time forcing them to adopt the Leninist pattern:

    (a) Within the Soviet bloc, leading to their subversion by electoral fraud and the *nomenklatura** patronage system;

    (b) Outside the Soviet bloc subordinating them to the Kremlin's purposes.

3. The evolution of democracies in many places was similarly subverted by electoral fraud, or they were overthrown by the military if they did not produce regimes acceptable to Washington or Moscow.

4. It provided a cover for the employment of world economic integration as a means for the rich and powerful in the leading Western nations to exploit the world's resources, untrammelled by interference in the interests of the peoples of those regions and their economies;

5. The evolution of science and technology was diverted to military uses, to the neglect of the pursuit of more useful goals.

6. It provided the pretext for economic growth in the USA and USSR to be diverted to the arms race and the military-industrial complexes, and hence to very wealthy (in the USA) and powerful interests whose position was secured by the arms race:

    (i) In the USSR the military-industrial complex became the priority section of the economy, and those associated with it became a privileged class, often living in special enclosed communities, enjoying privileges such as high-quality housing, access to special shops with western goods, etc.

    (ii) In the USA, the expensive arms programmes paid for by the taxpayer ensured the massive transfer of wealth from the general taxpayer to the owners and shareholders of the armaments (and dependent) companies. This has constituted a massive redistribution of wealth from poor and middle income groups to the rich through taxation and the use of tax money in paying defence contractors (the arms and electronics industries.)

7. It provided the pretext for the provision of social welfare, health, education, etc. to take second (at the very least) place to the requirements of the military-industrial complex.

8. In the USA the Cold War provided a mechanism for:

    (a) denouncing any support for the interests of working people, schemes for mutual social welfare and insurance, etc., to be denounced as "Communist" and therefore dismissed as evil;

    (b) and even for *consideration* of them to be rendered socially unacceptable.

9. It has had a distorting effect on history itself. In addition to the distortions of Western and Soviet propaganda about the Cold War, absorbed by historians on both sides of the divide, it led, for example, to the "burying" of the memory of the Armenian Genocide.

    (a) Russian Armenia was thoroughly Sovietized.

    (b) The US need for the Turks as allies in the Cold War led to their unwillingness to confront the facts of history. Thus in the face of sanctions threatened by the Turkish government against US businesses and military bases in their country, when resolutions formally acknowledging the Armenian Genocide were introduced into Congress in 1990, the

State Department secured that the resolutions would not pass as they were against US interests.

10. The thinking of the neo-conservatives makes quite explicit the function of the Cold War as a "myth," the truth or falsity of which is quite immaterial. Its primary function was to make the USA governable by the elite who control it, and to provide the justification for the maintenance and expansion of the US empire right across the world. Thus the neo-conservative dominated administration of George W. Bush, long after the end of the Cold War, seeks actively to increase US influence, and wherever possible military bases, in the countries of the former Soviet Union around the borders of Russia.

11. The arms race resulted in significant scientific discoveries and technological developments.
Great advances were made in rocket technology during the space race,
The rockets were based on military designs formulated during this period).
The money and resources given to the space race was due the propaganda value in the Cold War of being the first to put a man in space or on the moon.
Developments were made in missiles, military aircraft, chemical weapons, biological weapons, anti-aircraft warfare, anti-tank weapons, submarines warfare, electronic intelligence, reconnaissance aircraft and spy satellites.

12. Some ethnic and nationalist feuds were suppressed by the Cold War, only to reappear after it ended, e.g. in Yugoslavia and the Caucasus. Others were made worse by becoming proxy struggles between the superpowers, e.g. in Angola.

Some Basic Observations about the Cold War

The Balance of Power
1. Both sides accepted an initial share-out of the globe at the end of the Second World War.
    (a) The USSR exercised the predominant influence in the area occupied by the Red Army.
    (b) The USA exercised the predominant influence in:
        (i) The Western Hemisphere (since the Monroe Doctrine*);
        (ii) The capitalist world;
        (iii) The empires of the old imperial powers.
    These spheres of influenced were:
        (i) well-defined within Europe, e.g. by the agreement on the post-war administration of Germany and Austria, and by the terms of the Percentages Agreement;
        (ii) rather less well-defined outside Europe.
2. This was a very unequal division of power which reflected the realities of power politics in 1945.
    (a) The USSR:
    (i) At the beginning of the century Russia had been the most backward of the Great Powers, and the last to industrialize significantly.
    (ii) Since that time it had undergone:
        fighting on its soil during the First World War, with huge losses of manpower;
        revolution;
        civil war with foreign intervention;
        huge social upheaval under Stalin.
    (iii) In the Second World War it had suffered, in total, greater destruction than any state had ever undergone in world history, with unprecedented losses of manpower and infrastructure.

  (b) The USA:
   (i) had been the only Great Power to have made a profit out of the First World War without suffering any destruction of infrastructure.
   (ii) During the Second World War it had:
      suffered 3% of the manpower losses of life of the USSR;
      emerged wealthier than before;
      the undisputed world superpower;
      the world's only nuclear power.
3. Thus the main issues in 1945 were:
   (a) for the USSR: to preserve its independence from the world's only nuclear superpower;
   (b) for the USA: the maintenance of virtual world dominion. The Soviet threat against the USA was hardly genuine, due to:
      (i) the imbalance of power;
      (ii) the desperate state of the USSR after the destruction of the Nazi invasion;
      (iii) the Soviet government had turned away from Trotsky's belief in encouraging world revolution when Stalin took power in the late 1920s under the slogan "Socialism in one country".
4. Despite these realities, and despite the wartime propaganda which portrayed Stalin as the brave leader of a great democracy, the Truman administration in the USA chose to change this view and to portray:
   (a) Stalin as an evil dictator, like Hitler (despite having so recently been that great democrat and ally "Uncle Joe");
   (b) the USSR as a totalitarian* society;
   (c) the power of the USSR and Communism as dark, looming threats to the entire world, including the USA.
   Given the nature of Soviet society, the first two were easy to do, simply by revealing the state of Soviet society and relying upon the evidence. The only problem was embarrassment at claiming, in 1946, the opposite of what had been claimed during 1941-45. This last, was more difficult. Thus:
   (d) the extent of Stalin's ambitions;
   (e) the strength of Soviet conventional forces in Europe;
   were systematically exaggerated. This sustained and systematic exaggeration of Soviet power was to continue until the end of the Cold War.
5. Being portrayed by the Americans as a powerful rival, threatening the world superpower, suited the leaders of the USSR:
   (a) It flattered their vanity;
   (b) It enabled them to draw their own people together defensively against the real threat posed by the USA.
6. In time, the USSR was able to put up a reasonable show as a competing superpower. Under Stalin it acquired nuclear weapons, and under Khrushchev, ICBMs. In the space race it launched the first successful orbiting unmanned and manned satellites. Under Kosygin and Brezhnev it was able to project Soviet power across the world.
7. However, neither side tried directly to extend their hegemony into an area clearly in the sphere of influence of the other.
   Thus the USSR did not intervene to help the Communists in the Greek Civil War; and the USA did not intervene to help the Hungarians in the Hungarian Uprising, or the Czechs in the Prague Spring.

8. The two superpowers did compete:
    (a) in the area of the new post-colonial states;
    (b) in the oceans of the world.
9. Although the Cold War was in considerable part a public show, the nuclear arsenals were real, and the main danger to the world was of:
    (a) nuclear war by accident:
      (i) due to the misinterpretation of events by one side as an attack by the other, such as "reading" a mark on radar caused by a flock of migrating birds as an incoming nuclear missile;
      (ii) due to the misinterpretation of the intentions of one side by the other, e.g. Gorbachev subsequently revealed that during the early 1980s the Soviet leadership feared that Reagan and Thatcher were planning a first strike, on the basis of the hostility and bellicosity* of their speeches and actions.
    (b) Miscalculation by the leaders of one side seeking a propaganda victory over the other side by forcing them to back down on some issue in order to gain prestige at home. This use of the Cold War as a "virility test" was a problem mainly with the US leadership, because of presidents' desires to win re-election for a second term, e.g. Eisenhower's condemnation of the Truman administration as "soft on Communism" and the Kennedy's generation of the Cuban Missile Crisis to give him an opportunity to win a propaganda victory.
10. The real threat by the USSR to the USA was not military but political. Secretary of State John Foster Dulles privately observed to his brother, CIA director Allan Dulles, "The poor people are the ones they appeal to, and they have always wanted to plunder the rich." In other words, the USSR was a potential threat to the rule of the wealthy in the West. It presented an alternative economic system which prevented great inequalities of wealth, and which guaranteed to all its citizens a job, health care and educational opportunities. The ruling elite of the USA could not allow that to be evident to their own people, hence the systematic:
    (a) propaganda against Communism, socialism and calls for social justice;
    (b) state harassment of left wingers in the USA (often beyond what was permitted by US law);
    (c) economic warfare against the USSR and all other Communist countries except Yugoslavia (a thorn in Stalin's side).

The Arms Race

1. The only country actually to have used nuclear weapons is the USA, which used them twice, under the following conditions:
    (a) the USA was not directly threatened;
    (b) their use would not directly contribute to the significantly earlier ending of the war;
    (c) their use could not be described as intended for military targets (with some "unintended" collateral civilian damage);
    (d) their use was primarily for public relations effect.
2. Throughout the last half century the Soviet Union responded to US technological innovations after a time lag of about four or five years. The deployments resulting from their response were then used:
    (a) to fuel US fears of their gaining "superiority" in the arms race;
    (b) to justify a new level of spending to fuel a new phase of the arms race.
3. Thus it is now clear that the military strength and technological level of the Soviets during the arms race was never what it was claimed to be, and that US policy-makers were aware of that. By the time that the USSR had developed an atom bomb First, the US had 235 in its arsenal. By

and the time the Soviets had 120, the US had 1,436, By 1964, France had its first 4 and China its first one, the British had 310, the Soviets 5,221, and the USA 31,056.

The misconception that the US was falling behind was employed to justify defence spending:

(a) to maintain US superiority over the rest of the world;

(b) to "feed" the US military-industrial complex;

(c) to unite a disparate country, difficult to govern, by fear of a common enemy;

(d) to empower its leaders, as "those who deliver us from evil."

4. This raises the issue of whether the arms race was not so much a consequence of the Cold War, as its real *raison d'être*.*

The effect of the arms race, and this may have been one of its main purposes, was to move huge amounts of wealth from the general US taxpayer to the military-industrial complex, i.e. from the poor or less wealthy to the very wealthy.

This would explain behaviour which would otherwise be inexplicable, e.g. that US leaders have repeatedly failed to take advantage of opportunities presented to them to reduce the threat of confrontation:

(a) Stalin's peace offensive in 1946;

(b) Soviet proposals for the unification, neutralization and democratization of Germany in 1952;

(c) the Thaw generated by Stalin's successors in 1953-55;

(d) Khrushchev's unilateral reduction of Soviet armed forces by one third in two years in 1960.

(e) Gorbachev's proposals during 1985-6 to ban all nuclear tests, abolish NATO and the Warsaw Pact, and remove US and Soviet fleets from the Mediterranean Sea.

The Significance of these Observations

1. It has been recognised since the time of Plato that a state functions better if the thought of the people is dominated by a myth. Plato called such a myth a "noble lie."

2. Most state-propagated myths are provided by political ideologies.*

    [For political ideologies see the companion volume "Single-Party States"]

3. Some such myths, on the face of it, seem "noble" such as the liberal myth that people get very rich by working hard or being especially able, even though they are false, and in the long run cruelly deceptive to those they cheat. Some such myths, however, are by no means noble, even when taken at face value. The myth of an external or internal threat is perhaps the most effective type of myth for purposes of:

    (a) providing unity in a society which is very divided, e.g. by great differences of wealth, origin, culture, religion or race;

    (b) to empower the political leaders:

    (i) by creating a perceived need for unity against the common foe;

    (ii) by stifling criticism as disloyal;

    (iii) by enabling the leaders to pose as "protectors".

    Hitler's myths of the genetic superiority of the Aryan master-race, the "November criminals," and the genetic evil of the Jewish race were hardly "noble."

4. It is now a commonplace of psychology, by reference to the theory of cognitive dissonance,* that if such ideas are obviously false, as most are, they will be strongly and emotionally defended with quasi-religious zeal in compensation for their evidential weakness. Since the Cold War threat of the Soviet Union towards the USA was an unreal one, it had to be

backed up by all the emotions associated with patriotism. This explains what Eric Hobsbawm refers to as the quasi-religious Manichaean* and "apocalyptic tone" of much US propaganda, e.g. President John F. Kennedy in 1960: "The enemy is the communist system itself - implacable, insatiable, unceasing in its drive for world domination. ...This is not a struggle for supremacy of arms alone. It is also a struggle for supremacy between two conflicting ideologies: freedom under God versus ruthless, godless tyranny."

5. Such myths are frequently devised precisely to allow us to interpret what is happening in a way which is fictional, in order to preserve our sense of being right and good.

Thus the European imperialist powers interpreted their often bloody repression and ruthless economic exploitation of the indigenous peoples of Africa as "bringing to them the benefits of civilisation" or "bearing the white man's burden" - even when they were in the process of impoverishing, enslaving or killing them.

In just the same way, the myth of the Cold War enabled Americans to view their impoverishing, enslaving and killing of various Third World peoples as "saving them from Communism" or "bringing them "liberty."

6. Such myths are often electorally popular, since they are usually self-serving. Apparently US citizens *like* to have an enemy whom they can characterise as evil, as by implication it places them on the side of the godly and confers a pleasant feeling of righteousness. This is probably due to the strong US Christian evangelical tradition, with its Old Testament identification of one's own cause with God's, and one's own actions as essentially righteous, and as directed against evil (others with conflicting interests). This is evident in the traditional self-serving American concept of "manifest destiny."*

7. Such myths usually serve the interests of the existing social end economic elite. It is clear that the myth of the Cold War served the interest, in the USA, of the military-industrial complex, and of the political elite.

(a) for the military-industrial complex:
   (i) it ensures taxpayer support for research and development for high-technology industry;
   (ii) guaranteed taxpayer funds to guarantee a market for production;
   (iii) taxpayer funds to provide for large private profits.
(b) for the political class, it guaranteed the external threat necessary to:
   (i) unify support;
   (ii) ensure the marginalization or suppression of dissent.

8. It provided the pretext for the USA to support a very large number of brutal military despotisms which oppressed their people, and practised torture as a matter of course, whose rulers lived well off the diversion to their personal pockets of US "aid," throughout the Americas, Africa, the Far East and the Middle East.

9. The élites which create and propagate these myths may retain their own distance from them. It seems likely that Mussolini never came to believe in the myths he propagated - except perhaps the myth of his own god-like qualities. Hitler, on the other hand, really believed his own myths. This is perhaps the most dangerous situation of all, for the ruler, beset by mythical enemies becomes a fanatic in pursuit of fantastic goals, living in a world of the imagination but using real weapons against real people. Obviously, the more powerful the state whose rulers believe their own myths, the more dangerous for the rest of the world the situation would be. There is some evidence that US Presidents Kennedy and Reagan believed in the myths they propagated.

10. Curiously, the Soviet elite was less inclined to sit back and accept the benefits, several times making rebuffed attempts to bring the dangerous international nuclear standoff to an end. It was a Soviet leader within the Kremlin, Nikita Khrushchev, who was prepared to "tale a fall"

to avoid nuclear war when faced with irrational confrontation from the White House. And in the end it was Mikhail Gorbachev who used the media of communication publicly to bring the confrontation to a final conclusion, and so forced the myth-makes to look elsewhere for their "Satan."

11. With the disappearance of the so-called "evil empire", privileged gelites in the USA needed a substitute terror "threat" against which to:

(a) unite the country under their leadership;

(b) justify massive expenditure by the taxpayer on weapons to "defend" the strongest country in the world;

(c) so continue the movement of wealth from the US taxpayer to the military-industrial complex.

Glossary

bellicosity: the quality of being warlike

cognitive dissonance: a psychological explanation of the ability of people to maintain belief in some system of thought against all the facts by increasing their emotional commitment to it

ideologies: usually unquestioned systems of belief about society which determine the interpretation of experience and judgements of value. They usually exist to justify the existing social and economic arrangements in society, especially the privileges of the elite.

Manichaean: dividing the world into two contrasting camps, one (one's own, of course) being good, and the other evil.

manifest destiny: the US belief in their status as a "chosen people" with a God-given destiny to take the continent of North America from the native population; later expanded to include the entire American continent (embodied in the Monroe Doctrine), then control of the Pacific during the 1930s, after the Second World War extended to hegemony over the rest of the non-communist world, and today over the borderlands of the former USSR. It derives from the American Protestant identification of themselves with the claim of the Old Testament Israelites to be "God's chosen people" and to have divine right to take the "promised land" from its indigenous inhabitants by force.

military-industrial complex: the coalition of forces and interests which benefit from an arms race: e.g. the military, the industrialists who manufacture arms, their workers, the journalists and politicians who make capital out of raising the international temperature

Monroe Doctrine: a claim to exclusive US hegemony over the Western hemisphere, originally issued in 1823

nomenklatura: the lists of names by which the Communist party controlled appointments to politically sensitive posts in Communist countries

raison d'être: the real reason why something exists, or is the case

totalitarian: a regime which seeks to control all aspects of the lives of the citizens

21. Writing Essays about the Cold War

1. The Cold war is the name which is given for a state of hostile relations, or a breakdown of relations, between nations. It was *not* a war, although the stories of some wars form part of the history of the Cold War. Therefore the Cold War cannot form the subject of an answer to any question about "a war of your choice" or "a war you have studied."

2. The Cold War is a large and complex topic. In order to help yourself handle the material in writing a wide essay on this subject, it helps to have in your own mind a clear understanding of the *nature* of the Cold War, what it really was (discussed at the end of chapter 2 and in chapter 20). In this way, subsidiary material can better be "fitted in" to your plan, and a distinctive personal fingerprint be left upon your essay.

3. Unlike real wars, breakdowns of relationships frequently have no single starting point. Whereas a war may begin at a particular time, with a declaration of war, or an outright attack by one state upon another, the Cold War has no such beginning. Thus there is no single point at which it can be said that *this* is the point at which the Cold War began.

   This creates a difficulty in answering questions about the causes of the Cold War. It may not be clear whether a particular event which contributed to the worsening of relations between the superpowers constitutes a cause of the Cold War or an event within the Cold War.

   Within limits, this distinction is arbitrary. There are limits, because it is clear that problems at Yalta and Potsdam may unambiguously be considered causal factors, while the Berlin Blockade is too late to be considered among the causes of the Cold War.

   But there remains a doubtful area. Thus the question arises for the examinee, if I include a particular factor as a cause, will the examiner think that I am taking the notion of general causes of the Cold War too far into the story of the Cold War itself? On the other hand, if I exclude it, will the examiner think that I simply did not know about it, and penalise me?

   The best way to cope with this problem is to use the introduction to point the difficulty out to the examiner, and to stipulate (or specify) how far along the road you are going to consider factors as causal. You might also then mention that you will not go into those factors which become relevant immediately after the date at which you stop. Thus you let the examiner know that you know more than you are going to deal with in your essay.

   The more you know the more narrowly you should restrict the time span you will cover, in order to display the depth of your knowledge and insight to the examiner. If you do not possess any such depth, you should define the period you cover as widely as possible, so as to impress him/her with the extent of your knowledge over a wide sweep of time.

4. History is rarely a matter of "black and white" and to see it in black and white terms is a sign of intellectual immaturity. The Cold War was, on the surface, a confrontation between two super-powers, in which the propaganda of the victorious side was, and still is, almost all-pervasive. In your reading of books published during the Cold War, and in watching television programmes made during the Cold war, you should bear in mind that so all-pervasive was the propaganda on both sides, and so difficult was it entirely to evade its effects, that even the most apparently well-balanced works may be affected. Therefore you should be constantly aware of the likely presence of bias, and look for all the typical signs of propaganda: double standards, selective use of evidence, etc.

5. This all-pervading presence of bias particularly tempts students into a Manichaean, black and white stance, in which the USSR is portrayed as Mordor, the dark land, the source of all evil, while the USA is the noble champion of all that is good, true and worthwhile. For example, in contrasting the ideological bases of the two empires in examinations, many students are inclined to refer to the ideology of the USA and its "allies" as "democracy". Yet even a brief investigation will show that the USA and its "allies" always supported authoritarian regimes which terrorized their populations if they obediently accepted US hegemony, such as those of Suharto in Indonesia, the Shah in Iran, Ngo Dinh Diem in South Vietnam, the Colonels in Greece and Marcos in the Philippines. At the same time, they themselves readily undermined or destroyed democracies, such as those of Guatemala, Iran, and Chile which were likely to be disobedient; and widely interfered in the outcomes of elections to pervert the working of democracy in many other countries (*See page 28*). Therefore, *whatever their claims*, the ideology supported by the USA and its "allies" could not have been democracy. In fact it was capitalism and the supremacy of wealth and the wealthy. Similarly, the real ideology propagated by the USSR and its "allies" was not socialism, but the command economy, centrally controlled and planned. In any case, ideological concerns may always have played a poor second place to considerations of old-fashioned power politics as both sides manoeuvred for advantage against each other.

Books for the IB from Anagnosis

Theory of Knowledge

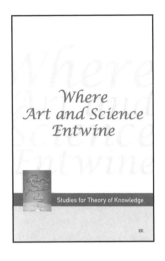

Theory of Knowledge
Visual Arts

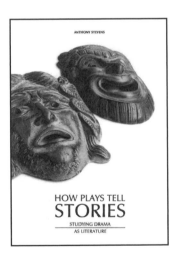

Language A1
Drama

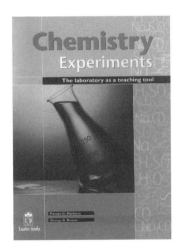

Chemistry

Study Skills

All Anagnosis books can be ordered online by credit card from:

www.anagnosis.gr

For up to date information about Anagnosis books
visit our website: www.anagnosis.gr
email: info@anagnosis.gr

Anagnosis, Deliyianni 3, Maroussi 15122 Greece
telephone: ++30-210-62-54-654
fax: ++30-210-62-54-089